Competition, Strategy, and Innovation

Understanding the latest trends and technologies and their impact on companies, organizations, or state administrations is essential to successfully develop a business in the age of Industry 4.0.

This book presents a unique selection of topics and offers the reader an understanding of the implications of the newest technologies such as artificial intelligence (AI), the Internet of Things (IoT), augmented reality (AR), and new trends like social media and sustainable competitiveness in business. It presents the impact of the newest trends on businesses, consumers, and the result on the economy. Contributions showcase the technical perspective of new technologies and provides an innovative and enriching perspective on the implementation of AI in e-commerce and the developmental barriers it can create, modern social media usage in businesses, the newest trends in innovation management, sustainable competitiveness in the business context, the influence and effect of augmented reality, and the privacy problem of the Internet of Things to consumers. This book illustrates how to develop innovation cooperation between business, academia, and public institutions through the example of the biopharmaceutical industry.

It will be of value to researchers, academics, professionals, and students in the fields of economics, management, and international business.

Rafał Śliwiński is Associate Professor at the Department of International Management, Poznań University of Economics and Business, Poznań, Poland.

Łukasz Puślecki is Assistant Professor at the Department of International Management, Poznań University of Economics and Business, Poznań, Poland.

Routledge Advances in Management and Business Studies

Trust, Organizations and the Digital Economy
Theory and Practice
Edited by Joanna Paliszkiewicz and Kuanchin Chen

Chinese Business and the Belt and Road Initiative
Institutional Strategies
Jerry J. Zhang

Management Control Systems, Decision-Making, and Innovation Development
The CDI Model
Dawid Szutowski

Competition, Strategy, and Innovation
The Impact of Trends in Business and the Consumer World
Edited by Rafał Śliwiński and Łukasz Puślecki

Critical Perspectives on Innovation Management
The Bright and Dark Sides of Innovative Firms
Edited by Patryk Dziurski

Operations Management in Japan
The Efficiency of Japanese Manufacturing
Hiromichi Shibata

Stakeholder Management and Social Responsibility
Concepts, Approaches and Tools in the Covid Context
Ovidiu Nicolescu and Ciprian Nicolescu

Japanese Business Operations in an Uncertain World
Edited by Anshuman Khare, Nobutaka Odake, and Hiroki Ishiruka

For more information about this series, please visit: www.routledge.com/Routledge-Advances-in-Management-and-Business-Studies/book-series/SE0305

Competition, Strategy, and Innovation

The Impact of Trends in Business and the Consumer World

Edited by Rafał Śliwiński and Łukasz Puślecki

Routledge
Taylor & Francis Group
NEW YORK AND LONDON

First published 2022
by Routledge
605 Third Avenue, New York, NY 10158

and by Routledge
2 Park Square, Milton Park, Abingdon, Oxon, OX14 4RN

Routledge is an imprint of the Taylor & Francis Group, an informa business

Library of Congress Cataloguing-in-Publication Data
Names: Śliwiński, Rafał, 1974- editor. | Puślecki, Łukasz, 1981- editor.
Title: Competition, strategy, and innovation : the impact of trends in business and the consumer world / edited by Rafał Śliwiński and Łukasz Puślecki.
Description: New York, NY : Routledge, 2022. |
Series: Routledge advances in management and business studies | Includes bibliographical references and index.
Identifiers: LCCN 2021025359 (print) | LCCN 2021025360 (ebook) | ISBN 9781032068909 (hardback) | ISBN 9781032068923 (paperback) | ISBN 9781003204343 (ebook)
Subjects: LCSH: Technological innovations--Management. | Technological innovations--Economic aspects. | Competition. | Strategic planning. | Business forecasting.
Classification: LCC HD45 .C626 2022 (print) | LCC HD45 (ebook) | DDC 338/.064--dc23
LC record available at https://lccn.loc.gov/2021025359
LC ebook record available at https://lccn.loc.gov/2021025360

ISBN: 978-1-032-06890-9 (hbk)
ISBN: 978-1-032-06892-3 (pbk)
ISBN: 978-1-003-20434-3 (ebk)

DOI: 10.4324/9781003204343

Typeset in Sabon
by MPS Limited, Dehradun

Contents

List of Tables vii
List of Figures viii
About the Contributors ix

Strategy, Innovations, and Consumers Under the Influence of Megatrends 1
RAFAŁ ŚLIWIŃSKI AND ŁUKASZ PUŚLECKI

PART I
Strategy and Competitiveness 13

1 Artificial Intelligence: A Prerequisite for Competitive Advantage in E-Commerce 15
RAFAŁ ŚLIWIŃSKI

2 Towards Sustainable Markets and Business Models – New Trends in Building Competitive Position 35
MAGDALENA ŚLIWIŃSKA

3 Digital Megatrends and the Management Barriers They Form 73
GRZEGORZ SOBIECKI

PART II
Consumer World 103

4 Understanding Consumer-Perceived Value in Augmented Reality – Implications for Marketing Activities 105
MAŁGORZATA BARTOSIK-PURGAT AND MILENA RATAJCZAK-MROZEK

5 Consumer Resistance to the Internet of Things: A Privacy Perspective 133
TOMASZ GRZEGORCZYK

6 The Effects of Social Media Tools' Usage in International Marketing Communication – Corporation Perspective 151
MAŁGORZATA BARTOSIK-PURGAT, MICHAŁ STASZKÓW AND MICHAŁ LEMAŃSKI

PART III
Innovation 173

7 Accelerating R&D with Knowledge and New Technological Solutions – From Innovation Cooperation to Translational Innovation 175
ŁUKASZ PUŚLECKI, MAREK DĄBROWSKI, MICHAEL CZEKAJLO AND MATEUSZ PUŚLECKI

8 Family Business Responsibility – Allocation of Profit and Innovation Planning 203
EWA WIĘCEK-JANKA AND ALICJA HADRYŚ-NOWAK

Looking Ahead 2030 223
RAFAŁ ŚLIWIŃSKI AND ŁUKASZ PUŚLECKI
Index 238

Tables

2.1 Fair Trade labels 56
3.1 The research model 75
3.2 Historical waves of technological progress 77
3.3 Timeline of the ten megatrends identified in 2011–2019 78
3.4 The amplified identity trend and its phases of development in 2011–2019 80
3.5 Management barriers mapped across trends 90
3.6 Key resources and their interdependence in addressing barriers 97
4.1 Results of the literature review concerning application of AR and consumer perception of value 113
6.1 Social media (SM) tools used by companies in international marketing communication in relation to geographical regions 161
6.2 Assessment of the characteristics of social media tools used by companies in international marketing communication 162
6.3 The influence of social media tools on the effects of international marketing communication 163
7.1 Digital health technologies addressing the Covid-19 pandemic in selected Horizon 2020 and Innovative Medicines Initiative (IMI) projects 180
7.2 Simulation tools 188
7.3 Outcomes of the innovation cooperation in the "ECMO for Greater Poland" HUB 193
8.1 Results of the first stage of the research – expert interview 209
8.2 Test results for auxiliary hypotheses ($\alpha = 0.05$; $n = 420$) 215
8.3 Results of testing the main hypothesis ($\alpha = 0.05$; $n = 420$) 217

Figures

2.1	Determinants of sustainable markets	41
2.2	Impact of sustainable strategies on the business model	52
3.1	Patterns X, Y, and Z identified for management barriers across trends	89
3.2	The data management strategy for business model transformation	95
4.1	Process of the papers' selection for the literature review	111
4.2	Main types of value perceived by the consumers in the context of AR and their implementation in companies' marketing activities	122
7.1	Translational innovation model	190
7.2	Ecosystem improvement and R&D development: "know-how and knowledge transfer" in the Artificial Life Support and Patient Safety Education Center, part of the "ECMO for Greater Poland" Innovation Ecosystem (HUB)	192
8.1	Model treatment of family business responsibility	207
8.2	Declared business line in the studied sample (n = 420)	210
8.3	Distribution of analyzed family businesses in Poland (n = 420)	210
8.4	Size of family businesses in the analyzed sample (n = 420)	211
8.5	Legal form of business activity declared in the analyzed sample (n = 420)	211
8.6	Managers in the studied sample according to gender (n = 420)	212
8.7	Managing generation in the studied sample (n = 420)	212
8.8	Distribution of answers for one of the variables describing family business responsibility (profit allocation, n = 420)	213

Contributors

Małgorzata Bartosik-Purgat – Poznań University of Economics and Business, Department of International Management, Poznań, Poland

Michael Czekajlo – Hunter Holmes McGuire Center for Simulation and Healthcare, Virginia Commonwealth University, Richmond, United States; Alliance for Innovation – Polish-American Foundation, United States; Polish Society of Medical Simulation, Poland

Marek Dąbrowski – Poznan University of Medical Sciences, Department of Medical Education, Poland; and Polish Society of Medical Simulation, Poznań, Poland

Tomasz Grzegorczyk – Poznań University of Economics and Business, Department of International Management, Poznań, Poland

Alicja Hadryś-Nowak – Poznań University of Economics and Business, Department of International Management, Poznań, Poland

Michał Lemański – Department of International Business and Management, University of Nottingham, Ningbo, China

Mateusz Puślecki – Poznan University of Medical Sciences, Department of Medical Rescue, Department of Cardiac Surgery and Transplantology, Poland; Polish Society of Medical Simulation, Poznań, Poland

Milena Ratajczak-Mrozek – Poznań University of Economics and Business, Department of International Marketing, Poznań, Poland

Magdalena Śliwińska – Poznań University of Economics and Business, Department of European Integration, Poznań, Poland

Grzegorz Sobiecki – Interim Managers Association, BMPS Consulting, Poland

Michał Staszków – Poznań University of Economics and Business, Department of International Management, Poznań, Poland

Ewa Więcek-Janka – Poznań University of Technology, Department of Marketing and Economic Control, Poznań, Poland

Strategy, Innovations, and Consumers Under the Influence of Megatrends

Rafał Śliwiński and Łukasz Puślecki

Global Changes as a Challenge for Enterprises and Consumers

Dynamic changes in the global economy pose a significant challenge for local and global enterprises – small, medium, and large. Changes seem equally difficult for consumers, for whom the future is marked by many questions: Will they have to give artificial intelligence (AI) control over driving? Will their privacy be a total pipe dream? Will technological development mean an easier life? The basis of these dynamic changes and emerging dilemmas are megatrends resulting from demographic changes, political and economic changes, globalization, greater restrictions on access to resources and their shrinking deposits, as well as attempts to rebuild the natural, social, and economic environment and, above all, from very dynamic changes in technology. The purpose of this chapter is to outline the major megatrends affecting business and consumer strategies.

Demography as the Basis of Changes

With regard to demographics, it is important to note the rapidly increasing population in developing countries and the aging of societies in highly developed economies. In 2021, the world's population is approximately 7.8 billion (Worldometer, 2021). In 2050, the world's population is projected to reach 9.8 billion, and in 2100, around 11 billion (Gaub, 2019). Considering the fact that in 1800 there were about 1 billion people in the world, it can be concluded that the dynamics of development over the last centuries were extremely high, unprecedented in the history of mankind. For businesses, the key news is that the main gains were in Africa and Asia. Developing these markets seems to be the first strategic challenge. The second, in turn, is the simultaneous maintenance or development in markets that are shrinking due to an aging population, such as Europe. For enterprises, from a strategic point of view, the dynamic population growth is a great opportunity for development, increasing market shares in developing countries and improving

DOI: 10.4324/9781003204343-101

competitiveness. For consumers, population growth means dwindling resources, often associated with an increase in prices and crowds in physical, virtual, and mental space. Nevertheless, thanks to the large number of potential customers, many very important investments in innovation in products or services for consumers may take place.

Shift in the Political and Economic Balance of Power in the World

In 2008, George Bush, as a representative of the G7 group, invited the G20 group to jointly solve the world's political and economic problems (Stolberg & Landler, 2008). It was a symbolic moment of changing the balance of power in the world. In terms of world presidency, the dynamic development of China is putting the hegemony of the United States to the test. In practice, this means tougher competition in global markets, which Chinese companies have entered with great success. While the 20th century was characterized by setting the tone for economic development in the world by several countries, today a large group of countries provide incentives for development. Countries such as China, India, Indonesia, Brazil, Russia, and Mexico are gaining economic importance in the international arena (PWC, 2015) and are beginning to play a leading role in the global economy. For companies, this means increased competition not only in the low-tech area, but also in the high-tech area, as rapidly developing countries invest heavily in the latest technologies. For consumers, this means an increase in the number of products offered, and to a large extent, also a partial drop in prices, but also perhaps the loss and uncertainty of tomorrow caused by, for example, overload of information, the pace of changes, the need to constantly learn new things, lack of understanding of certain technologies, and fear of abuse e.g. from hackers or scammers.

Scarce Resources as a Global Problem

The consequence of the existence of many centers of dynamic economic growth and demographic growth is fewer natural resources. This applies to both vital resources, such as fresh water, food, and clean air, as well as resources necessary for production, such as oil, antimony (necessary for the production of semiconductors), tantalum (necessary for the production of capacitors and resistors), zinc (important metal in the production of batteries), as well as palladium, cobalt, or rare earth elements (key to the production of many high-tech products). The growing demand due to increased world population, which has ever greater life aspirations, and consequently the demand pressure from industry, can very quickly lead to rising prices, exhaustion of resources, competitive struggle, and even wars. Already, the global resource market is dominated by companies from the richest countries in the world, and a progressive increase in the prices of natural resources can also be observed. From the point of view of strategic challenges for enterprises, the key problem is gaining long-term access to resources and guaranteeing a price level of production resources, which is difficult to obtain. Many companies, and even countries, may be excluded from world production, in particular of high-tech products, due to the gradual depletion of resources, or their high price level in the future. For consumers, shrinking resources will mostly mean problems with access to clean and essential resources (water, food, air), a gradual increase in the price of ecologically clean food, and price pressure on many other products dictated by shrinking production resources. This will also apply to high-tech products, which will often determine the development potential of consumers.

Artificial Intelligence as a Source of Growth and Change

Another key megatrend is technological progress, which significantly determines the pace of economic development, as well as the intensity of competitive struggle. First of all, AI should be mentioned, the development of which transforms the economic landscape of the world (Castrounis, 2019; Diamandis & Kotler, 2020; Lee, 2018). Self-learning intelligence is a tool that changes the rules of the game in competition at the level of companies, industries, or countries (Iansiti & Lakhami, 2020). There are even statements, such as by Vladimir Putin, that the leader in AI will control the world (CNBS, 2017). AI for enterprises offers significant opportunities, but not everyone can afford to invest in this new technology. The experience with AI so far shows that the involvement of this technology in, for example, e-commerce may mean winning the competition and taking over market shares. This is described in more detail in Chapter 1, devoted to building a competitive advantage in e-commerce thanks to AI. For enterprises, AI creates opportunities to lower costs and increase efficiency (Cordes & Stacey, 2017), as well as the possibility of building better products or finding products that have not existed before. This revolution is already happening, and some results are already visible, for example, AI winning the GO game versus Lee Se-Dol, autonomous cars, and the talking and joking robot Sofia, who even obtained honorary citizenship of Saudi Arabia and has become the subject of various controversies (Parviainen & Coeckelbergh, 2020; Stone, 2017). For consumers, AI may mean an increased risk of job loss and the need to change industries. The scale of this phenomenon in pessimistic scenarios may be massively and relatively concentrated in time. Optimistic scenarios include a significant spread of this process over time and the emergence of new types of work for people that did not exist before. Probably like any revolution, it causes fear, but the spread of computers also caused fear in the last century when they were first introduced.

Augmented and Virtual Reality Changing Cooperation Habits and the Way of Education

Another important technology classified as key in the world is augmented reality (AR), the marketing aspects of which are discussed in Chapter 4, and virtual reality (VR). This technology has changed the way people work, learn, research, and design in many professional and private areas, increasing the possibilities of its users. VR means, among other things, that two or more people can cooperate with each other remotely on tasks that require personal meetings, which is very useful during for example the Covid-19 pandemic. A perfect example is the Hololens 2 product from Microsoft, which combines AR and VR. This product is a tool that, on the one hand, is very practical, and on the other hand, is a window to another world that will change the lives of millions, if not billions, of people. In terms of professional life, Hololens 2 allows for collaboration of any number of people from any location, allowing for virtual teleportation anywhere in the world. In practice, this allows, for example, repair of a broken machine in real time that requires the knowledge of a high-class specialist, for example, in Europe who is normally difficult to access, and thanks to a virtual meeting, the specialist can manage the movements of an employee in a remote factory in the Philippines, repairing the machine with his hands. In addition, the process of designing new, even very complex architectural or mechanical projects, such as a motorbike or car, is significantly simpler. VR eliminates the limitations of people's imagination thanks to the constant three-dimensional display of, for example, a vehicle structure with internal systems marked with different colors. It also allows for a virtual meeting of several designers working together. In technical terms, the method of creating, for example, a new vehicle – adding new systems, controls, etc. – is much easier than designing in computer-aided design (CAD)/computer-aided manufacturing (CAM) programs.

At the same time, VR and AR have radically changed education. This is a breakthrough that mankind has long been waiting for. It enables, for example, three-dimensional and faithful-to-reality displays of complex systems or ecosystems that previously were difficult to envision and hard to teach with mock-ups, models, etc. Medical students can learn about the human body by viewing virtual organs, their sections, individual body elements, or body parts at a different level of detail than previously available. Moreover, this technology enables students to perform virtual patient surgeries or participate in actual patient operations with a specialist doctor from another part of the world. The development of virtual, augmented, and mixed-reality solutions has caused significant advances in healthcare technologies. Advances that we could only dream of a decade ago are now being implemented – from educating new students with modern medical simulation to planning procedures. The use of AR and VR in healthcare offers serious promise. By rendering three-dimensional information on real-world scenes, AR enables surgeons and doctors to stay grounded in actual procedures simultaneously, providing ready access to all the data available through other emerging technologies. Medical students have an opportunity to use overlays to access information in an interface where they can quickly explore and verify different solutions. Thanks to AR, in order to make diagnoses and plan for procedures, doctors can compare data to what they are seeing in the real world. Certainly, healthcare is capable of becoming one of the essential influences on the development and future of AR (Jeffery, 2020). Thanks to VR and AR, you can also learn carpentry, mechanics, and chemistry by performing various experiments or trials. This is a real revolution.

From a strategic point of view, businesses face the challenge of participating in a brand new, extremely broad market and also of adapting this technology in their business to collaborate, problem-solve, and create. As always, such adaptation will require investments, and without them, it may not be possible to build a future competitive position. From consumers' point of view, AR and VR create new opportunities to spend free time, to entertain themselves, and to communicate. These changes should be assessed positively; however, they can also lead to health problems. There is research that people who spend a lot of time in VR lose their sense of whether they are in a physical or virtual world at a given moment. In addition, such people may also have problems with the self-balance, headaches, or nausea (Lee et al., 2017). Therefore, this technology may also have a negative impact on physical health. This does not change the value of AR or VR, but it indicates that excess use of this technology can be problematic, at least without getting used to it. The various consumer attitudes in the field of AR, its perceived value, and its implications for the sphere of marketing are presented in Chapter 4.

The Internet of Things as a Driver of Change

Another key technology is the Internet of Things (IoT). In short, the IoT means devices that have sensors that transmit various types of data to other electronic cooperating devices or, for example, a control center that can be located in a computing cloud, etc. The IoT is directly related to big data because the IoT generates gigantic amounts of data that can be used in various ways e.g. by AI. The IoT has many potential uses. The first one is creating cooperating ecosystems of devices that achieve a specific effect, e.g. a field with many humidity sensors communicating wirelessly with an irrigation system. If the soil moisture level drops below a certain level, the system will autonomously react, thanks to the IoT, by irrigating the soil. Another example is a system of light sensors in a city that turns off street and road lighting, or a home ecosystem that, thanks to sensors, regulates access to fresh air, humidity, and temperature. Another example is a car, which, as an ecosystem of related sensors, reacts to the skidding of one wheel or to sleeping driver by stopping the car. All such autonomous ecosystems receive the term "smart", indicating their intelligent behavior. Another use of the IoT is to check the level and condition of certain products and provide information to the user or performer of a specific activity. In practice, this could mean a refrigerator that checks the level of food or drink, and when it sees them missing, it either notifies the owner or makes purchases on its own. So, this means making purchasing decisions, creating a huge market for virtual purchases of food, drinks, and stimulants. Very often, a virtual assistant, which communicates with the user using human speech, is introduced to mediate between the devices and the user. Examples of such interactions are also described in Chapter 1.

The use of the IoT, however, goes far beyond the examples presented above. Using, for example, Apple Watch or applications for smartphones (e.g. Pulse Oximeter) in conjunction with the built-in heart rate sensor, it is possible to obtain detailed health data of the user, even information about the level of oxygen saturation in the blood, which in the Covid-19 era can save many people's lives. Combining IoT development with telemedicine and telehealth technologies, a new Internet of Medical Things (IoMT) has emerged. This approach takes into account the use of a number of wearables, including ECG and EKG monitors, as well as medical measurements, such as skin temperature, glucose level, and blood pressure readings. According to Frost and Sullivan (2017), by 2017, nearly 60% of operations in the healthcare field had already adopted IoT or IoMT systems. This trend has resulted in improvements in everything from patient experience to profitability. According to Allied Market Research (2020), the global IoT in the healthcare market is anticipated to reach $332.67 billion by 2027 (Jeffery, 2020).

Due to its monitoring capabilities, the IoT can constantly and reliably control life processes. It can also monitor production processes in businesses, from cooperation and delivery monitoring, through the production process, until the product reaches the customer or even during the entire life of the product at the customer level. From a strategic point of view, companies wishing to keep pace with the development of modern factories and methods of coordinating the value creation process should join the IoT and big data trends, creating an efficient production ecosystem. Sometimes, this means replacing a lot of production equipment and making a lot of investments. However, companies should remember that the IoT is an important element of Industry 4.0, which, thanks to data and precision, contributes to companies' achievement of high and repeatable quality, reliability, and predictability of production to an unprecedented degree. From the consumer's point of view, the IoT brings many amenities. It enables remote supervision and management of home devices as well as management of remote access to rooms. Uses arise in many areas. The dark side of this technology is also no less. By downloading large amounts of data, sensors raise questions about privacy. Many consumers choose not to buy new smart devices to maintain privacy. This issue is dealt with in more detail in Chapter 5, dealing with the privacy perspective of the IoT. This is because the feeling of overall tracking and lack of privacy is becoming a problem for many consumers.

Ubiquitous Digitization

As part of the technological megatrend, digitization should also be discussed. It allows for productive use and benefits from digital data resources collected in various formats, e.g. audio documents, video, databases, spreadsheets, graphics, etc. Digitization has many benefits: better traceability, organization, faster processing time, reduced workload, lower costs, and reduced use of paper. Digitization in everyday life means communication using digital technologies such as email, Skype/Zoom/Microsoft Teams, listening to music from digital devices, online shopping, watching movies from digital resources, or reading e-books. In business, it means reaping the benefits of data (IoT, big data) and optimization of the delivery process (time, place, quantity), production process (inputs, quality, quantity, repeatability, minimization of waste and losses, etc.), distribution, and many other less crucial activities. Thanks to digitization, many trends that are part of it, such as social media, VR, AR, and AI, have developed. Chapter 6 describes how a company, e.g. a producer of consumer products, can use social media to communicate with the consumer in an effective way and maximize a marketing strategy. Digitization also means a permanent presence on various digital platforms e.g. via a smartphone. Thanks to this device, people are constantly available for digital communication with others, which lead to the phenomenon of social media. As a consequence, society is transforming and digitizing. Chapter 7 describes an example of the use of digitization, describing innovations related to the application and use of digital technologies and modern medical simulation in the field of patient healthcare. It describes the latest solutions that can be a source of inspiration for many environments and social groups, and it emphasizes the importance of innovative cooperation, R&D innovation ecosystems, open innovation, and translational innovation in the development of modern therapeutic solutions.

From the point of view of corporate strategy, digitization creates many dilemmas, e.g. how should the company be present in digital media; moreover, to what extent should the company be digitized in order to capture opportunities from the environment, and what investments must be made to use digital tools. Another important question is whether or not and how to convert the company's operating model to digital. These are just examples of dilemmas, but some of them may pose significant problems for managers. Chapter 3 describes digital megatrends and the barriers they create for management. Digitization also poses significant challenges for management staff, who are not always prepared to meet these challenges.

From the consumer's point of view, digitization brings many benefits in terms of communication, acceleration of banking online, shopping online, and free communication, even on an international scale. However, there are costs associated with it, especially in terms of loss of privacy, addiction to social media, e.g. Facebook or Instagram, sometimes mental health problems, or even suicides. This is not an argument against digitization, but rather for training, especially for the younger part of society, on how to deal with the new digital reality. Recently, there have even been companies offering drug rehabilitation programs for young people addicted to the Internet and the digital world. Progressive digitization, especially among young people, is leading to the development of a "head down" generation that constantly looks at their smartphones. Perhaps one of the challenges in the future will be the attempt to develop at the international level common principles of "digital hygiene" for young people, taking into account the issues of their addiction to the digital world. On the other hand, one of the important challenges related to the rapid digitization of societies is the sustainable access to technology, so important in the future education of all young people, aimed at combating digital exclusion and the digital divide in the world.

Sustainable Development as a Remedy for the World's Ills

An important and relatively new, but powerful, megatrend is sustainable development, the need for which was manifested, among other things, by the UN Sustainable Development Goals (SDGs). It results from global environmental, economic, and social challenges and the growing awareness that further economic development must be carried out with respect for the welfare of all market participants and the natural environment. In the environmental dimension, this means, e.g. protection of the natural environment and growing food in an organic way without the use of harmful pesticides, which, for example, lead to the extinction of bees and many other species of insects. All natural resources should be used in a way that enables their quantitative and species reconstruction. In economic terms, sustainable growth means producing without polluting the environment, focusing on reducing polluting transport and therefore increasing local production instead of global supply chains. Sustainable economy also means using renewable energy sources and searching for technological solutions, such as electric or hydrogen technology for an ecologically clean source of power, heating, fuel, etc. In the social dimension, sustainable development means, above all, seeking a fairer distribution of global income. This means fighting poverty in all its dimensions. This also applies to the liquidation of still-existing slavery, also among children. An example in this area is the company Tony's Schocolonely, which for several years has been trying to produce chocolate completely free from slave labor, especially among children (tonyschocolonely.com). Moreover, this trend also applies to the equal rights of women, equal access to education, and thus equal development opportunities for people around the world. There are many grassroots social movements, an example of which is Fair Trade, which, on the one hand, tries to support poor producers in the Global South countries and, on the other hand, makes the societies of developed economies, e.g. in Western Europe, aware of how they can contribute to sustainable social development throughout the world.

In practice, the sustainable development megatrend has found a significant resonance in the societies and economies of many countries. It has become so important that a company now has to take it into account in order to develop and survive in the market. Businesses include this megatrend in their development strategy and compete with various ideas and solutions in the field of sustainable development. These issues are discussed in detail in Chapter 2, pointing to the various strategies that companies can choose to differentiate themselves from competitors with sustainable products and solutions, and attract more informed consumers. Precisely in terms of the strategy, the issue of sustainable development requires some thought, and sometimes small – and sometimes significant –changes. This is certainly a challenge, especially in the face of past megatrends also requiring strategic responses and adjustments. Family business is also important for sustainable development, its responsibility, and at the same time planning and implementing innovations in many dimensions. These issues are dealt with in Chapter 8, which sheds light on profit allocation, innovation, and development, as well as the latest research in the field. In the consumer dimension, this megatrend aims to improve the quality and availability of food and clean air, preserve the natural environment, and provide equal access to education and work for various social groups. In practice, sustainable development has a very positive effect on the consumer. Perhaps that is why it is so important for consumers and why it has become such a necessity for businesses.

Summing up, the above-mentioned megatrends have permanently changed reality. They cannot be stopped. You can only adapt to them and possibly use them to achieve your goals. If you want to do this, as a business or as a consumer, you need to get to know them. For this reason, the remaining chapters discuss these megatrends. Without a doubt, modern technologies are driving unimaginable changes – in terms of pace and scope – in all areas of human activity. Technology influences how we live and work, how we learn, and how we heal ourselves. The world is evolving exponentially. With regard to this issue, it is also worth paying attention to the Conclusion, which discusses the development of megatrends for technology, sustainable development, demography, and globalization in the context of strategic and consumer challenges until 2030. We hope that reading all chapters will be fruitful and that they will provide valuable inspiration for scientists, practitioners, students, employees of state administrations or supranational organizations.

References

Allied Market Research. (2020). *Internet of Things in healthcare market*. https://www.alliedmarketresearch.com/iot-healthcare-market

Castrounis, A. (2019). *AI for people and business: A framework for better human experiences and business success*. O'Reilly Media.

CNBS. (2017). Putin: Leader in artificial intelligence will rule world. *CNBC*. https://www.cnbc.com/2017/09/04/putin-leader-in-artificial-intelligence-will-rule-world.html

Cordes, F., & Stacey, N. (2017). *Is UK industry ready for the fourth industrial revolution? BCG*. Retrieved from https://media-publications.bcg.com/Is-UK-Industry-Ready-for-the-Fourth-Industrial-Revolution.pdf

Diamandis, P. H., & Kotler, S. (2020). *The future is faster than you think: How converging technologies are transforming business, industries and our lives*. Simon and Schuster.

Frost & Sullivan. (2017). Internet of Medical Things, forecast to 2021. *Growth opportunities, challenges, and future perspectives in healthcare*. https://store.frost.com/internet-of-medical-things-forecast-to-2021.html

Gaub, F. (2019). Global trends to 2030. Challenges and choices for Europe. *ESPAS*. https://ec.europa.eu/assets/epsc/pages/espas/ESPAS_Report2019.pdf

Iansiti, M., & Lakhami, K. R. (2020). *Competing in the age of AI: Strategy and leadership when algorithms and networks run the world*. HBR Press.

Jeffery, N. (2020) White paper – the importance of IOT and the cloud in drug development, clinical diagnostics and patient interaction. Director International Revenue and Strategy, Beyond.pl Linkedin profile, pp. 1–15.

Lee, K.-F. (2018). *AI superpowers: China, silicon valley, and the new world order*. Houghton Mifflin Harcourt.

Lee, J., Kim, M., & Kim, J. (2017). A study on immersion and VR sickness in walking interaction for immersive virtual reality applications. Symmetry, 9(78), 1–17. https://doi.org/10.3390/sym9050078

Parviainen, J., & Coeckelbergh, M. (2020). The political choreography of the Sophia robot: Beyond robot rights and citizenship to political performances for the social robotics market. *AI & Society*. https://doi.org/10.1007/s00146-020-01104-w

Price Waterhouse Coopers. (2015). The World in 2050. Will the Shift in Global Economic Power Continue?. https://www.pwc.com/gx/en/issues/the-economy/assets/world-in-2050-february-2015.pdf

Stolberg, S. G., & Landler, M. (2008, October 22). Bush calls 20 nations to summit on markets. *The New York Times*. https://www.nytimes.com/2008/10/23/business/economy/23bush.html

Stone, Z. (2017). Everything you need to know about Sophia, the world's first robot citizen. *Forbes*. https://www.forbes.com/sites/zarastone/2017/11/07/everything-you-need-to-know-about-sophia-the-worlds-first-robot-citizen/?sh=683297c246fa

Worldometer (2021). World population. *Worldometer*. https://www.worldometers.info/

Part I

Strategy and Competitiveness

1 Artificial Intelligence: A Prerequisite for Competitive Advantage in E-Commerce

Rafał Śliwiński

Introduction

The subject of artificial intelligence (AI) has been known for decades. However, only in recent years has the emergence of the associated technologies, such as big data or the achievement of high-performance computer processors, influenced AI and its practical applications, leading to a spectacular victory for the computer (Google DeepMind) in 2016 on the Korean master, Lee Se-Dol, of the most difficult strategic game in the world, GO, and in 2014 on the Chinese world champion of GO, Kie Jie. Since then, the Google DeepMind algorithms have been improved several times (AlfaGo Lee, AlfaGo Master, AlfaGo Zero), and all the GO masters have been beaten by AI. Kie Jie's post-defeat comment is highly telling; the seasoned player recounted that he had never before felt such psychological pressure during a game. This event opened the door for AI to enter the economic arena, showing the potential to replace lawyers, accountants, stock traders, and many other intellectual professions that have not been threatened by competition so far. It also paved the way for AI to penetrate e-commerce and traditional commerce. Thanks to AI, commercial solutions for acquiring new customers or increasing customer satisfaction with the purchasing process or with purchased items have been substantially improved, and it seems that traditional solutions in the field of marketing and sales techniques are not able to cope with modern AI solutions.

The literature on the subject quite selectively treats the areas of e-commerce and their links with AI. E-commerce firms engage in fierce competition with other e-commerce participants, and they also take up the fight against traditional trade stores, such as Walmart. The literature usually describes one aspect, but there is lack of broad overviews of solutions that will create a bigger picture of using AI to increase the competitiveness of e-commerce. For the above reasons, the purpose of this chapter is to show how an e-commerce company can increase its competitiveness through the use of AI. By grouping the benefits of using AI, we can help readers visualize the advantages a business can derive

DOI: 10.4324/9781003204343-1

from this technology and how AI can strengthen or create a competitive edge. A scoping literature review was used to determine the scope of the body of literature (Munn et al., 2018). This type of review answers broad questions, especially in terms of issues that are still under-researched or at an early stage of research. The purpose of this scoping review is to provide an overview of the new methods of AI application to e-commerce with an in-depth analysis.

E-Commerce Competitive Advantage Thanks to AI

Retail e-commerce is expected to reach almost USD 6.5 billion globally in 2024, which is 55.5% more than in 2020 (Statista, 2021). In 2020, approximately 85% of all customer interactions were handled by AI, without human interference (Schneider, 2017). Furthermore, Servion predicts that by 2025, AI will handle 95% of all customer interactions (Nirale, 2018), including live phone calls and online calls, so realistic that it will be virtually impossible for customers to detect the bot. Commercial companies that are unable to prepare for this reality face serious risks of being left behind by their competitors. Prior research has confirmed a positive correlation between e-commerce and business performance, and the relationship between the use of modern technologies in e-commerce and positive business results (Jehangir et al., 2011; Syam & Sharma, 2018).

AI has made its way into e-commerce for good, and many researchers describe various aspects of this process (Kietzmann et al., 2018; Nadimpalli, 2017; Turban et al., 2018). Kumar et al. (2019) and Rossi (2016) describe ways AI helps customers by e.g. improving search results, helping buyers to understand their preferences, and serving as a personal assistant to shoppers. Many examples of AI in marketing are provided by Davis (2016), Davar (2018), and Venkatesan and Lecinski (2021). The use of chatbots in marketing is described by Mah (2016), among others. Salesforce's AI Einstein Service facilitates sales transactions (Womack, 2016). Kohl (2016) describes the use of AI to boost customer engagement, which is particularly important since shopping is evolving to transactions that will take place without human interaction, with the use of technology, such as the Internet of Things (IoTs). IBM's Watson AI is learning about people from their tweets. This will help companies predict consumer behavior, deciding what to offer and when (Russell, 2014). In general, AI is believed to have a big role in retailers' future (Arthur, 2016).

The basic concept associated with AI is its ability to learn and, as a result, to innovate. Thanks to this skill, AI can find patterns of use of given products and, using accumulated knowledge that is often of a broader scope than their human counterparts, propose a creative innovation that meets the expectations of customers to a greater extent than before, and even propose a completely new solution that did not exist before, to a problem that human counterparts could not deal with. In addition, AI is better than humans at repetitive activities or activities that require patience. For this reason, in a trade where every customer expects to be served with enthusiasm and patience, AI alone can meet or surpass these customer expectations.

Another central concept in achieving a competitive advantage in trade thanks to AI is the network. An AI-powered network includes a group of subnets, supply chain networks, networks of Facebook customer accounts, purchase histories from trading partners, etc. These networks have at least five things in common. They consist of digital connections between network nodes, carry data, are shaped by increasingly powerful software algorithms, ignore traditional industry boundaries, and are becoming increasingly important to our economy and social system (Iansiti & Lakhami, 2020).

The competitive advantage in trade built thanks to AI can therefore be defined as, first, the ability to innovate based on the use of AI to improve the basic, useful properties of trade in the context of a product/service or process, and second, as the ability to shape and control networks based on the accumulation of quantities and the diversity of their transactions as well as using AI to analyze this data to capture key information that is used to expand business activities, both in scale and in scope. In the first sense, a competitive advantage means a better designed website or a well thought-out and effective purchase/sales process. It involves differentiation of products and services, adding features that give the firm an edge over the competition. A firm with competitive advantage thanks to AI sees a greater number of goods sold in a given period, a greater percentage of first-time buyers, increasing market share in trade in products of a given type, etc. In relation to sales management, the advantages of AI may include more effective sales analysis in terms of quantity, space, time, and connection with seemingly insignificant facts that a human would be unlikely to make. For instance, AI may associate an influx of arriving ferries with more customers for a beach goods store, quickly prompting a decision to increase store inventory and initiating a highly coordinated, strategic effort to maximize store sales. Such systems, capable of performing quick market analyses and choosing the proper course of action, allow firms to function better in the economic reality than they would with traditional analytics. Additionally, the highly customizable nature of AI technology meets the needs of individual clients to an extent that was previously impossible to achieve. In other words, the second way of using AI to create a competitive advantage is based on its ability to innovate, as a result of gathering industry knowledge and creatively processing it.

In the second sense, the competitive advantage therefore depends on the amount of data flowing through the organization. Thanks to the aggregation of big data and the ability to extract value from it using advanced AI analytical tools, companies gain a significant advantage over competitors that are unaware of certain dependencies. Obtaining the second dimension of competitive advantage, however, requires a completely digital business and operational model (Iansiti & Lakhami, 2020), thanks to which AI can derive data from a data flow that is undisturbed by human action, from which AI acquires and then creatively uses key information necessary to implement tasks set before it.

The implications for the strategy are significant. First of all, it should be noted that the "blood" that nourishes the whole "body" of a company is data, and the "bloodstream" is information flow, which, just like in the human body, must be properly and very logically coupled with processes in order to be able to bring the desired benefits. In the case of firms, these benefits come in the form of innovation or pattern recognition, e.g. the most frequent purchasing behavior in a given period of the year, etc. As a consequence, the company's priority must be to change the operating model to a digital one by first identifying places from which data can be obtained, such as sales figures, history of customer behavior on the website (even if it did not end with a purchase decision), customer product usage data, or industry trend data, and then changing the company so that this data flows to the analytical center in the form of code to AI so that the competitive advantage can be created on this basis.

Second, instead of focusing on the structure of the industry, as suggested by the positional theory, businesses should focus on the structure of the network and the importance of the links that the company creates in different industries and at different levels by analyzing the data flow through the networks and the resulting consequences. As Iansiti and Lakhami (2020) point out, the strategy is now becoming the art of company development by deriving the energy from the networks' management to which the company has access, using data that flows through the company. The stronger the network effects used by the company, the fewer competitors the company will have, and it can achieve a greater concentration on the market, gaining a much stronger competitive advantage. These changes will gradually affect any traditional company that either adapts or dies. At best, traditional businesses will sell through large digital intermediaries like Amazon or Alibaba. In this respect, a lot is likely to happen on the world market. In short, due to AI, the nature of competition has changed from a predictable game with stable offerings and competitors, to a complex, dynamic game that is played across many dimensions. Leaders who understand this and re-equip their organizations accordingly will be best positioned to win in the next decade (Kimura et al., 2019).

Practical E-Commerce Solutions Increasing Sales

AI provides companies with a competitive advantage in e-commerce solutions, ranging from large platforms, such as Alibaba, Amazon, to smaller systems, such as Allegro or Pinterest, or the websites of individual companies. In this competitive advantage-building process, AI enables e-commerce sellers to analyze millions of interactions each day and ultimately target offers to one customer. By using AI, sales teams now have access to information that was not previously available. They can personalize the sales cycle with AI-powered applications that help sellers reach the right potential customers with the right message at the right time. AI will certainly have a huge and beneficial impact on the e-commerce industry in the coming years (Gupta et al., 2020; Kumar et al., 2019; Rust & Huang, 2014). So how can a firm create a competitive advantage in e-commerce thanks to AI? Below are some examples illustrating the emergence of an advantage and its sources.

Customer-Oriented Search

AI has the ability to orient search results to the preferences and needs of the searcher to a greater extent than before. This applies to both searching for products desired at a given moment and using the results from previously obtained preferences. This also applies to searching for previously impossible-to-specify preferences resulting from the ephemeral moment. A prime example is Pinterest's upgrade to a Chrome extension, which allows users to search visually (Novet, 2017), thus selecting an item in any photo online and then asking Pinterest to display similar items using image-recognition software (Griffith, 2018; Pinterest Labs, 2018; Wilson, 2018). The update offers significant opportunities with great commercial potential, while increasing the attractiveness of Pinterest, thus increasing its competitive advantage in the market. In addition to searching for matching products, AI enables buyers to discover complementary, related products in size, color, shape, material, or even brand. The visual possibilities of such software are unique, making the competitive advantage of Pinterest even bigger.

Another example of a company helping its customers make choices is the firm The North Face. The company uses AI to first recognize what jacket customers are looking for, and then provide hints to guide online shoppers to discover their perfect jacket from the presented options (Harris, 2016). One way that this is achieved is through AI voice technology, which asks the customer, "Where and when will you use your jacket?" Having the answer, the system then scans hundreds of products to find the perfect matches based on real-time customer input and its own research, such as local weather conditions (Asling, 2020). Thanks to AI, clients will receive products better suited to their needs, whether they are aware of these needs or not. At the end of the purchase process, thanks to AI, both the number of products sold and customer satisfaction are greater (Marshall, 2006).

By relying on data such as high buy rate, high basket values, and other indicators derived from AI, The North Face can develop future trading strategies and gather important information and patterns for suggestions that work for most customers. In the long run, as this technology evolves, the business can acquire more customers, increase conversions over time, and reduce the costs necessary to serve each customer (Faggella, 2018). Thanks to AI, The North Face has the potential to dominate the outdoor apparel industry. This example demonstrates how AI aids firms in achieving and even surpassing their sales goals to a greater extent than traditional solutions.

Efficient Sales Process Thanks to AI and CRM Integration

Many sales opportunities are not taken by human sales teams for various reasons. Thanks to AI coupled with Customer Relationship Management (CRM) systems, BI (business intelligence) can be used to a much greater extent to take advantage of opportunities, including those that for various reasons have not been taken before (Silva, 2019). Research has shown that the implementation of AI in the company's CRM increases the competitive advantage of the organization (Lassinantti et al., 2014; Shadbolt et al., 2012). Moreover, many companies are often overloaded with an excess of customer data with which they do little or nothing. This type of situation can be transformed into another competitive advantage thanks to AI. Predictive marketing systems of companies like Mintigo acquire such company data and, thanks to AI, generate additional sales opportunities that, over time, turn into an additional inflow of income (Asling, 2020). Such solutions increase the sales efficiency of companies by increasing their effectiveness and financial results. Moreover, AI accelerates and generates more precise updates on the company's future profitability based on current data (Martínez et al., 2018).

The times when customers were acquired by telephone contact are long gone. If a company wants to realistically acquire customers and create a strong sales message that reaches consumers at the right time on the right platform, the best solution is to integrate AI with a CRM system. What is more, AI will allow a firm to assess a group of potential or current customers and select those who can contribute to the company's profitability (Homburg et al., 2008; Zeithaml et al., 2001) by paying attention to their quality (Verhoef & Donkers, 2005) or focusing on those who will help create or consolidate a strategic advantage (Fader, 2012).

AI not only enables sales professionals to eliminate manual data entry, but it also increases their ability to centralize various customer databases and thus record the entire customer life cycle – whether it was via email, chat, phone calls, chatbots, etc. Moreover, it enables managers to make better predictions based on hard data and to minimize subjectivism (Agrawal et al., 2019). CallMiner Eureka, for example, uses AI and machine language to capture, transcribe, and extract content from customer interactions (phone calls, chat, email, Twitter). Transcripts are tagged according to key words and a rich categorization scheme. When this data is automatically entered into CRM, it can reveal key insights, including disclaimers, specific data about competitors, and ideal use cases. Sellers can search the transcription metadata for key words, phrases, and even acoustics, such as increased voice intonation, which can signal excitement and increased interest. In the arrangement of thematic groups and frequency maps, sellers are better prepared than before to detect significant trends among customers (Fatemi, 2019). Moreover, AI now has the advanced ability to effectively convert speech (spoken by clients) into text and vice versa, with accurate results (Wang et al., 2020). Many customer product inquiries are related to product specification issues. If AI is involved in handling all these questions, it is possible to significantly relieve employees and satisfy customers, who quickly receive accurate information. When combined with consultancy based on customer reviews, such sales information systems can significantly entice customers and increase sales.

Today, many AI systems allow natural language learning and voice input, such as Siri or Alexa. For example, thanks to AI, the CRM system can respond to customer inquiries, solve their problems, and even identify new opportunities for the sales team. AI can identify high-quality leads, which can give sales teams a competitive advantage in winning new jobs. Practical information about sales is delivered by the system on a large scale, sometimes counted in millions of records of potential customers. Moreover, AI can detect anomalies, duplicates, and other errors among the entered data that put customer relationships at risk. By integrating with external databases, AI can also interpolate missing records and update records in real time as contacts and other data change. Based on these analyses, AI makes predictions and recommendations for sellers in terms of a specific customer. The right data and timing mean a lot in sales. Without AI and machine learning, the company would not be able to use the entire, currently very large, data source to identify new customers and undertake mass communication with them using artificial bots or by generating recommendations for sellers. In a traditional system, customer acquisition would not be possible with these volumes of customers' data.

In addition, AI allows a company to perform sentiment analysis in real time during a conversation with the client (Smith, 2019). For example, Cogito provides phone call analytics that help salespeople understand and best respond to customer emotional states. The color-coded gauge serves as an indicator of the success of a given conversation. If the customer or salesperson reacts too sharply, the color changes from green to yellow or red. Cogito evaluates several key aspects of each conversation, including energy, interruptions, empathy, participation, tone, and pace. Analytics as sophisticated as this enable salespeople to proactively redirect calls (Fatemi, 2019). The possibilities of using these systems go far beyond the appropriate response to the customer's mood during a telephone conversation. They can provide data to train salespeople and identify best practices when dealing with different types of customer sentiment and in various situations. When all this historical call data is integrated with CRM systems, the benefits are far-reaching. At a minimum, salespeople and managers can use the results for training purposes to improve conversations and relationships with customers.

High Level of Personalization on Multiple Devices

Personalization is no longer anything new in e-commerce. However, with the increasing advances in AI, new deep levels of customization began to seep into the rapidly evolving world of e-commerce. Currently, AI-driven personalization adopts a multi-channel approach. Whether through a mobile app, website, or email campaign, the AI engine constantly monitors all devices and channels to create a universal customer profile. This unified customer profile enables e-commerce sellers to provide seamless customer experience across all platforms (Kumar et al., 2019). When entering a website multiple times to browse for a tablet case, for example, a consumer might receive a push notification on his or her mobile phone, informing the consumer about available promotions on this item. By making a purchase directly on the phone, the customer can save time and effort.

Moreover, thanks to AI's understanding of natural speech, the system can successfully personalize recommendations for consumers seeking vacation spots, hotels, cruises, and tours. Personalizing the results means that much of the overwhelming information that frequently appears to travelers is filtered out. As a result, consumers can make decisions faster and with more confidence. The system will search the results, taking into account the preferences of the seeker, who can express them in everyday language, e.g. "where can I surf during my honeymoon?" AI systems can then deliver personalized recommendations of points of interest and local insights, achieving hit levels never seen before (Wayblazer, 2020). The new dimension of personalization may also result from greater integration of sales systems with data from mobile devices. Some mobile technologies can register what products a user is browsing, determine the user's taste, and immediately recommend personalized products. Moreover, if a business integrates the customer's physical data from smartphones, such as vital statistics, measurements and pupil dilation factor, and frequency of visits to certain websites, then the level of personalization to which recommendations can be adapted can be surprising. Forward-thinking e-commerce retailers will certainly want to make greater use of data on preferences and health from devices such as smartphones or smartwatches, like the Apple Watch – the latest version even measures blood oxygen saturation.

Provide a Personal Relationship with Chatbots

High-tech trading is now focused on building individual experiences, not mass markets. Many modern e-commerce marketers are already getting more sophisticated with their AI's ability to attract attention, and one of the approaches being widely developed is known as "conversational trading". In the world of e-commerce, it is a combination of visual, vocal, written, and predictive capabilities. Consumer needs are rapidly evolving to the point where retailers struggle to keep up. If brands want to survive, they should make the use of chatbots one of their developmental priorities; AI will conduct an individual conversation with thousands of potential customers in a tireless, impeccable, and effective manner (Adam et al., 2020). Thanks to this, sales opportunities and the level of customer visits on virtually every platform that the store uses will significantly increase. Moreover, chatbots as a tool can be more effective than humans and can also help save up to 30% in customer support services (Techlabs, 2017).

Chatbots are a valuable customer service solution for e-commerce sellers (Forbes, 2018), more than alternatives such as contact forms, phone calls, and email. However, online, face-to-face contact is a medium that remains available when the customer needs it. Moreover, it remains the fastest and, in many cases, the most convenient way of getting answers to visitors (Asling, 2020). Nevertheless, 63% of customers prefer messaging an online bot to communicate with a business or brand (Gigante, 2019). This statistic means that the customs are changing, and face-to-face interaction in some situations is becoming obsolete. In practice, chatbots can actively take over operational and marketing sales tasks (Marr, 2018). They can automate ordering processes and are an effective and inexpensive way to service your customers. Customer support via social media is starting to become a requirement rather than an option. Today, most customers are permanently logged into one or more platforms, such as Facebook. Taking advantage of this fact, you can integrate the chatbot with the shopping cart of an online store and use the messaging function, such as Messenger, to confirm orders or provide immediate online support (Asling, 2020). It is also possible to integrate the chatbot system with the shopping cart, which can work with all stores based on the platform. The more shopping carts a company chatbot supports, the more potential customers it can have. Additionally, certain systems require shopping cart integration to obtain information such as product details, quantities, and shipping terms that chatbots can use to provide accurate answers to customers. The experience of companies implementing chatbots shows that their use results in a significant increase in sales, in particular through chatbot assistance throughout the entire sales process. Additionally, chatbots reduce the number of so-called abandoned shopping carts in online stores (Digiteum, 2019).

Implementation of Virtual Assistants

A virtual assistant, like Amazon's Alexa, can be an important support for commerce. Integrating such an assistant into your own products may soon become a necessary condition for selling. For example, the Amazon Echo product allows you to interact with the computer in a way that has never been seen before, e.g. by obtaining information about the weather, getting the latest news, and even joking with Alexa. In terms of more practical uses, customers can order food through the Amazon Echo. The IoT makes sure that Alexa knows about it and waits for confirmation of the purchase need or does it automatically. Alexa as a virtual assistant can order Uber, order catering, offer entertainment for the weekend, and order tickets to the cinema, the theater, or a match (Ordoñez, 2018). Alexa personalizes the choices, but there is room for suggestions – in addition to those resulting from personalization. Using a virtual assistant, a company has a chance to be in the sales channel, which may turn out to be very important in the near future. It is like buying or renting premises in a newly built shopping center; we are not sure yet how many customers it will attract, but we suppose very many.

Virtual assistants, like Amazon's Alexa, Apple's Siri, Microsoft's Cortana, or Google's Assistant, influence the way customers make purchases and provide e-commerce sellers with a creative opportunity to use them. For these reasons, AI in this version can again give the company a competitive advantage. An example of a company that has integrated Alexa (Amazon) and Waze (Google) is Ford (O'Kane, 2018). Thanks to this, the driver and passengers can use their experiences with the virtual assistant in the car. Another example is the LG company, which has integrated the virtual assistant of Google and Amazon (LG, 2020) with many manufactured devices (LG ThinQ), such as washing machines, refrigerators, TVs, dryers, dishwashers, etc. This allows the customer to have full information about the device and its work progress (e.g. laundry status, prepared ice cubes), as well as information that e.g. consumables like filters should be replaced. For instance, when food runs out, a refrigerator with an incorporated virtual assistant can make purchases automatically; the user can set the purchasing rules in advance. Virtual assistants take customer purchases and company sales to another level.

Improve Customer Recommendations

AI uses pop-ups, texts, and emails to provide product recommendations to buyers, and tracks user searches to understand consumer behavior. Search engines and other social media platforms also display images and advertisements for products related to the user's interests, which are also tracked by AI in e-commerce. For example, Amazon uses data from customers' previous purchases to recommend new products. Netflix, on the other hand, uses consumers' view histories in order to recommend various movies and series. High-quality recommendations were always important for B2C websites or e-shops (Nilashi et al., 2016) Therefore, AI can offer appropriate, individualized, and helpful recommendations for different types of consumers. In this way, it can direct personalized purchase recommendations to the consumer. AI does not guess; rather, it uses a variety of data like products the customer recommended on social media, location, dwell time, or customer segments/buyer personas. The main source of data in e-commerce is the website of the store. This applies to both anonymous and identified (logged in) clients. By monitoring customer behavior, AI can analyze the most popular purchasing paths and divide them by interests. The system knows what is being added to the cart, even if the transactions have not been completed (Sroczyński, 2019). This is important for what will be presented to customers in recommendations and what AI can do to increase customer purchases. Out of these data sources, transaction data plays a crucial role in forming recommendations. AI collects all information about products (prices, categories, variants) and customer purchases (accompanying products, complementary products, frequency of purchases, etc.), and imports historical transaction data into a recommendation system, which, when integrated with current data, forms the basis for various types of recommendations and helps distinguish the products that sell best. Accurate recommendations can effectively enhance the customer's trust, satisfaction, and loyalty in e-commerce (Nilashi et al., 2016; Yoon et al., 2013).

Highly personalized retail recommendations are based on big data. As more data comes in, AI becomes increasingly capable of generating the most relevant recommendations for customers (Lopukhina, 2020). Thanks to the knowledge about the user, AI can formulate various recommendations and express them in different ways (Sroczyński, 2019). The most common ways are personalized recommendations. Matching the displayed products to the interests of the user helps to attract attention and encourage further purchases. Personalized recommendations are dynamically adjusted to the amount of information businesses have about the user. Another type of recommendation is based on similar products in terms of the purpose of use, technical or visually similar data, and complementary products (Sroczyński, 2019). Recommendations expressed by AI can be found in the product finder. The in-store search engine is an important sales tool, especially if the assortment is broad. When AI is applied to search engines on store websites, typing in popular product names yields personalized search results, which often translates into higher sales. Moreover, the AI recommendation system can also connect with advertising systems and initiate automated retargeting advertisement campaigns for customers who acquired particular products and might therefore be interested in buying similar items (Lopukhina, 2020).

In almost every case above, a search engine that incorporates AI has a role to play on a website before and after checkout, and even during the checkout process (Lopukhina, 2020). AI-generated recommendations display products most suited to individual consumers' tastes and preferences, adjusting them in the real time, starting from the moment the customer starts typing subsequent letters into the browser (Sroczyński, 2019). This provides a win-win situation because there is a high probability that the customer will find the searched item, which also increases the chance that the store will record additional sales. Generally, AI recommendation systems create higher sales rates from an average order value; they positively influence the profits and increase customer satisfaction at the same time.

Use of Intelligent Agents

New intelligent agent negotiation systems have become a popular tool used in e-commerce as a result of the development of AI. An intelligent agent is a software unit that performs some set of operations on behalf of a user or other program with a certain degree of independence or autonomy (Pivk & Gams, 2000). Intelligent agents will search a myriad of information on the Internet and select specific information of interest to the user. Agents speed up the process of finding items on the Internet and leave users more time for other tasks. Many buyers outsource the search to their agents, so online stores wishing to increase profits should equip themselves with their own agents that can handle the buying tasks for the benefit of the store. Intelligent agents can be a significant support for online sales. An automated agent has three main functions: matching buyers and sellers, facilitating transactions, and providing institutional infrastructure. Agents are completely automated and have full control of their activities. They have their own language of communication and not only react to the environment, but are also able to use their initiative, for example, to generate their own goals (Asling, 2020).

Use of AI to Manage Your Inventory

AI can make a significant contribution to the financial success of a business through intelligent inventory management. The resource planning agent, such as the Divo system, performs several functions that significantly accelerate the market reaction. First, it constantly monitors key data and, based on it, suggests changes to the decision maker. For example, when selling beach flip-flops, AI monitors temperature levels and weather data, as well as the frequency of ferry trips along the coast. As temperatures in a region increase, weather conditions improve, and/or the frequency of ferry trips increases, the demand for beach sandals can increase rapidly. The system then contacts a responsible person in the firm and presents data on increased demand and the number of flip-flops remaining in stores. At the same time, it analyzes the delivery route and storms occurring in this area, indicating, for example, the need to order transport immediately if the company wants to avoid the lack of salable goods. Second, the system can show the assortment categories with the highest sales in the period of time selected by the manager, e.g. last week. Third, AI analyzes internal data on an ongoing basis and, for example, when a company has a network of 100 stores, it can reveal that five stores provide 45% of the business's turnover, drawing the manager's attention to these locations. The analysis may contribute to a greater use of profitable locations and an additional increase in turnover. It may also assist in finding what makes stores profitable and perhaps increase the profitability of the other stores in the network. The potential benefits may exceed expectations, and the already mentioned examples indicate a significant potential usefulness of AI in assortment management.

Optimizing the product range for the next season is a difficult task that takes a lot of time for managers. Creating a sales plan for the next season determines the purchasing plan. Very often, in the traditional model, it is done based on a simple extrapolation of historical data. In practice, this is a highly inaccurate approach that leaves space for many surprises and a lot of stress. AI, on the other hand, approaches the forecast methodically. It can show managers the current demand determinants, correlated with current fashion trend data, forecast weather, or even competitors' sales data, allowing company leadership to better manage the uncertainty and complexity of the assortment, providing data in real time, and making predictions that take into account a much larger number of criteria than company analysts used in the past. At the same time, the system presents current data on stocks and sales levels, indicating the reasons for a bull market or bear market. AI also allows the manager to approximate customer data, their profiles, demand constraints, etc. In short, AI manages the company's assortment and sales faster and more successfully than in the traditional model. It shows the consequences of decisions made in real time, allowing for quick adjustments or optimization. In addition, AI provides detailed monitoring and insight into the assortment of competitors, which may provide additional information that is important from the sales point of view.

The competitive advantage resulting from the use of AI for assortment management can significantly contribute to the sales success of both traditional and online stores. Taking into account the broad context affecting sales in real time allows an inventory manager to make better decisions, and the ongoing analysis allows for a quick response that cannot be underestimated, and can guide a firm to take advantage of an opportunity or avoid a threat.

The Problem of Fake Product Reviews

Research confirms a positive correlation between reading positive online reviews and purchasing decisions (Chen et al., 2004; Floyd et al., 2014; Helversen et al., 2018). False reviews are quite important in the product review system, and they often discourage customers from buying (Purnawirawan et al., 2015). Recent research provides data that 52% of online consumers use the Internet to search for products, and 24% do so before a purchase decision (Ha et al., 2015). As a result, reviews play a substantial role in how consumers decide to spend their money. Recognizing fake reviews is crucial in fighting this unethical practice, and with help of AI, this can be done on a mass scale (Berthon et al., 2018; Horne & Adali, 2017; Paschen, 2019). AI uses language processing methods to detect unusual text patterns, writing styles, and formatting. Self-learning systems are getting smarter thanks to more data, so, ironically, the more fake reviews the better. To find a fake review, AI compares each product's reviews against industry standards and competitors. If an anomaly is detected, then AI ignores suspicious reviews when calculating the sentiment analysis (Elad, 2019).

Therefore, machines that understand the dual sentiment based on a specific product and branch patterns are more accurate than verifiers (Biondi et al., 2017) because people are responsible for about 90% of sentiment analysis errors (Elad, 2019). Technically, it is very difficult to apply human-trained machine learning to help AI to understand dual sentiment because things like sarcasm are complicated in code. However, self-learning systems search through all products and industry categories to identify general feelings and tone, and to better understand instances of double sentiment such as sarcasm in reviews (Elad, 2019). These systems are becoming more and more difficult to cheat and can really help to prevent the fake reviews from appearing in online stores. Of course, the question arises to what extent it will be possible to manipulate reviews thanks to AI, but it is expected that sooner or later the disproportion between the described product and the actual product will see the light of day one way or another.

Moreover, the same technology allows for the detection of counterfeit products, which are a problem for producers and also for trade. For example, 3PM Marketplace Solutions adds a layer of protection for brands by applying machine learning algorithms that detect counterfeit products and help companies understand how consumers discover their products. AI then uses data from multiple online markets and analyzes it to determine which products are actually counterfeit, a fascinating and effective way to use technology to solve the painful problem of counterfeit products.

Conclusions

As this chapter shows, the methods of using AI in e-commerce presented above represent a real revolution. On one hand, firms who leverage these solutions can become leaders in their industry. On the other hand, firms that are slow to implement these innovations will sooner or later become marginalized. The described applications of AI are rarely introduced simultaneously, but nevertheless the presence of each of them creates synergy that translates into sales results. The mere fact that AI can search through millions of potential sales leads, select the most promising accounts, contact them, and finally win new customers in a number much bigger than salespeople would achieve in the traditional way completely changes the rules of the game. The new sales and marketing methods discussed in this section do not exhaust the topic, but they are a thorough collection of the most important changes that have been developed and implemented over the past decade. Some of them, such as virtual assistants, are still new to customers. All the methods described are constantly evolving and improving.

The discussed innovations have significant practical implications. A traditional online store or website through which sales take place cannot and will not be able to compete with a website or online store powered by the above-mentioned AI tools. The difference is visible in many dimensions like establishing contact, evoking interest in the product, bringing the customer to the store, using customer information to periodically direct personalized offers, or collecting customer information to modify the store's offer, for example, by increasing the number of product variants. These are, of course, only selected implications, and there are many more of them, as shown in the chapter's contents.

An interesting question is the AI's future in e-commerce in the 2030 perspective. There will certainly be further digitization of businesses, and presumably most of them will already have a fully digital operating model. Moreover, it can be assumed that human interaction will be rare in online stores, and 95–98% of shopping interactions will take place with bots that perfectly imitate human behavior. It is likely that competition without AI tools will be virtually impossible for traditional online stores. At the same time, from the customer's point of view, shopping will be a great pleasure thanks to a high degree of personalization. People will also spend more on shopping than they do now, due to the fact that systems suggesting complementary products matching customers' preferences will work really perfectly. Moreover, in 2030, in all likelihood, online stores will dominate traditional commerce. This is conjecture, of course, but it could come true even before 2030.

Future research should demonstrate the effectiveness of the various methods described in this chapter with respect to the traditional methods as well as other modern methods. In addition, it would be worth analyzing the extent to which, in order to maximize sales efficiency, a firm should convert the operating model into a digital one depending on the size of its store or the level of online sales.

References

Adam M., Wessel M., & Benlian A. (2020). AI-based chatbots in customer service and their effects on user compliance. *Electronic Markets*, *31*, 427–445. https://doi.org/10.1007/s12525-020-00414-7.

Agrawal, A., Gans, J., & Goldfarb, A. (2019). Economic policy for artificial intelligence. *Innovation Policy and the Economy*, *19*(1), 139–159.

Arthur, R. (2016, June 15). Future of retail: Artificial intelligence and virtual reality have big roles to play. *Forbes*.

Asling, D. (2020). 19 powerful ways to use artificial intelligence in eCommerce. https://www.linnworks.com/blog/artificial-intelligence-in-ecommerce.

Berthon, P., Treen, E., & Leyland, P. (2018). How truthiness, fake news and post-fact endanger brands and what to do about it. *GfK Marketing Intelligence Review*, *10*(1), 18–23, doi: 10.2478/gfkmir-2018-0003.

Biondi, G., Franzoni, V., Poggioni, V.(2017). A deep learning semantic approach to emotion recognition using the IBM Watson Bluemix alchemy language. In O. Gervasi (Ed.), *Lecture notes in computer science, computational science and its applications* – ICCSA 2017, 10406 (pp. 718–729). Springer.

Chen, P. Y., Wu, S. Y., & Yoon, J. (2004). The impact of online recommendations and consumer feedback on sales. ICIS 2004 Proceedings, 58.

Davar, N. (2018, May-June). Marketing in the age of Alexa. *Harvard Business Review*.

Davis, B. (2016, April 19). 15 examples of artificial intelligence in marketing. *Econsultancy*. https://econsultancy.com/blog/67745-15-examples-of-artificial-intelligence-in-marketing/.

Digiteum. (2019). Chatbots and AI in the E-commerce industry, digiteum.com. https://www.digiteum.com/artificial-intelligence-chatbot-e-commerce/.

Elad, N. (2019). How AI beats fake reviews. *Mycustomer*. https://www.mycustomer.com/community/blogs/niveladrevuze/how-ai-beats-fake-reviews.

Fader, P. (2012). *Customer centricity: Focus on the right customers for strategic advantage*. Wharton Digital Press.

Faggella, D. (2018, October 29). Artificial intelligence in retail. *Tech Emergence*. https://www.techemergence.com/artificial-intelligence-retail, accessed December 2020.

Fatemi, F. (2019). 5 ways artificial intelligence is transforming CRMs. *Forbes*. https://www.forbes.com/sites/falonfatemi/2019/08/10/5-ways-artificial-intelligence-is-transforming-crms/?sh=6488aeb25354, accessed 10 January 2021.

Floyd, K., Freling, R., Alhoqail, S., Cho, H. Y., & Freling, T. (2014). How online product reviews affect retail sales: A meta-analysis. *Journal of Retailing*, *90*(2), 217–232.

Gehrmann, S., Strobelt H., & Rush A. M. (2019). GLTR: Statistical detection and visualization of generated text, *arXiv* preprint arXiv:1906.04043, arxiv.org, https://arxiv.org/pdf/1906.04043.pdf.

Gigante M., (2019). 30+ Artificial intelligence statistics for 2019. https://learn.g2.com/artificial-intelligence-statistics.

Griffith, E. (2018). Pinterest is a Unicorn. It just doesn't act like one. *New York Times*. https://www.nytimes.com/2018/09/09/technology/pinterest-growth.html

Gupta, S., Leszkiewicz, A., Kumar, V., Bijmolt, T., & Potapov, D. (2020). Digital analytics: Modeling for insights and new methods. *Journal of Interactive Marketing*, 51, 26–43.

Ha, S. H., Yong Bae, S., & Son, L. K. (2015). Impact of online consumer reviews on product sales: Quantitative analysis of the source effect. *Applied Mathematics*, 9(2L), 373–387.

Harris, R. (2016, January 12). The North Face brings AI to Ecommerce, marketing mag. http://marketingmag.ca/brands/the-north-face-brings-ai-to-ecommerce-165328, accessed April 2021.

Helversen B., Abramczuk K., Kopeć W., & Nielek, R. (2018). Influence of consumer reviews on online purchasing decisions in older and younger adults. *Decision Support Systems*, *113*, 1–10.

Homburg, C., Droll, M., & Totzek, D. (2008). Customer prioritization: Does it pay off, and how should it be implemented? *Journal of Marketing*, *72*(*5*), 110–130.

Horne, B.D., & Adali, S. (2017). This just in: Fake news packs a lot in title, uses simpler, repetitive content in text body, more similar to satire than real news. *Published at the 2nd international workshop on news and public opinion at ICWSM*. https://arxiv.org/abs/1703.09398.

Iansiti M., & Lakhami, K. R. (2020). *Competing in the age of AI: Strategy and leadership when algorithms and networks run the world*. HBR Press.

Jehangir M., Dominic, P. D. D., Downe, A. G., & Naseebullah (2011). Technology resources and e-commerce impact on business performance. In V. Snasel, J. Platos, & E. El-Qawasmeh (Eds.), *Digital information processing and communications*. ICDIPC 2011. Communications in Computer and Information Science. (189). Springer. https://doi.org/10.1007/978-3-642-22410-2_38.

Kietzmann, J., Paschen, J., & Treen, E. (2018). Artificial intelligence in advertising. how marketers can leverage artificial intelligence along the consumer journey. *Journal of Advertising Research*, *58*(3), 263–267. https://doi.org/10.2501/JAR-2018-035.

Kimura, R., Reeves, M., & Whitaker, K. (2019). The New Logic of Competition, Boston Consulting Group . https://www.bcg.com/publications/2019/new-logic-of-competition.

Kohl, R. (2016, February 18). 2 ways artificial intelligence is changing customers engagement. *The Future Customer Engagement and Commerce*. https://www.the-future-of-commerce.com/2016/02/18/commerce-artificial-intelligence/.

Kumar, V., Bharath, R., & Venkatesan, R. (2019). Understanding the role of artificial intelligence in personalized engagement marketing. *California*

Management Review, *61*(4), 135–155. https://doi.org/10.1177/000812561 9859317.

Lassinantti, J., Bergvall-Kareborn, B., & Stahlbreost, A. (2014). Shaping local open data initiatives: Politics and implications. *Journal of Theoretical and Applied Electronic Commerce Research*, *9*(2), 17–33.

Lopukhina, D. (2020). AI-based product recommendations: How to reach today's customer. *Business 2 Community*. https://www.business2community.com/ecommerce/ai-based-product-recommendations-how-to-reach-todays-customer-02358602.

Mah, P. (2016, November 4). The state of chatbots in marketing. *Enterprise Innovation*.

Marr, B. (2018). How artificial intelligence is making chatbots better for businesses. *Forbes*. https://www.forbes.com/sites/bernardmarr/2018/05/18/how-artificial-intelligence-is-making-chatbots-better-for-businesses/?sh=eaaa6a14e724.

Marshall, M. (2006, March 4). The North Face to launch insanely smart Watson-powered mobile shopping app next month. VentureBeat. https://venturebeat.com/2 016/03/04/the-north-face-to-laun ch-insanely-smart-watson-powered-shopping-app-next-month.

Martínez, A., Schmuck, C., Pereverzyev Jr, S., Pirker, C., & Haltmeier, M. (2018). A machine learning framework for customer purchase prediction in the non-contractual setting. *European Journal of Operational Research*, *281*(3), 588–596.

Munn, Z., Peters, M. D. J., Stern, C. (2018). Systematic review or scoping review? Guidance for authors when choosing between a systematic or scoping review approach. *BMC Medical Research Methodology*, *18*, 143. https://doi.org/10.1186/s12874-018-0611-x.

Nadimpalli, M. (2017). Artificial intelligence – Consumers and industry impact. *International Journal of Economic Management Science*, 6, 429. https://doi.org/10.4172/2162-6359.1000429.

Nilashi, M., Jannach, D., bin Ibrahim, O., Esfahani, M. D., & Ahmadi, H. (2016). Recommendation quality, transparency, and website quality for trust-building in recommendation agents. *Electronic Commerce Research and Applications*, *19*, 70–84.

Nirale, S. (2018, June 18). The next-gen experience: How emerging technology is changing customer service. *Futurescot*. https://futurescot.com/the-next-gen-experience-how-emerging-technology-is-changing-customer-service/.

Novet, J. (2017). Pinterest improves visual search in its Chrome extension. https://venturebeat.com/2017/04/21/pinterest-improves-visual-search-in-its-chrome-extension/.

O'Kane, S. (2018). Alexa and Waze add depth to Ford's improving SYNC infotainment system. *The Verge*. https://www.theverge.com/2018/1/28/1693273 8/alexa-waze-ford-sync-ecosport-suv-hands-on.

Ordoñez, L. (2018). Virtual assistants: Are they the future of eCommerce? Oleoshop Blog. https://www.oleoshop.com/en/blog/virtual-assistants-are-they-the-future-of-ecommerce.

Paschen, J. (2019). Investigating the emotional appeal of fake news using artificial intelligence and human contributions. *Journal of Product & Brand Management*, *29*(1), 223–233, doi: 10.1108/jpbm-12-2018-2179.

Pinterest Labs. (2018). The latest in AI & machine learning at Pinterest, *labs.pinterest.com*. https://labs.pinterest.com/projects/.

Pivk, A., & Gams, M. (2000). Intelligent agents in E-commerce. *Electrotechnical Review, Ljubljana, Slovenija*, 1–16.

Purnawirawan, N., Eisend, M., De Pelsmacker, P., & Dens, N. (2015). A meta-analytic investigation of the role of valence in online reviews. *Journal of Interactive Marketing*, *31*, 17–27.

Rossi, B. (2016, July 18). 3 ways artificial intelligence is transforming e-commerce. *Information Age*. https://www.information-age.com/3-ways-artificial-intelligence-transforming-e-commerce-123461702/.

Russell, K. (2014, February 4). IBM is using Watson to psychoanalyze people from their tweets. *Business Insider India*. https://www.businessinsider.in/ibms-is-using-watson-to-psychoanalyze-people-from-their-tweets/articleshow/29878188.cms.

Rust, R. T., & Huang, M. H. (2014). The service revolution and the transformation of marketing science. *Marketing Science*, *33*(2), 206–221.

Schneider, C. (2017, October 16). 10 reasons why AI-powered, automated customer service is the future. *Watson Blog*. https://www.ibm.com/blogs/watson/2017/10/10-reasons-ai-powered-automated-customer-service-future/.

Shadbolt, N., O'Hara, K., Berners-Lee, T., Gibbins, N., Glaser, H., Hall, W., & Schraefel, M. (2012). Linked open government data: Lessons from data.gov.UK. *IEEE Intelligent Systems*, *27*(3), 16–24.

Silva, M. (2019). The relationship between organizational commitment, knowledge transfer and knowledge management maturity. *Journal of Knowledge Management*, *23*(3), 489–507.

Smith, C. (2019). An employee's best friend? How AI can boost employee engagement and performance. *Strategic HR Review*, *18*(1), 17–20. https://doi.org/10.1108/SHR-11-2018-0092.

Sroczyński, O. (2019, April 30). Jak sztuczna inteligencja zwiększa konwersję w sklepie internetowym. *Magazyn E-commerce*, 5. https://www.magazyn-ecommerce.pl/artykul/jak-sztuczna-inteligencja-zwieksza-konwersje-w-sklepie-internetowym.

Statista. (2021). Retail e-commerce sales worldwide from 2014 to 2024, statista.com. https://www.statista.com/statistics/379046/worldwide-retail-e-commerce-sales/.

Syam, N., & Sharma, A. (2018). Waiting for a sales renaissance in the fourth industrial revolution: Machine learning and artificial intelligence in sales research and practice. *Industrial Marketing Management*, *69*, 135–146. https://doi.org/10.1016/j.indmarman.2017.12.019.

Techlabs, M. (2017). Can chatbots help reduce customer service costs by 30%? How chatbots may offer automation of customer service / sales positions. *Chatbots Magazine*. https://chatbotsmagazine.com/how-with-the-help-of-chatbots-customer-service-costs-could-be-reduced-up-to-30-b9266a369945.

Turban, E., Outland, J., King, D., & Lee, J. K. (2018). *Electronic commerce*. Springer Texts in Business and Economics. 249–283. https://doi.org/10.1007/978-3-319-58715-8_7.

Venkatesan, R., & Lecinski, J. (2021). *The AI marketing canvas: A five stage roadmap to implementing for customer*. Stanford University Press.

Verhoef, P. C., & Donkers, B. (2005). The effect of acquisition channels on customer loyalty and cross-buying. *Journal of Interactive Marketing*, *19*(2), 31–43.

Wang, S., Kang, B., Ma, J., Zeng, X., Xiao, M., Guo, J., Cai, M., Yang, J., Li, Y., Meng, X., & Xu, B. (2020). A deep learning algorithm using CT images to screen for corona virus disease (Covid-19). *medrxiv*. https://doi.org/10.1101/2020.02.14.20023028, https://www.medrxiv.org/content/10.1101/2020.02.14.20023028v5.full.pdf.

Wayblazer. (2020). IBM case study. https://www.ibm.com/case-studies/g754268s52509l83.

Wilson, M. (2018, March). The world's most innovative companies. *fastcompany.com*. https://www.fastcompany.com/company/pinterest.

Womack, B. (2016, September 18). Salesforce Unveils Artificial Intelligence 'Einstein' Service. *Bloomberg News*. https://www.bloomberg.com/news/articles/2016-09-18/salesforce-unveils-artificial-intelligence-einstein-service.

Yoon, V. Y., Hostler, R. E., Guo, Z., & Guimaraes, T. (2013). Assessing the moderating effect of consumer product knowledge and online shopping experience on using recommendation agents for customer loyalty. *Decision Support Systems*, *55*(4), 883–893.

Zeithaml, V. A., Rust, R. T., & Lemon, K. N. (2001). The customer pyramid: Creating and serving profitable customers. *California Management Review*, *43*(4), 118–142.

2 Towards Sustainable Markets and Business Models – New Trends in Building Competitive Position

Magdalena Śliwińska

Introduction

In recent years, we have witnessed growing global challenges of an economic, social, and environmental nature. More than 10% of the world's population is affected by hunger (WHO, 2019), income inequalities constitute a major problem (Cingano, 2014; The International Fair Trade Charter, 2018), and degradation of the natural environment is progressing at an alarming rate, causing not only a decline in natural resources that are crucial for the development of industry, but above all threatening the future of humanity by depleting resources essential for life: air and water, as well as fauna and flora. The negative consequences for the climate are well known. Highly developed countries use resources as if they had several planets at their disposal, which means that we live at the cost of future generations. The current crisis resulting from the coronavirus pandemic only confirms the weaknesses in the existing system that led to the world's current state, showing them as if through a magnifying glass.

Therefore, further economic development can undoubtedly only take place in a sustainable manner, i.e. in such a way that it first takes into account the well-being of people and the environment. This growing awareness of the need for sustainable development is evidenced by the UN Sustainable Development Goals (SDGs) and the policies of an increasing number of countries working towards implementation of these goals, as well as the emergence and growth of sustainable markets thanks to strong social and business interests. It appears that global challenges are so serious that there is no longer any choice for the economy but to transform towards a "sustainable market economy". This is also confirmed by the academic discussion around these issues, stressing the need for "inclusive globalization" (Gorynia, 2019), or finding the appropriate relationship between the state and the market (Ratajczak, 2017), reform of capitalism, and even change of the paradigm of economics (Fiedor et al., 2016; Mączyńska, 2011; Porter & Kramer, 2011).

This raises several questions. What do global challenges and the need for sustainability mean for businesses? How do companies adapt to the

DOI: 10.4324/9781003204343-2

new situation? How can they improve their competitiveness in a sustainable way or create new sustainable business models? According to Aras (2015, p. 1) "today sustainability risks and opportunities have become a global imperative and a megatrend for business". Indeed, companies must reckon with the expectations of increasingly aware consumers who wish to take some responsibility for global problems. An increasing number of consumers expect pro-environmental and pro-social behavior from a company. Therefore, companies are beginning to compete with each other in this field, too. Increasingly, they not only want to demonstrate that they are socially and environmentally responsible, but they are consciously beginning to raise the bar for the social and environmental goals they pursue in an effort to become the "sustainable leader".

On the other hand, companies must take into account the regulatory requirements of countries and international organizations, which are increasingly incorporating various types of obligations related to sustainable development into the legal framework of market operations. For example, the European Union intends to achieve a climate neutral economy by 2050 and has announced the 7th environmental action program to guide European policies for innovation, circular economy, and sustainability (ec.europa.eu). This means that by 2050, all companies will have to comply with new rules that constitute on the one hand new requirements to meet, but on the other hand an opportunity to enter new areas of business. The European Commission is also considering ways in which it will integrate human rights due diligence (HRDD) into EU law following the idea of the Modern Slavery Act 2015 introduced in the UK (Modern Slavery Act, 2015). Moreover, it is becoming increasingly clear to all that the implementation of the SDGs is not possible without the active participation of society and business. Taking responsibility for global problems has become increasingly important not only to nation states and international organizations, but also to the market. Therefore, the development of sustainable markets will likely be supported in various ways by governments, which are not able to solve all environmental, social, and economic problems on their own. This is important for businesses insofar as one can expect to see an increasing number of different incentives and programs supporting sustainable entrepreneurship in its broadest sense as well as the development of sustainable markets. Taking advantage of them can be an important part of building a firm's future competitive position. The transformation towards a "sustainable market economy" is a fact, and the stages towards building sustainable markets, as well as the role and challenges for businesses at each stage of this process, are aptly identified by Simons and Nijhof (2021). Therefore, for those companies that are aware of the changes taking place and the challenges involved, being a "sustainable enterprise" may turn out to be not only a necessary condition for survival in the coming years, but an important element in increasing their competitiveness. Those companies that will be the first to notice, understand, and translate these changes into their operations will win their future competitive position.

For the above-mentioned reasons, this chapter will focus on different ways of entering sustainable markets and including sustainability in companies' business model, which has become a new trend in building firms' competitive position. It will first discuss the notions of sustainable markets and sustainable business models, as many companies and consumers as well as researchers may feel confused with different understandings and approaches to these new phenomena. Second, it will outline different ways of entering sustainable markets and analyze their impact on the company's business model. Furthermore, the nature of sustainable certification schemes and different aspects of their development will be discussed using the example of Fair Trade labels. Last, three cases of Fair Trade companies constituting "born sustainable" business models will illustrate how social aspects of sustainable development may account for the basis for building a strong competitive position.

Defining Sustainable Markets

In recent years, sustainable markets have constituted an emerging field of research. However, dynamic development and different approaches to this topic may make businesses, consumers, as well as researchers and politicians confused about how they should be interpreted or what the differences are between such terms like "sustainable", "ethical", or "fair". Therefore, this section will first focus on the distinction among the notions of sustainable, ethical, and fair markets. Second, the determinants of sustainable markets will be identified. Finally, this section will conclude with deriving the definition of sustainable markets from their determinants.

Sustainable, Ethical, or Fair?

In recent years, there has been a growing popularity of the notions of sustainable and ethical markets. These terms are mostly used in the context of sustainable development and responsible consumption. However, they are understood in different ways, and there is a lack of unambiguous definition and classification of these concepts.

Sustainable markets are mostly defined as those that contribute to the protection of the environment and to stronger livelihoods of the poorest participants of the market. This refers to the concept of sustainable development, understood as economic development putting the welfare of people and the planet as a priority, as well as to the implementation of the SDGs. It can be said that sustainable markets aim to reflect externalities, or the true costs of natural resource degradation and environmental pollution, and that they promote just and safe labor practices (Sustainable Markets).

Quite often, the notion of sustainable markets is used interchangeably with the notion of ethical markets, deriving from the concept of ethical consumption. Ethical products are commonly considered to support small producers, protect animals and the environment, and ensure that their production did not use child labor, slave labor, or animal testing.

Moreover, the notion of ethical products is often used interchangeably with the notion of fair products. This may be due to the fact that the latter is the oldest of the mentioned terms and is closely related to the dynamically developing Fair Trade initiative, which for several decades has been aimed at fighting extreme poverty, and which initially included handicraft products of producers from the Global South and was gradually extended to food and other products. The concept of ethical products and markets, in turn, initially began to emerge in the context of improving working conditions in the garment industry, and over time has come to be applied in the context of many other branches. In a narrower sense, it therefore includes goods that have been produced in a socially responsible manner, whereas in a broader sense, it also includes the environmental aspects of sustainability. An example of this broader understanding is the annually issued Ethical Consumer Markets Report. This report covers a wide range of goods and services, including ethical food and drink (e.g. Organic, Fairtrade, Rainforest Alliance of Sustainable Fish), clothing and cosmetics, various products and services that contribute to the creation and operation of green homes (e.g. energy-efficient appliances, boilers or light bulbs, sustainable timber and paper, or green electricity tariffs), or eco-travel and transport (e.g. alternative fuel vehicles or bicycles) and local shopping or charity shops (Ethical Consumer, 2020). It is therefore noteworthy that ethical markets include not only goods whose production methods prioritize human welfare (workers, producers) or environmental protection, but also a wide range of products and services that contribute in various ways to sustainable development and the creation of a green or blue economy.

Therefore, ethical markets can be characterized not only by socially and environmentally responsible modes of production, but also by products and services whose characteristics and applications contribute to sustainable development. This term could also be a description of sustainable markets, which are often associated with fresh, local, and sustainably grown products and no food waste, no GMOs, and no chemicals (https://sustainablemarket.ca/). For the above-mentioned reasons, it seems impossible at present to draw a precise line between ethical and sustainable markets, nor determine which of them is superior. It could be the first one, as it is not only the real global threats, but also certain ethical values that have resulted in the concept of sustainable development. However, it seems that nowadays, most often "sustainable markets" is treated as an umbrella term, which may be the result of the popularization of the concept of sustainable development and the wide recognition of the SDGs.

Determinants of Sustainable Markets

Individual sustainable markets do not cover, however, all aspects of sustainable development. This is well illustrated by one of the more easily identifiable determinants of these markets, sustainable product labels. They inform the customer which elements crucial for sustainable development were ensured during the production or distribution process of a given product. Therefore, sustainable, ethical, or fair markets are usually understood as markets of certified products that meet at least one of the criteria important for sustainable development. This is how sustainable markets are perceived, for example, in the report of Meier et al. (2020), who share the data for 14 of more than 400 sustainability standards. They define these standards as third-party-assessed norms relating to environmental, social, ethical, and food safety issues that are adopted by companies to show how their organizations or products perform in specific areas. These standards may be developed by organizations from the public and private sectors at the local, national, or international level, and they are often perceived – along with private voluntary standards and sustainability metrics and reporting, as well as innovative laws and policies – as examples of market governance mechanisms (MGMs) (IIED). When a product is certified, it becomes possible to identify the aspects of sustainability that it follows. This could be, for example, the protection of forests in the case of Rainforest Alliance (www.rainforest-alliance.org), ecological farming methods in the case of "Euro-leaf" (www.eu-organic-food.eu), or countering extreme poverty and marginalization of small producers and workers in the case of Fair Trade certifications. For example, a product may be considered sustainable because the producer has obtained a certificate informing that the product was made without the degradation of rainforests, or another certificate that proves the climate-neutrality of the production method. The type of product is therefore of great importance, as different characteristics will indicate sustainability in each case. Hence, when we speak of sustainable markets, we generally mean goods that meet some, but not necessarily all, of the sustainability criteria that are often, but unfortunately not always, central to the production process of a given product.

In reality, distinguishing different kinds of sustainable markets according to the criterion of a particular aspect of sustainable development is not easy, as they permeate each other. This happens for two reasons.

First, sustainable certification schemes are trying to cover more and more aspects of sustainability by expanding the scope of certification. Thus, for example, some Fair Trade certifications include ecological aspects to a greater or lesser extent. In turn, certification systems of a more ecological nature are evolving to include social aspects as well (e.g. the previously mentioned Rainforest Alliance). Second, many companies choose to have several certifications at once to show their customers that their product is sustainable in every possible way. Therefore, drawing clear lines between different types of sustainable markets is becoming increasingly difficult. However, this provides another argument that the concept of a market for sustainable products should be treated as superior to other terms such as markets for ethical, organic, or fair products and all their variations.

It is also important to note that product certifications are not the only determinants of sustainable markets. Companies can convince their customers of the sustainable nature of their production and operations by means of private voluntary standards, sustainability metrics, or reports. Local markets are also considered to be sustainable markets, allowing local food producers to sell their products directly to consumers at specially adapted places or online platforms, saving environmental costs of transportation. The distribution channel can therefore also be one of the ways to define sustainable markets. Fair Trade shops or World Shops show that the distribution channel determines whether a specific product may be considered sustainable, in this case a Fair Trade product. Fair Trade companies, such as members of the World Fair Trade Organization (WFTO), ensure that their entire operation and the whole supply chain are subordinated to the overarching social objective of Fair Trade – improving the living and working conditions of marginalized producers. These are companies that were created for this purpose and therefore can be categorized as an illustration of "born sustainable" business models. Thus, in this case, it is primarily the sustainable business model (SBM) of an individual firm, rather than other determinants, that makes the goods it sells sustainable. However, due to the broad framing of the concept of SBMs and the impossibility of establishing clear boundaries for it, as will be discussed in the section on SBMs, only "born sustainables" have been included as a determinant of sustainable markets.

For the above-mentioned reasons, it is not easy to clearly define the concept of sustainable market and to precisely delineate its boundaries. One of the main reasons is that there are different determinants of these types of markets, which are, first, features and uses of products and services; second, economically, socially, and environmentally responsible ways of production and distribution; third, a wide range of sustainable product certification schemes; and fourth, "born sustainable" business models (Figure 2.1). As the figure shows, only the combined application

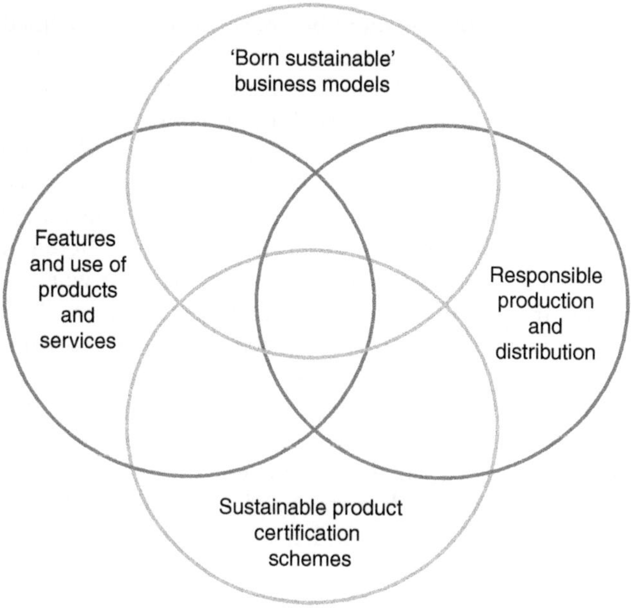

Figure 2.1 Determinants of sustainable markets.

of the various determinants allows boundaries of sustainable markets to be drawn. Products that contribute to the green economy will not necessarily be produced in a responsible manner, or will not necessarily have one of the product sustainability labels. Responsible production, on the other hand, does not necessarily translate into product features and use that contribute to sustainability, as the responsible production process itself contributes to it. The same is true for sustainable product certification systems or "born sustainable" business models, which can translate differently and to varying degrees into commodity characteristics and sustainable ways of producing them.

Figure 2.1 also demonstrates that the determinants can overlap. The features and purposes of the product may be reflected in obtaining one or more sustainable certificates, associated with the adoption of a responsible way of production, or result from the fact that the company constitutes a "born sustainable" business model. Similarly, socially and environmentally responsible production may translate into product features, may be reflected in obtained certificates, or may result from the adopted business model. Most of the time, "born sustainable" business models certify all or part of the products they sell, but sometimes, for a variety of reasons, they do not.

Definition of Sustainable Markets

For the above-mentioned reasons, sustainable markets could be defined as those that include products (or services), which, due to their characteristics or intended use, or socially and environmentally responsible way of production (providing) and/or distribution, contribute to sustainable development. Their external, differentiating features that are easily identifiable by consumers may be sustainable product or service labels or "born sustainable" business models. However, this immediately raises the question of to what extent the goods (and services) offered in these markets should contribute to sustainable development, or whether it is enough that they are merely neutral from that point of view. This involves, among other factors, the aforementioned question of to what extent particular products considered to be sustainable actually are, or whether their qualification as sustainable is indeed determined by key features of the product or its manufacturing process. This refers to situations when a product, e.g. chocolate, obtains one of the sustainable certificates, but the cocoa from which it was produced was collected by children and it is sold in plastic packaging harmful to the environment.

The definition of sustainable markets is based on the determinants identified above and reflects the current perception of sustainable markets, trying to cover their various aspects as broadly as possible. However, sustainable markets are a new dynamic phenomenon that requires further research to detail and clarify their definitions and classification criteria. The above-defined sustainable markets do not fit, for example, into the existing market divisions into industries and products, as they are somehow independent from individual branches. Thus, they constitute a new type of market requiring further research, not matching the existing classification schemes drawn up on the basis of the transaction subject criterion. This new type of market is emerging within already existing markets for individual products and services according to a new criterion – contributing to sustainable development. It may be already expected that future research on sustainable markets will attempt to classify markets according to their degree of sustainability, especially in the face of the fact that they are increasingly perceived as a temporary stage of a systemic transition towards a "sustainable market economy".

Looking for a Sustainable Business Model

Like sustainable markets, sustainable business models (SBMs) also represent an emerging field of research and become an important topic for all kinds of businesses, as "being sustainable" becomes an important element of building firms' competitive position. Therefore, this chapter will focus on different understandings and approaches towards SBMs in the context of the fundamental definitions of business models, which will constitute a basis for further analysis of how sustainable strategies, derived from determinants of sustainable markets, may influence business models and enhance competitiveness.

Defining Business Models

In literature, there are many definitions of business models, which mostly relate to how companies do business; how they make a profit; and how they create, deliver, and capture value (Clauss, 2017; Richardson, 2008; Teece, 2010, p. 172; Zott et al., 2011, p. 1021). Osterwalder and Pigneur (2010, p. 12) define business models as the rationale behind the way an organization creates value and provides and creates returns on that value. Their Business Model Canvas (BCM), a tool for designing, describing, analyzing, and changing business models, constitutes one of the most common business model frameworks. The authors divide business models into nine elements (Osterwalder & Pigneur, 2010, pp. 20–21):

1. Customer segments
2. Value proposition that seeks to solve customer problems and satisfy customer needs
3. Customer communication, distribution, and sales channels
4. Customer relationships
5. Revenue streams resulting from value propositions successfully offered to customers
6. Key resources required to offer and deliver the previously described elements
7. Key activities
8. Key partnerships
9. Cost structure

Johnson et al. (2008, pp. 52–54) perceive a business model differently, identifying only four main elements, "which taken together, create and deliver value". However, they cover most of the elements of the previous framework, approaching them in a different way. In their opinion, the most important element is the customer value proposition (CVP). They understand it as the way to help customers get an important job done. Only once the firm understands how to solve an important problem or fulfill an important need for the target customer, can it make an offer that satisfies the desire or solves a problem and that is defined not only by what is sold but also by how it is sold. The second element defined by the authors is the profit formula, which is "the blueprint that defines how the company creates value for itself while providing value to the customer". It contains four elements: 1. revenue model, which means price multiplied by volume; 2. cost structure, which implies how costs are allocated (includes cost of key assets, direct costs, indirect costs, economies of scale); 3. margin model, which means the contribution needed from each transaction to achieve desired profits; and 4. resource velocity, meaning how quickly resources need to be used to support the target volume. The third crucial element of a business model according to this concept is key resources, like the people, technology, products, equipment, channels, partnerships, alliances, and branding required to deliver the value proposition to the targeted customer (contrary to the generic ones that do not create competitive differentiation). The fourth element constitutes the key processes that allow a firm to deliver value in a way it can successfully repeat and increase in scale. These may include training, development, manufacturing, budgeting, planning, service, and the company's rules, metrics, and norms.

The authors stress that the first two buildings blocks define value, respectively, for the customer and the company, and the third and fourth describe how that value will be delivered to both the customer and the company. They perceive the power of their framework in the complex interdependencies of its parts, as major changes to any of them affect the others and the whole. That is why this approach to the business model may be very useful when thinking about sustainable business models. Such an approach to the problem can make it easier for companies to understand how making certain elements of the business model sustainable and entering sustainable markets in different ways, as defined in the previous section, may enable and accelerate the transformation process of a "conventional" business model towards a sustainable business model. This is particularly important in the face of the lack of an unequivocal definition of a sustainable business model.

Sustainable Business Models as a New Field of Research

Sustainable business models constitute without a doubt a "new and emerging field of research" (Schaltegger et al., 2016, p. 4), especially in the context of their role in the implementation of SDGs and contribution to the transition towards a "sustainable market economy", as well as in the context of different aspects of their functioning and challenges they encounter. The term "sustainability" is, however, "frequently mentioned as central to corporate activity without any attempt to define exactly what sustainable activity entails. This is understandable as the concept is problematic and subject to many varying definitions" (Aras, 2015, p. 1). In combination with the diversity of approaches to the notion of the business model, it is therefore not surprising that there are a variety of understandings of the concept of the sustainable business model, different approaches to it, and different notions used, like e.g. the business model (innovations) for sustainability or sustainable business model innovation (Predenville & Bocken 2017; Schaltegger et al., 2016; van Bommel, 2018).

The forerunners of the term "sustainable business model" are considered to be Stubbs and Cocklin. They defined an "ideal type" of sustainability-oriented business model, which comprised different structural and cultural attributes of an organization. They included developing community spirit, investing in employees' trust and loyalty, and engaging in sustainability assessment and reporting, which related among others to the organization's purpose and goals, its performance measurement approach, the need to consider all stakeholders, how nature should be treated, or whether the organization's leaders drive the necessary cultural and structural changes to implement sustainability (Schaltegger et al., 2016, p. 3). Nowadays, most frequently sustainable business models are perceived as business models relating to sustainable development understood as economic development facing people and the natural environment in the first place. However, they can also be understood differently, as models that are resistant to uncertainty and risk (Brillinger et al., 2020) or models that intend to continue their existence into the future (Aras, 2015, p. 1). Sometimes, the sustainable business model is used to describe companies whose activities do not adversely affect the environment or actively contribute to its protection, but more and more authors recognize that sustainable business models need to be based on all economic, social, and environmental elements (Høgevold et al., 2014; Lüdeke-Freund, 2009; Peter & Smith, 2011; Vos, 2007). Høgevold et al. (2014, pp. 362–364) argue that numerous recent business sustainability frameworks, like the Dow Jones Sustainability Index, FTSE4Good, Global Reporting Initiative (GRI), or Social Accountability International (SAI), address a range of issues and do not cover the same aspects. Although there is no unity to observe among these indicators and reporting systems, it is evident that these frameworks consistently address economic, environmental, and social aspects of business sustainability. Bocken et al. (2014, p. 47) stress, however, that sustainability rankings such as the Guardian Green and Sustainable Business Awards or Forbes top 100 sustainability leaders, which are often based on the GRI or similar sets of indicators, do not specifically look at business model innovation. In their opinion, these rankings tend to focus on relatively narrow ranges of indicators, such as carbon emissions and water use, social indicators such as health and safety, and other employee-related measures, corporate governance ratings, and Corporate Social Responsibility (CSR) contributions. It implies that these indicators and reporting systems do not necessarily cover all relevant aspects related to sustainable development, nor do they identify business models that are sustainable in all their dimensions.

Sustainable Versus Conventional Business Models

There are different types of sustainable business models recognized in the literature, such as social enterprises (Brugmann & Prahalad, 2007; Doherty et al., 2014; Grassl, 2012), product service systems (PSS) (Tukker, 2004), hybrid organizations (Haigh et al., 2015), and closed-loop, circular models or industrial symbiosis (Chertow, 2000; Manninen et al., 2018; Wells & Seitz, 2005). Bocken et al. (2014, p. 48) developed eight sustainable business model archetypes, which link the theoretical concept of business model innovation to the practical transformation mechanisms emerging for delivering industrial sustainability. The authors divided them into three groups: technological archetypes (1. maximizing material and energy efficiency, 2. creating value from waste, and 3. substituting with renewables and natural processes); social archetypes (4. delivering functionality rather than ownership, 5. adopting a stewardship role, and 6. encouraging sufficiency); and organizational archetypes (7. repurposing for society or environment, and 8. developing scale-up solutions). Thanks to the categorization of these eight archetypes and the mechanisms related to them, companies can develop business models that may be perceived as fully or partially sustainable (van Bommel, 2018, p. 830). Another useful approach delivers the definition of a business model for sustainability of Schaltegger et al. (2016, p. 6), which relates to the fundamental idea of a business model: "A business model for sustainability helps describing, analyzing, managing, and communicating (i) a company's sustainable value proposition to its customers, and all other stakeholders, (ii) how it creates and delivers this value, (iii) and how it captures economic value while maintaining or regenerating natural, social, and economic capital beyond its organizational boundaries". Unlike the archetypes mentioned above, which sometimes refer to only one aspect, this approach views the environmental, social, and economic elements together, which is justified from the point of view of sustainable development combining all three elements.

All of these elements help clarify the main differences between sustainable and conventional business models. It is the "extension and the emphasis given to organizational, market and societal transformations that distinguish the discourse on business models for sustainability from their conventional antecedents, which focus on organizational value appropriation, that is, one-dimensional profit maximization, without considering the consequences for the wider social and ecological contexts" (Schaltegger et al., 2016, p. 5). Therefore, using the business model perspective for developing sustainable competitive strategies offers the firms the possibility to meet the expectations of both the consumers and governments, to contribute to sustainable development, and to maintain simultaneously their own business goals. This approach seems to be crucial in the process of building a firm's competitive position. As Bocken et al. (2014, p. 42) stress, sustainable business models are important in driving and implementing corporate innovation for sustainability, can help embed sustainability into business purpose and processes, but can also serve as a key driver of competitive advantage.

The Dichotomy of SBM Perception

All of this implies that SBMs can be perceived in two ways. On the one hand, they refer to companies that transform their businesses towards a sustainable business model. They may, for example, want to become more sustainable in different aspects of their activity. They may want to develop in a sustainable way and/or enhance their competitive position in a sustainable way. They may also look for a way to build their competitive position on different sustainability elements, or to enter new markets of products or services perceived as sustainable. In other words, they include increasingly sustainable elements in their business models, transforming them into sustainable business models. On the other hand, the term "SBM" is used to refer to firms or organizations that are "born sustainable". For "born sustainable" businesses, Dicuonzo et al. (2020, p. 2) consider companies "that have chosen, since their establishment, to build a business model focused on the sustainability principles" and in their research they examine those companies that have chosen to base all production on respect for the environment since their foundation. "Born sustainable" business models could be defined more broadly as businesses that from the outset were created in order to implement one of the purposes related to sustainable development. In other words, the sense of their foundation, development, and whole activity is subordinated to the implementation of a specific social, economic, and/or environmental goal meeting sustainable development challenges. It is also important that they may take various organizational and legal forms, ranging from foundations and Non-Governmental Organizations (NGOs) engaged in business, to cooperatives and companies (e.g. Ltd.). Understood in this way, the concept of the "born sustainable" business model refers also to a large degree to the understanding of sustainable and inclusive business models of the report "Mind Our Business" (Concord, 2020, pp. 3–11), where they are perceived as businesses "going beyond profit to include participatory governance structures and clear environmental and social impact". It implies that they are driven by a social and environmental mission, led by a long-term vision, and governed inclusively, as well as creating decent work opportunities, empowering women and youth, reaching out to marginalized people, and contributing to the green transition. Using the business model perspective for developing sustainable competitive strategies may be very useful for "born sustainables". First, despite the fact that they put social or environmental goals first, they have to make profits in order to survive and achieve their goals. Second, like all other companies, they often develop in different directions and different aspects of their activity, and expansion should include all the elements of sustainable development or be carried out in a sustainable way, since the sense of their creation and functioning is to contribute to sustainable development.

For the above-mentioned reasons, the concept of the sustainable business model should not be considered only statically. A dynamic approach would make it possible to perceive this concept as a process concerning all those companies that aim to develop and compete in a sustainable way by transforming one or more elements of their business models. This view is supported by the empirical findings of Høgevold et al. (2014, p. 357), who indicate evolutionary changes as companies move on a continuum from superficial to embedded sustainable business models and the application of sustainable business practices. The authors conclude that the planning, implementation, and evaluation of sustainable business models evolves over time within companies and their supply chains, as well as in the marketplace and society. Therefore, in the next section one of the possible ways of looking at this evolutionary process and possible strategies approaching it will be presented.

Entering Sustainable Markets – Towards Sustainable Strategies and Changing Business Models

Identifying the determinants of sustainable markets implies that there are different ways to enter these markets. These multiple pathways can be perceived as sustainable strategies, which may lead to the transformation of conventional business models into sustainable business models. A useful basis for analyzing how this occurs can be seen in the juxtaposition of the concept of the business model proposed by Johnson et al. (2008), which embraces most of the elements of Osterwalder's vision discussed in the previous section, with determinants of sustainable markets summarized in Figure 2.1. Therefore, first, sustainable strategies deriving from determinants of sustainable markets will be presented, and second, their impact on different elements of business models will be discussed. It is argued that following one or more strategies identified in this section affects all elements of a company's business model.

Sustainable Strategies

Determinants of sustainable markets previously defined in this chapter enable the identification of "sustainable strategies", which may be chosen by companies in order to enter sustainable markets and transform their businesses from conventional business models or superficial sustainable business models towards embedded sustainable business models. Depending on the industry in which the company operates and its market position, as well as its initial business model, i.e. the current value offered to customers, profit formula, key resources, and key processes, it is necessary to select such ways of entering sustainable markets that would contribute to strengthening the company's competitive position. Every firm should start from evaluating strategies given its strengths and weaknesses, resources, actual competitive position, and goals to find one that is most beneficial. The perspective of determinants of sustainable markets allows a company to analyze and choose the best strategies from the perspective of that particular company to increase competitiveness in a sustainable way or to build on sustainability it's competitive advantage, as well as to choose the degree of sustainability. This analysis can take place within the framework of single, some, or even all of the determinants of sustainable markets. Taking these determinants as a starting point, four sustainable strategies can be distinguished:

1. Product/service strategy
2. Certification strategy
3. Responsible production/distribution strategy
4. "Born sustainable" strategy

Product/service strategy implies that the companies may start or develop the production of goods, which in different ways, thanks to their features and use, contribute to sustainable development. These may be e.g. elements of green homes or green and circular economy, such as energy-efficient appliances or alternative fuel vehicles. This strategy may be an important way of building a competitive position in the face of the plans of the EU to be a climate-neutral economy by 2050. By that time, all firms and organizations in the EU will have to adjust to the new rules, which may offer an enormous chance for all businesses that can predict in advance which goods and services will be in greatest demand in this area and that succeed at offering them.

The second type of sustainable strategy is the certification strategy, which involves certifying one or multiple production lines using one of more sustainable certification schemes. They can, for example, meet the needs of consumers who are increasingly choosing products that are organic, are fair, do not contribute to rainforest destruction, or whose packaging is biodegradable or recyclable. Certifying the first product line may constitute a good starting point for all those businesses that want to start their journey towards building a competitive position in a sustainable way without making major changes in their current business model in the short term.

The third sustainable strategy deriving from determinants of sustainable markets, responsible production/distribution strategy, entails ensuring that production processes and ways of sourcing products and their ingredients, as well as distribution, are responsible from a sustainable development perspective. This can be done by using one of the above-mentioned certification schemes, but there are also other ways to achieve this. Many firms choose their own "sustainable program", aimed at convincing consumers about their socially or environmentally responsible ways of production, which will be discussed in the next section. Making the supply chain more transparent to the public may also play a crucial role in this respect. Companies are even starting to compete in this respect with concrete benefits. According to Traidecraft Exchange (2020, pp. 01–05), finding out and publicly reporting on who is in the firm's supply chain had a lot of benefits, such as building brand reputation, enhancing consumer trust, leading to better business relationships, helping to win new contracts, minimizing a range of risks, or supporting compliance. It is also expected that in the aftermath of the British Modern Slavery Act of 2015, which required large commercial organizations doing business in the UK to annually report the steps taken to ensure that modern slavery is not taking place in their organization and supply chains, the EU and other countries around the world will increasingly include HRDD in their legislation. Being proactive in the integration of human rights into supply chains can therefore contribute not only to a firm's competitive position, but also promote increased implementation of rules in international trade that may become mandatory in the near future. Yet another example of socially and environmentally responsible production and distribution is local markets or online platforms that enable people to buy locally produced food. Such markets contribute to reducing environmental costs of transport thanks to shortening of the supply chain, and they strengthen the resilience of local food chains, which has proved to be an extremely important element in building a sustainable economy in the face of, for example, the coronavirus pandemic.

The "born sustainable" strategy, as the fourth sustainable strategy, involves a company or organization being created in order to achieve a specific social or environmental goal; all their activities are subordinated to that goal, and their profits (or surpluses) are reinvested or directly financed to that primary goal. Different kinds of cooperatives or Fair Trade companies are a good example of this. Most often, they combine two or more SBM archetypes defined by Bocken et al. (2014). From the perspective of building a competitive position, the perspective that Brillinger et al. (2020, p. 122) take seems to be important. Namely, they suggest that different business models for different products and services may exist as a portfolio within one firm. This implies that transforming business models into sustainable models or the creation "born sustainable" models by e.g. bigger companies or capital groups may occur parallel to each other. This means that companies may follow different sustainable strategies for different products or groups of products and transform their business models towards SBMs at different speeds and in different ways.

Impact on Business Models

All four strategies affect the crucial elements of a firm's business model. A useful basis for analysis of these relations may be the juxtaposition of the concept of the business model proposed by Johnson et al. (2008) with the sustainable strategies discussed above (Figure 2.2). In particular, it seems crucial that each of the entry routes into sustainable markets, described above as sustainable strategies, may offer a specific Customer Value Proposition (CVP), which constitutes a fundamental element of every business model. Choosing the first strategy offers consumers a product with features or uses that promote sustainability (e.g. green building, clean energy, products and services that build a circular economy). Choosing the second strategy offers customers the value of reassurance offered by third-party certification organizations about the sustainability of the production process or distribution in one or more aspects or about other important product attributes that support sustainability (e.g. Fair Trade certifications ensuring that the producers of a product have been adequately compensated for their work). The third strategy offers consumers the belief about the sustainability of the production and distribution process of goods they purchase, in a different way, through for example, private sustainability programs, different sustainable reporting systems, ensuring the transparency of the whole value chain or shortening their value chain and being present on local markets. The adoption of the fourth strategy, in turn, allows the creation of value in such a way that the purchase of any goods or the benefit of any service of a particular company or organization contributes directly to the realization of a specific social or environmental objective, as the entire economic activity of the entity offering them is subordinated to the realization of this objective (e.g. production cooperatives of people with disabilities, Fair Trade companies). All four strategies affect the most important element of the business model, according to Johnson et al. (2008) – the CVP. They offer the possibility to fulfill in different ways important needs of those customers who care about sustainable development, and to adjust the firm proposition to specific customer expectations regarding the features of the product or service and the way it is produced or sold.

Similarly, all four strategies impact the other elements of the business model. For example, with regard to profit formula, it should be stressed that socially responsible ways of production mostly mean higher production costs (e.g. organic food demands more labor-intensive production methods, whereas Fair Trade cooperates with the poorest producers, whose labor efficiency, due to their marginalization, may be lower than average and requires support, training, etc.), which affects the other elements of the profit formula, like the revenue model and margin model. Adopting the first strategy, in turn, may require significant

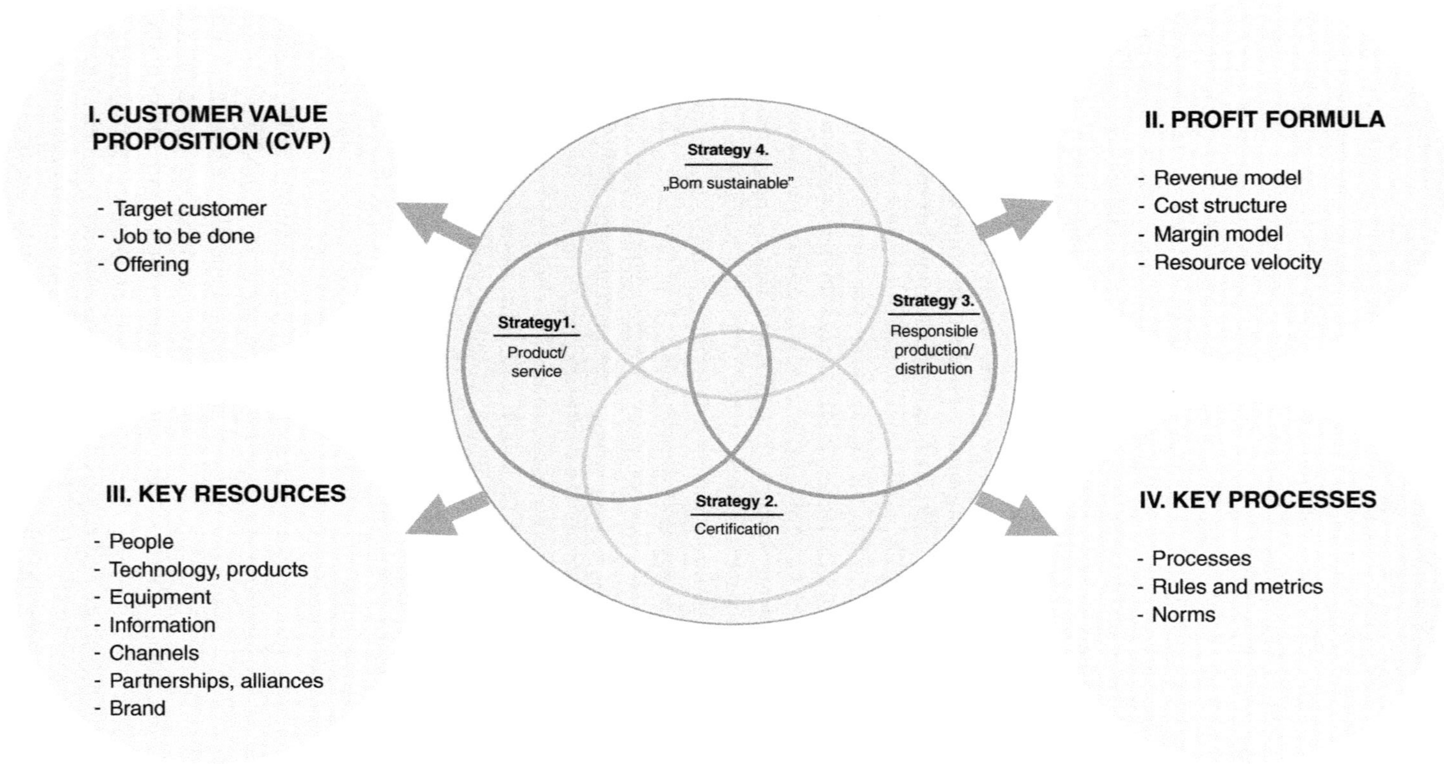

Figure 2.2 Impact of sustainable strategies on the business model.

investment in innovation, which also generally translates into a higher price for sustainable products and affects other elements of the profit formula.

Regarding key resources, the first strategy may specifically affect technologies and partnerships, although it may affect all other key resources. The fourth strategy may especially affect people, distribution channels, or partnerships as they are crucial for "born sustainables". With the first and fourth strategies, companies can build their brand, reputation, and image from the ground up, whereas the second and third strategies are more about improving their existing image and reputation.

Regarding key processes, the first strategy may affect design and product development or hiring new specialists, whereas the second and third strategies may affect more manufacturing and marketing, as both of them relate to responsible production and distribution. Developing as "born sustainable" affects all processes, rules, and norms, as all processes in the firm are subordinated to a concrete sustainable goal. The adoption of each of the strategies listed above results in the permeation of sustainable elements through all four business model elements defined by Johnson et al. (2008). This means that, depending on a company's commitment to sustainable transition, all of its dimensions of business can be affected through entry into sustainable markets.

The more sustainable market entry strategies a company adopts and the better it matches them to its offerings and the way it operates, the more embedded its sustainable business model will be. This also applies to "born sustainables", who have sustainability written into their business model from the outset. The remaining three strategies enable them to become even more sustainable, "more deeply embedded SBM", because raising the bar for "sustainability" is never-ending. There will always be a space for improvement from a sustainability perspective, so it would be difficult to set boundaries for the notion of 100% SBM. Much closer to reality at present seem to be the notions of superficial, embedded, or "born sustainable" business models, all of which may be advanced further by the above-mentioned strategies.

The fact that all four strategies of entering sustainable markets affect the most important elements of a business model means that the juxtaposition of the determinants of sustainable markets with a business model may constitute a useful tool for firms creating their competitive position in a sustainable way or, looking at this process otherwise, using the sustainability to enhance their competitiveness. Therefore, the next two subsections will use the example of Fair Trade to outline sustainable certification schemes and developments in the area of socially and environmentally responsible production and "born sustainable" business models in order to show how this process may look in reality and how sustainability may become a competitive advantage.

Sustainable Certification Schemes and Beyond: The Case of Fair Trade

Because sustainable ways of production are a key characteristic of sustainable markets and sustainable business models, this section is devoted to most popular ways used by companies to assure their consumers that the products they offer were produced in a sustainable way. Therefore, using the example of Fair Trade, this section will focus on different aspects of using sustainable certification schemes and on what goes beyond them, e.g. private sustainable programs. On the one hand, it will more precisely show the ways in which the second and third of the abovementioned strategies may be implemented, and on the other hand, it will present one dimension of the dynamics of the development of sustainable markets influencing sustainable strategies.

Diversity of Certification Schemes and Product Labels

Sustainable certification schemes constitute a useful tool to show consumers that products (or services) meet some of the sustainable development requirements. After a successful certification process, firms are allowed to carry a product label on the packaging of their product to distinguish these products from the "conventional" ("non-sustainable") ones. Companies may certify one or more of their production lines, which allows them to gradually adjust to their individual situation, including the sustainable criteria in their development and competition strategies. In recent years, a growing number of different sustainable certification schemes have been developed, which offer companies increasingly more ways to introduce sustainable elements into their development strategies. The flagship example of sustainable certification schemes is Fair Trade labelling, which has been dynamically developing in the last two decades. Fair Trade stands out from other sustainability approaches "thanks to a common vision, which is reflected in the key fair trade commitments, integrated into the labels' specifications" (Commerce Équitable et al., 2019, p. 6). Among others, these commitments include payment of fair prices; long-term direct trading relationships; no child, forced, or otherwise exploited labor; workplace non-discrimination; gender equity; democratic and transparent organizations; safe working conditions and reasonable work hours; investment in community development projects; and environmental sustainability (Fair World Project). It means, that Fair Trade certification schemes break down the meaning of product "sustainability" and "quality" by principles, criteria and indicators. Moreover, they base on monitoring the implementation of these required standards by an external party and potentially provide opportunities for use by a range of different types of organizations (Commerce Équitable et al., 2019, p. 12).

Fair Trade labels are the only sustainability initiatives to implement precise economic commitments with regard to commercial relations between buyers and producers. In particular, producers' organizations are their main target, and their requirements address issues related to a more equal relationship between producers and buyers. However, the dynamic development of Fair Trade in the last years has progressively led to the emergence of differing standpoints, and the variety of labels matches the diversity within the Fair Trade movement (Commerce Équitable et al., 2015, p. 113, 2019, p. 13). On the one hand, these differences can lead to confusion about what Fair Trade really means, but on the other hand, it can be perceived as an indicator of the Fair Trade market trends, influencing the extension of the Fair Trade product definition and the boundaries of the Fair Trade market (Śliwińska, 2021). Moreover, this enormous diversity offers companies the opportunity to choose the certification scheme most suitable for them, taking into account the most important elements of sustainable development from their point of view, and they can use their development towards sustainability for strengthening their competitive position.

An example of differences between Fair Trade certification schemes is their geographical scope. Some Fair Trade labels (e.g. Fair for Life, Fair Trade USA, Naturland Fair) are currently global, which means that they certify not only North-South production – which was the traditional approach of Fair Trade – but also "domestic" production (North-North or South-South) (see Table 2.1). This development is based on the idea that marginalized communities are everywhere, not only in the Global South, because the inequality gap is widening globally. Another example of differences is the fact that some of the labels combine Fair Trade and organic characteristics of products, which is becoming an important development in the Fair Trade market. For instance, actors in the organic sector, such as Naturland Fair, have created Fair Trade labels that are restricted to producers already committed to organic agriculture (Commerce Équitable et al., 2019, p. 13, 98).

There are different opinions within the Fair Trade movement regarding whether it should include only small-scale producer organizations or other actors, like coffee plantations. This dilemma was the reason for splitting between Fairtrade International (FI) and Fair Trade USA (FTUSA) in 2012, when the former chose to work exclusively with small-holder producer cooperatives in some products such as coffee, whereas the latter decided to follow its Fair Trade For All Initiative, expanding certification to large estates with hired workers in those products and to more small-scale farmers that were not organized (Commerce Équitable et al., 2019, pp. 47–59). For example, Fair for Life does not make small producers a priority, as today, producers' organizations only represent 27% of the Fair for Life certified organizations, whereas plantations reach 27% and contract farming 46% (Commerce

Table 2.1 Fair Trade labels.

Name	*Geographical Scope*	*Specific Requirements*	*Type of Organization*
ATES – Association for Fair and Sustainable Tourism	• developing countries • OECD countries	• social requirements	• European tour operators • tourist circuits in other countries
Fair for Life	• developing countries • OECD countries	• social responsibility	• producer's organizations • contract farming/ production • plantations • hired labor
Fairtrade International	• developing countries	x	• small producer's organizations • contract farming/ production • hired labor/plantations
Fair Trade USA	• developing countries • OECD countries	x	• producer's organizations • contract farming/ production • hired labor/plantations
Naturland Fair	• developing countries • OECD countries	• social responsibility • organic certification	• producer's organizations • contract farming/ production • hired labor/plantations
SPP – Small Producers' Symbol	• developing countries	• organic certification	• producer's organizations
WFTO – World Fair Trade Organization	• developing countries • OECD countries	x	• producer's organizations • contract farming/ production • hired labor/plantations

Source: Adapted from International Guide to Fair Trade Labels 2020 (Commerce Équitable et al., 2019)

Équitable et al., 2019, p. 33). Certification schemes differ also in the threshold for the use of the label. For example, FTUSA has a relatively weak one, requiring just 20% of certified ingredients for the use of a front panel seal, which is comparable to the low threshold of e.g. FI (Commerce Équitable et al., 2019, p. 59). There are also differences to observe concerning the use of Fair Trade premiums, the purpose of which was to be used by the collective organization to build sustainable communities. The FTUSA criteria state, however, that it can be used for cash payments to individuals, payment of certification fees, and investment by the owner of a medium or large farm (Commerce Équitable et al., 2019, p. 58).

In the context of diversity of Fair Trade certification schemes, it is worth saying a few words about two of the biggest Fair Trade organizations, which are important pioneers in the Fair Trade market, Fairtrade International (FI) and World Fair Trade Organization (WFTO). The first one is the oldest and globally best-known Fair Trade label, and it remains the primary actor in this sector, acting as the main point of reference. Among other things, many Fair Trade labels use or reference FI minimum prices (Commerce Équitable et al., 2019, p. 46). FI-sealed products constitute also a substantial part of the whole Fair Trade market. For example, in 2018 they generated about 80% of all Fair Trade sales in Germany, one of the biggest Fair Trade markets (Śliwińska, 2021). According to ITC Report (Meier et al., 2020, p. 32) the Fairtrade-certified (FI) area expanded 93% in 2011–2018 and remained stable (+0.7%) in 2017–2018. In 2018, more than 2.6 million hectares were Fairtrade-certified, which represented 0.05% of the global agricultural area, where the share of Fairtrade cocoa area of global cocoa area is 10.0%, and for coffee it is 9.1%. Along with the WFTO, it is one of the few Fair Trade labels that effectively relies on a network to implement proper advocacy and awareness-raising of citizens and consumers and constitutes an ever-evolving label that reinvents itself to address contemporary challenges (Commerce Équitable et al., 2019, p. 46). In that sense, it can be perceived as a leader in this sector, designing the new trends. One of the last developments is the policy to allow companies to use an "ingredient label" on multi-ingredient products sourced with only one Fairtrade-certified ingredient. It modified the previous fundamental rule, which said that all ingredients of a product that can be Fairtrade-certified, must be certified (Commerce Équitable et al., 2019, p. 46). One of the aims of this new certification strategy is to expand farmers' access to world markets and enhance the sale volumes by making it easier for companies with a lower level of commitment to use the Fairtrade label, as numerous producers' organizations still live below the poverty line.

A different approach to labeling constitutes the Guarantee System of WFTO, which constitute a global community of over 1,000 social enterprises and 1,500 shops in 76 countries that fully practice Fair Trade, which means that they put people and the planet first in everything they do. The WFTO plays a crucial role in developing and integrating the Fair Trade movement internationally. Its Guarantee System is the only international verification model focused on social enterprises that put the interests of workers, farmers, and artisans first, and through peer-reviews and independent audits, the Guarantee System verifies if its members are mission-led companies fully practicing the ten Principles of Fair Trade across their business and supply chains (https://wfto.com). Therefore, the WFTO Guaranteed Fair

Trade product label informs the consumer about the whole business model of a particular company or an organization, its structure, its operations, and its supply chains, in contrast to other Fair Trade product certification schemes mentioned before, which enable companies to extend their product range by one or a few Fair Trade products without changing their business model substantially or subordinating it to the idea of Fair Trade.

The considerable diversity of Fair Trade labels presents difficulty not only for consumers, but also for companies, who are faced with the problem of which scheme they should choose. Therefore, the certification strategy requires a deeper understanding of the certification market, both in terms of its scope and price and how it fits into the company's operations, as well as in terms of how it is perceived by consumers in a given market, since different labels, which are proof of having gone through a certification process, are perceived differently in different geographic markets. Table 2.1 constitutes a simple presentation of the above-mentioned differences between the most available or significantly credible Fair Trade labels, which are thoroughly compared in the International Guide to Fair Trade Labels 2020.

The situation is further complicated by the dynamic development of new, non-Fair Trade, sustainable schemes in recent years. There are more than 400 such standards at the moment (Meier et al., 2020, p. xii). They often do not meet key Fair Trade commitments regarding the economic issues faced by producers, such as fair price or fair compensation for workers, premium for group projects, access facilitated to finance or prefinancing, and long-term commitment for buyers. However, mobilizing social and environmental vocabulary in their communications, they can make consumers confuse these initiatives with Fair Trade labels. According to the International Guide to Fairtrade Original (2019, pp. 110–115), these are, for example, Bonsucro, Utz-Rainforest Alliance, or Better Cotton Initiative (BCI). These labels have been growing rapidly in recent years. Bonsucro's total certified area increased by 79.7% in 2011–2018 and by 10.2% in 2017–2018, achieving in 2018 1.3 million hectares, which represents 0.03% of the global agricultural area and 3.2% of the global sugarcane area. The area where Better Cotton grew increased almost tenfold in 2011–2018 and by 17% in 2017–2018. BCI Farmers grew Better Cotton on more than 4.1 million hectares in the 2018–2019 season, which represents 0.09% of the global agricultural area and 12.9% of the global cotton area. The share of Utz and Rainforest Alliance area of global agricultural land in 2018 was 0.17%, but Utz and Rainforest Alliance area of global cocoa area was 31.5%, and for coffee it was 11.8% (Meier et al., 2020, pp. 29–39).

Private Sustainability Programs

On the one hand, this enormous diversity of sustainable certification schemes offers companies great opportunities to choose the certification scheme most suitable for them. However, on the other hand, it may lead both to their confusion in deciding which certificate to choose and to lowering the bar for the implementation of social and environmental goals. Individual certificates differ in scope and detail of requirements and thus in the level of realization of sustainable goals, and therefore also in price, which the final consumers are often not aware of. In this context, an important development constituting one of the effects of this diversity, is the emergence of their own sustainability programs by multinational companies, which is an example of the third sustainable strategy discussed above. By creating their own programs, companies become independent of external certification schemes and realize their own idea of sustainable development, which allows them to differentiate from their competitors using the same labels. "This shows that these businesses are becoming aware of the need to reinvest in the sectors of agricultural production, often in order to ensure the security of their supply chains. However, most multinationals are creating their own specifications rather than utilizing external labels. In this case, we are seeing that a commitment to fair prices is rarely the priority" (Commerce Équitable et al., 2019, p. 6). The renunciation of third-party certification may thus lead, although not necessarily, to lowering the bar for achieving a social goal. Companies using this strategy have to be aware of this threat, as the consumers are increasingly more aware of this aspect of private sustainability programs. The two examples of such programs shown below seem to represent well the problem outlined above.

One of the multinationals pursuing their own sustainability program is Mondelēz International, the owner of brands such as Cadbury, Milka, Oreo, and Toblerone. This company displays their commitment to sustainability as the first and most important information on its homepage: "Introducing Sustainable Futures. People and planet impact with social investment and partnerships." Most information on the homepage refers to sustainability issues, such as Mondelēz's work supporting its communities, people, and customers; taking a stand for gender equity and equality; joining the Uncycled Food Association; or committing to the reduction in virgin plastic use to combat plastic pollution (www.mondelezinternational.com). In 2012, Mondelēz launched a Cocoa Life program focusing on its cocoa supplying farmers in six key cocoa growing countries: Ivory Coast, Ghana, Indonesia, India, the Dominican Republic, and Brazil (www.cocoalife.org). According to Commerce Équitable et al. (2019, p. 111), 35% of Mondelēz International's cocoa is sourced with Cocoa Life guidelines. One of their brands, Cadbury, informs its consumers that all of its products will proudly carry the Cocoa Life logo and that this program of USD 400 million is aiming to reach 200,000 farmers and a million community members by 2022. It convinces consumers that despite their renouncement of Fairtrade certification, their farmers do not lose out and that they will further work together with Fairtrade and its third-party certification body to launch programs that help farmers. They pledged that from 2017, five times more Cadbury products will be made with sustainably sourced cocoa (www.cadbury.co.uk). However, as Commerce Équitable et al. notes (2019, p. 111), the standards are not available online, so the average consumer cannot verify them.

Another example of a multinational company maintaining its own sustainability program is Starbucks. In 2004, it launched the Coffee And Farmer Equity C.A.F.E. Practices that seek to ensure that Starbucks sources sustainably grown and processed coffee by evaluating the economic, social, and environmental aspects of coffee production. According to Commerce Équitable et al. (2019, p. 111), in 2016, nearly 65% of tea was Tea Practices sourced, and in 2018, 99% of coffee was C.A.F.E. Practices sourced, as the guidelines were later developed also for tea and cocoa. C.A.F.E. practices' standards are available online, and controls are made by SCS Global Services. From the Starbucks webpage, the consumer learns about Starbucks's new environmental sustainability commitment and may join (by giving their phone number) to stay up to date on Starbucks's commitment to sustainability. This renewed focus on sustainability means "giving more than we take from the planet." Chief executive officer Kevin Johnson explains this ambitious goal: "Our aspiration is to become resource positive – storing more carbon than we emit, eliminating waste, and providing more clean freshwater than we use" (Warnick, 2020).

Both examples show that multinationals are beginning to compete on sustainability and are integrating this aspect into their core activities, influencing crucial elements of their existing business models. The companies are well aware of the need to develop in this direction. Regarding the new Starbucks sustainability commitment, its CEO wrote: "Now, it's time to create an even broader aspiration – and it's work that requires visionary thinking, new ways of working, investment of resource and urgent action". In both above-mentioned cases, these programs do not focus specifically on Fair Trade principles, but they try to comprise different social and environmental aspects of sustainable development and stress their positive impact on farmers and their communities. Therefore, it may become difficult for consumers to assess whether their favorite brand, which is e.g. no longer certified by one of the Fair Trade schemes, cares better for the poorest farmers and the environment thanks to its own sustainable program than it did before, and whether it is more sustainable than before. Pursuing private sustainability programs instead of costly certification procedures and label fees is on one hand a way of distinguishing oneself in the marketplace from competitors when rivals use the same or similar labels, and an opportunity to convince customers that one's company is more sustainable than the competition. However, on the other hand, in the face of strong price competition, it may reduce costs by lowering the bar for social and environmental goals, especially in the case of lack of externally framed and externally audited standards. Consumers are more and more aware of these threats. Therefore, being forced to compete on both price and corporate social responsibility practices, the multinationals are themselves starting to champion the idea of mandatory global public regulation on social and environmental issues (Commerce Équitable et al., 2019, p. 6.). To what extent sustainability issues should be regulated and standardized, however, is a subject of current political and scientific debate.

Can Sustainable Be Competitive? The Case of Fair Trade "Born Sustainable" Business Models

In the previous sections, the focus has been mainly on how companies can enhance their competitiveness in a sustainable way and build their competitiveness on the different elements of sustainability, consequently transforming their business models towards increasingly embedded sustainable business models. It was argued that the transformation towards SBM can enhance the competitiveness of companies in various ways and that firms are competing with each other in a growing number of sustainability dimensions. Since "born sustainables" are a particular example of SBM, taking a different organizational form, from NGOs to Ltd., it seems important to provide evidence that they can be also competitive. Their establishment for the purpose of achieving a concrete social or environmental goal, and their successful development proves that grounding on and subordinating to sustainability all firm's activities can constitute an excellent basis for building a competitive position. Therefore, three cases of successful "born sustainables" are presented below.

GEPA

The GEPA mbH (Society for the Promotion of Partnership with the Third World) is an example of a thriving organization that, from its creation in May 1975, has been fully committed to the idea of Fair Trade, and constitutes one of the biggest members of WFTO. GEPA has not only contributed to the development of the market for Fair Trade products in Germany, but also to the dynamic development of the Fair Trade movement in Europe, as it is one of the co-founders of the WFTO and European Fair Trade Association (EFTA), as well as the Forum Fairer Handel – a network of German Fair Trade organizations and actors. It constitutes a great example of an ambitious "born sustainable" business model, and has spent the 40 years of its existence constantly trying to not only find new ways to make consumers more familiar with Fair Trade, but also to raise the bar for Fair Trade, among other things, by extending it to include environmental issues. That was always the essence of its customer value proposition. For instance, in 1986, GEPA introduced Café Orgánico, the first fair organic coffee in Germany. One year later, it launched the world's first organic tea – the foundation for successful cooperation with Naturland. Its activities have contributed to the inclusion, by the guidelines of Naturland, not only of ecological but also of social criteria regarding fair life and working conditions for ecological cultivation. In 2000, GEPA launched the first fair-bio chocolate in Germany, and since 2012, it has been using organic faires palm fat. In addition, around 77% of the GEPA's foods come from organic cultivation. GEPA also uses aluminum-free coffee packaging and renewable raw materials for its tea bags and new chocolate assortment (GEPA [1]). GEPA describes itself in the following way: "We do more in many areas than the general fair trade criteria demand. We are working as a pioneer to work together with our partners in the south for a better life – with respect for man and nature" (GEPA [2]). True to their mission, they recently introduced a real, fair climate chocolate "#choco4change". GEPA not only holds a "Fair Trade Company Guaranteed" certification from the WFTO, informing that its business model is fully devoted to all principles of Fair Trade (its central purpose), and uses profits exclusively for the goals of Fair Trade, but it is also involved with all its products in the different monitoring and certification Fair Trade systems to ensure the fulfilment of international criteria in that respect. All this shows the development strategy of GEPA, which is raising the bar for Fair Trade products and companies and which is reflected in the "fair+" mark. In this way, GEPA has built a very strong position in the German Fair Trade market, and it can be stated that it constitutes a trendsetter in this market. By constantly adding new elements to its original SBM, GEPA differentiates itself from the competition by being innovative, making its position in the market very strong and gaining the trust of more and more consumers. The numbers speak for themselves. The GEPA's overall turnover raised by 1,8% in 2018 in comparison to 2017, achieving 73.75 million EUR, and by 9.5% in 2019, achieving 80.73 million EUR (GEPA, 2018, 2019).

Fairtrade Original

Another example of a successful "born sustainable" business model that is fully devoted to Fair Trade and is one of the European pioneers of this idea is the Dutch company Fairtrade Original. Its roots date back to 1959, when the association S.O.S. – Komitee Steun Onderontwikkelnde Streken (Committee Support Underdeveloped Regions), the precursor of the current Fairtrade Original – was founded. From the outset, its aim was to help people in underdeveloped countries become self-reliant, and after a few years of dynamic development, in 1967, the S.O.S. made the switch from fundraising to trade (van der Stelt, 2009, pp. 7–14, 133). From an importer of wooden statuettes, it grew to become one of the most important Fair Trade companies in Europe, contributing to the development of the Fair Trade movement and market. Its mission is to make fair food and drinks available for everyone by developing local supply chains. Therefore, its offer covers more than 100 products available in supermarkets, and all profits are reinvested in projects that help accomplish its mission (www.fairtradeoriginal.com). What distinguishes Fairtrade Original in the market is its priority to build sustainable and fair value chains. That is why its development managers cooperate very closely with local partners in order to farm, prepare, and package products locally and prevent the value of those products from being monetized outside the countries of origin. In the face of intensive price and quality competition in the European food and drinks market, this constitutes a substantial challenge. Assisting the poorest farmers and processors in building a supply chain, ensuring that products are of the right quality, ensuring that workers are productive, and making sure that they get certified means a huge effort and risk for the company. Conscious consumers, however, appreciate this, choosing these products in supermarkets, so the company is growing, entering new product and geographical markets, and its operating revenues are systematically increasing (Fairtrade Original, 2019, p. 43). Implementing its ambitious mission to build sustainable supply chains with partners from the Global South and raising the bar for Fair Trade products, Fairtrade Original also extends the range of its offer, going beyond traditional Fair Trade products. A notable development was when Fairtrade Original entered the market of cooking products of Asian, South American, and African cuisine, which so far were hardly available as Fair Trade products. These are e.g. Mexican enchiladas or tortilla soup, Tunisian shakshuka, Maroccan harira soup, or Thai massaman curry (Fairtrade Original). In 2019, it introduced the first young jackfruit in the Dutch retail market. It seems that this company bases its customer value proposition and builds its competitive position both on raising the bar for achieving a concrete social goal, which is the aim of its existence, and on catering to the sophisticated tastes of Western consumers, who want not only to know "who is behind the product", but also to meet new flavors and to easily prepare meals of different cuisines of the world.

Tony's Chocolonely

Another great example of a "born sustainable" business being spectacularly successful in the market is the Dutch company Tony's

Chocolonely. It was created by the journalist Teun van de Keuken in order to eliminate slavery from the chocolate industry, after he was shocked to discover that much of the chocolate sold in supermarkets is made by people, often children, working as slaves. From the beginning, in 2006, Tony's Chocolonely carries out its mission to "make 100% slave free the norm in chocolate". And it has in mind not only its own chocolate, but "all chocolate worldwide". Because of the modern slavery and illegal child labor on cocoa farms in West Africa, the main source of cocoa in the world, "Tony's Chocolonely exists to change that" (Tony's Chocolonely [1]). This is its customer value proposition.

To achieve this ambitious goal, it developed a roadmap that outlines its long-term goals and consists of three pillars: creating awareness, leading by example, and inspiring to act. Raising consciousness concerns, on the one hand, the cocoa farmers that should learn where to draw the line between illegal child labor and helping out on the farm after school and learning how cocoa is grown. On the other hand, it concerns Northern societies and the chocolate industry that have to become aware of the problem of modern slavery, understood as any form of forced labor or exploitation of adults or children (including the worst forms of illegal child labor outside the immediate family, which are not acceptable under any circumstances). This is a major issue, for instance, in West Africa's cocoa supply chains, where there are over 30,000 cases of modern slavery and over 1.56 million cases of illegal child labor (Tony's Chocolonely annual fair report, 2019/2020, p. 70, 152). Tony's "leading by example" refers to five sourcing principles that include investing in long-term partnerships with farmers cooperatives, helping them to professionalize, paying cocoa farmer a higher price, investing in agricultural knowledge and training to help them improve productivity on their farms so they can earn a decent income, and ensuring the traceability of cocoa beans (Tony's Chocolonely [2]). It also involves removing anonymity from the supply chain. It meets the Fairtrade standards, but by carrying for traceable cocoa and paying, in addition to the Fairtrade-premium, Tony's additional premium to the farmers cooperatives (which significantly exceeds the first one) Tony's Chocolonely raises the bar for Fair Trade products, going beyond the standard requirements of already high-quality Fairtrade International requirements (Tony's Chocolonely annual fair report, 2019/2020, pp. 15–20, 86). It also tries to inspire other firms to apply its model and maintains an ongoing dialog with politicians, NGOs, and academia to increase the pressure on the industry to adopt its five sourcing principles for slave-free cocoa. Tony's Chocolonely also considers the environment, prohibiting deforestation and encouraging farmers to implement more environmentally friendly production methods and minimize the use of pesticides. However, for the moment it is not seeking to make its entire supply chain organic, as it noticed that organic farming does not guarantee a positive social impact, which is the first priority of the firm (Tony's Chocolonely [3]).

It seems that the consumers appreciate this focused approach very much, as in recent years Tony's Chocolonely has experienced dynamic growth. In 2017, it became the leading chocolate brand in the Netherlands, with 18.8 % of the market and 53% increase in sales on the previous 12 months (Traidecraft Exchange, 2020, p. 5). In 2019, it began successfully expanding into other markets. In its annual report 2019–2020, Tony's shows e.g. that in the US, it nearly doubled sales from € 5.6 to € 10.3 million, and its second year in the UK resulted in € 8.7 million in sales, what means more than doubling its launch year of the € 3.2 million (Tony's Chocolonely annual fair report, 2019/2020, p. 80). The Supply Chain Consulting Group concludes in 2019, that "the brand's success reflects growing consumer demand for a transparent supply chain, with customers willing to pay more to guarantee ethical sourcing" (Traidecraft Exchange, 2020, p. 5). Therefore, it can be said that Tony Chocolonely owes its dynamic development and the current competitive position particularly to the main objective for which it was created – one of important social aspects of sustainable development, which is eliminating modern slavery in its supply chain and the whole chocolate industry, to which its whole business model was from the outset subordinated. It constitutes proof that doing financially well and doing good for people and the planet can go hand in hand (Tony's Chocolonely annual fair report, 2019/2020, p. 75).

All three above-mentioned cases constitute examples of entire subordination of all key elements of a business model to a specific social objective, which is one of the most important aspects of sustainable development. Although they differ somewhat in their customer value propositions and raise the bar for Fair Trade products in different ways, it is notable that they all succeed in the market, and their market success is accompanied by a commitment to a social purpose that goes beyond business. Their social involvement in conveying the idea for which they exist, both to society and to other companies as well as governments, is a notable aspect of these organizations. They can do it, among others, thanks to the fact that they have subordinated their entire activity to the goal of sustainable development, accepting the costs associated with it and treating profits as a means to achieve their mission. They all constitute proof that building one's competitive advantage on sustainability and implementation of the SDGs through business activities is not only possible, but can also constitute an effective growth strategy and can go hand in hand with financial success.

Conclusions

This chapter was devoted to sustainable markets and business models, which in recent years constitute an emerging field of research and an important topic for all kinds of businesses, as "being sustainable" becomes an important element of building firms' competitive position. Because of dynamic development and different approaches to the sustainable markets and business models, many consumers and companies, as well as researchers, may feel confused about how the notions of sustainable products, markets, firms, or business models should be understood and what are the differences between such terms as "sustainable", "ethical", and "fair". Therefore, this chapter aimed to outline the different understandings of these notions and proposed an approach for analyzing sustainable business models and their evolution, which may constitute a framework for further research. Defining the determinants of sustainable markets (Figure 2.1), enabling identification of four sustainable strategies and the juxtaposition of them with basic business model elements (Figure 2.2), provides a tool that may be useful both for researchers as well as for managers for analysis and development of competitive strategies that are based on sustainability or aim to include some sustainable elements. It also displays that all discussed strategies of entering the sustainable markets influence in different ways the main elements of the traditionally understood business model. As including sustainability in competitive strategies and even competing on sustainability becomes a norm in high-developed economies, this chapter devoted special attention to sustainable certification schemes and private sustainable programs of multinationals, as well as to "born sustainable" business models, which constitute different and to some extent contradictory approaches to entering sustainable markets. Various aspects of these approaches were discussed, and it is argued that companies need to choose a specific approach according to their individual situation and goals. Presented cases show that "sustainable" may mean "competitive".

There is no doubt that in order to be competitive in the near future, firms will have to increasingly care both for the quality of their products and services as well as for their sustainability, even if it still will be understood in different ways. A big challenge for many "born sustainables" is to care for the highest physical quality of their products and satisfy the needs of demanding consumers. The leaders in "conventional" markets face the challenge of transforming their businesses towards sustainable business models while simultaneously maintaining and increasing their competitive position. Because of the efforts of many civil society organizations and governments, the social awareness of the global social and environmental challenges and the need to promote sustainable development has grown rapidly in recent years. Companies must take this into account and expect growing consumer pressure, which will cause competition in sustainability to grow over time. As responsible consumption evolves, it can be expected that the degree of sustainability, along with price and quality, will become a critical and permanent determinant of consumer choices. It may be of crucial importance for future research, which includes sustainability in increasingly broad areas of management in recent years. An important example of it constitutes the concept of shared value, arguing that there are numerous ways in which addressing societal concerns can yield productivity benefits to a firm (Porter & Kramer, 2011, p. 8). It is becoming increasingly clear, however, that CSR and sustainable business relates not so much to the question of how to improve competitive position and bring more money to shareholders in a sustainable way, but much more about how business can take on the role of contributing to economic development and simultaneously contributing to the public good (Borglund et al., 2021).

The above-mentioned developments may also result in the popularity growth of different sustainable certification schemes and rankings, reports, or competitions for the most sustainable business models, firms, or practices, such as The Global 100 Most Sustainable Corporations in the World (www.corporateknights.com) or the Common Good Matrix (www.ecogood.org), as well as the growing number and diversity of platforms and organizations integrating and supporting "sustainable companies". To be sustainable in one aspect may not be enough to win with competitors in the near future, and companies will look for possibilities to convince their consumers that they are sustainable in every possible dimension. Companies will not only prove that they are socially or/and environmentally responsible, but will consciously raise the bar for their sustainable goals, and this trend will undoubtedly intensify.

An important aspect of sustainability is that it is not always reflected in the physical characteristics of the product, which is especially the case when social goals relating to such values as altruism and helping the weakest and marginalized participants of the market are pursued. Therefore, building a competitive position when entering sustainable markets relies to a large degree on consumer trust in the company and what it claims about its sustainable practices. On the one hand, this can lead to increasing the role and popularity of different ways of demonstrating the companies' transparency in their value chains, which already now constitutes an important trend and strategy of building sustainable business models, and on the other, can raise the importance of sustainable products and business model certification schemes, as well as reporting systems, which provide an external audit.

The discussion about including sustainability in building the competitive position of firms is a part of a wider debate on the role of government in the economy; in particular, to what extent is the market able to take over the responsibility for social and environmental global challenges, and in which way should the government support the evolution of the capitalistic system towards a "sustainable market economy". Nowadays, there is a wide consensus that all parties – business, government, and civil society – are responsible for implementing necessary changes, and it can be expected that the need for strong collaboration between all of them will become even stronger in the face of the Covid-19 pandemic. Several entities are working on fostering this collaboration, including the Sustainable Markets Initiative, the Sustainable Trade Initiative, the Mistra Centre for Sustainable Markets, the Green Economy Coalition, and Sustainable Brands. Raising social awareness and pressure, as well as the commitment of many governments to the SDGs set by the United Nations, like the EU priority to work towards "An economy that works for people – working for social fairness and prosperity" and the European Green Deal (CONCORD Europe, Cooperatives Europe, FTAO, 2020, pp. 8–10), are the reason that the legal, regulatory, policy, and institutional reforms to mainstream sustainability and corporate accountability across all businesses may accelerate in the near future. This effort will rely on imposing some new obligations regarding sustainable ways of production or distribution, as well as physical features of products, but it may mean new support and incentive policies for development strategies based on sustainability. Also, local authorities are more and more involved in supporting the development of sustainable business models. A notable example is the Sustainable Trade Champions, distinguished in the EU Cities for Fair and Ethical Trade Award (https://www.trade-city-award.eu). However, one should not expect that any government regulation will solve the problem of the transition towards sustainable markets. On the contrary, first, this process will have a perennial character, and second, some legal standards will be set on a basic level, leaving a lot of space for competition on sustainability. Social movements and ambitious companies will always raise the bar and make way for sustainable innovations constituting a base for building a firm's competitive position. This means that consumer attitudes and their expectations towards companies will largely determine the extent to which the market will take responsibility for counteracting global challenges.

References

Aras, G. (Ed.). (2015). *Sustainable markets for sustainable business. A global perspective for business and financial markets*. Gower Publishing Limited.

Bocken, N. M. P., Short, S. W., Rana, P., & Evans, S. (2014). A literature and practice review to develop sustainable business model archetypes. *Journal of Cleaner Production*, *65*, 42–56.

Borglund, T., De Geer, H., Sweet, S., Frostenson, M., Grafström, M., Lerpold, L., Nordbrand, S., Sjöström, E., & Windell, K. (2021). *CSR and sustainable business*. Sanoma Utbildning.

Brillinger, A.-S., Els, C., Schaefer, B., & Bender, B. (2020). Business model risk and uncertainty factors: Toward building and maintaining profitable and sustainable business models. *Business Horizons*, *63*, 121–130.

Brugmann, J., & Prahalad, C. (2007, February). Co-creating business's new social compact. *Harvard Business Review*, *85*(2), 80–90, 156.

Chertow, M. R., (2000). Industrial symbiosis: Literature and taxonomy. *Annual Review of Environment and Resources*, *25*(1), 313–337.

Cingano, F. (2014). *Trends in income inequality and its impact on economic growth*. OECD Social, Employment and Migration Working Papers, No. 163, OECD Publishing. https://doi.org/10.1787/5jxrjncwxv6j-en.

Clauss, T. (2017). Measuring business model innovation: Conceptualization, scale development, and proof of performance. *R & D Management*, *47*(3), 385–403.

Commerce Équitable France, FWP, FairNESS, Forum Fairer Handel, Arnold, N., Bennett, E., Blendin, M., Brochard, M., Carimentrand, A., Coulibaly, M., De Ferran, F., Durochat, E., Gautrey, G., Geffner, D., Leyssene, C., Lorenz, J., Maisonhaute, J., Pulsen, O., Ripoll, J., Sidrey, N., & Stoll, J. (2019, November). *International guide to fair trade labels. Edition 2020*. www.commercequitable.org.

Commerce Équitable France, FWP, FairNESS, Durochat, E., Stoll, J., Frois, S., Selvaradj, S., Lindgren, K., Geffner, D., Carimentrand, A., Pernin, J.-L., Dufeu, I., Malandain, E., & Smith, A. (2015, May). *International guide to fair trade labels. Edition 2015*. www.commercequitable.org.

CONCORD Europe, Cooperatives Europe, FTAO. (2020). *Mind our business. Amplify the transformative power of sustainable and inclusive business models through EU external action*, CONCORD Europe. https://concordeurope.org/2020/12/01/mind-our-business-amplify-the-transformative-power-of-sustainable-and-inclusive-business-models-through-eu-external-action/.

Dicuonzo, G., Galeone, G., Ranaldo, S., & Turco, M. (2020). The key drivers of born-sustainable businesses: Evidence from the Italian fashion industry. *Sustainability*, *12*(10237), 1–16. https://doi.org/10.3390/su122410237, www.mdpi.com/journal/sustainability.

Doherty, B., Haugh, H., & Lyon, F. (2014). Social enterprises as hybrid organizations: A review and research agenda. *International Journal of Management Reviews*, *16*, 417–436. https://doi.org/10.1111/ijmr.12028.

Ethical Consumer. (2020, December 21). *Ethical consumer markets report 2020. Ethical consumerism in the pandemic*. https://www.ethicalconsumer.org/research-hub/uk-ethical-consumer-markets-report.

Fairtrade Original. (2019). *Jaarverslag 2019*. https://indd.adobe.com/view/27b1b55f-f9d0–45f3-b76b-8bcaa63c7750.

Fairtrade Original. (n.d.). *Ontdek onze producten uit Azië, Afrika & Zuid-Amerika*. https://www.fairtradeoriginal.nl/producten/wereldkeukens/page/3

Fair World Project. (n.d). *Fair trade principles*. https://fairworldproject.org/get-informed/movements/fair-trade/principles.

Fiedor, B., Scheuer, B., & Dokurno, Z. (2016). Paradygmat zrównoważonego rozwoju a współczesna makroekonomia – ujęcie epistemologiczne. *Ekonomista, 2016*(1), 11–31.

GEPA [1]. *Fairness mit Tradition.* https://www.gepa.de/gepa/geschichte.

GEPA [2]. *100% fair: Wer ist die GEPA?.* https://www.gepa.de/gepa/mission/wer-ist-die-gepa.html.

GEPA. (2018). *Facts and figures. Business year 2018.* https://www.gepa.de/fileadmin/user_upload/Info/GEPA/ZahlenDatenFakten_E_06–18.pdf.

GEPA. (2019). *Facts and figures. Business year 2019.* https://www.gepa.de/fileadmin/user_upload/Info/GEPA/ZDF_E_10–2020_web.pdf.

Gorynia, M. (2019). Competition and globalization in economic sciences. Selected aspects, *Economics and Business Review, 5*(3), 118–133.

Grassl, W. (2012). Business models of social enterprise: A design approach. *ACRN Journal of Entrepreneurship Perspectives, 1*(1), 37–60.

Haigh, N., Walker, J., Bacq, S., & Kickul, J. (2015). Hybrid organizations: Origins, strategies, impacts, and implications. *California Management Review, 57*(3), 5–12.

Høgevold, N. M., Goran, S., Wagner, B., & Petzer, D. J. (2014). Sustainable business models. Corporate reasons, economic effects, social boundaries, environmental actions and organizational challenges in sustainable business practices. *Baltic Journal of Management, 9*(3), 357–380.

IIED-International Institute for Environment and Development. (n.d). *Shaping sustainable markets. A research initiative that seeks to ensure markets work to support, rather than undermine, sustainable development.* https://pubs.iied.org/sites/default/files/pdfs/migrate/G03703.pdf.

Johnson, M. W., Christensen, C. M., & Kagermann H. (2008, December). Reinventing your business model. *Harvard Business Review.*

Lüdeke-Freund, F. (2009). *Business model concepts in corporate sustainability contexts from rhetoric to a generic template for 'business models for sustainability.* https://www.researchgate.net/publication/228134074_Business_Model_Concepts_in_Corporate_Sustainability_Contexts_From_Rhetoric_to_a_Generic_Template_for_'Business_Models_for_Sustainability', https://doi.org/10.2139/ssrn.1544847.

Manninen, K., Koskela, S., Antikainen, R., Bocken, N. M. P., Dahlbo, H., Aminoff, A. (2018). Do circular economy business models capture intended environmental value propositions? *Journal of Cleaner Production, 171*, 413–422.

Mączyńska, E. (2011). Dysfunkcje Gospodarki w kontekście ekonomii kryzysu (The Economy's Dysfunctions in the Context of the Economics of Crisis). *Zeszyty Naukowe nr 9, PTE Kraków, 9*, 43–70.

Meier, C., Sampson, G., Larrea, C., Schlatter, B., Voora, V., Dang, D., Bermudez, S., Wozniak, J., & Willer, H. (2020). *The state of sustainable markets 2020: Statistics and emerging trends.* ITC. https://www.intracen.org/publication/Sustainable-Markets-2020.

Modern Slavery Act. (2015). https://www.legislation.gov.uk/ukpga/2015/30/pdfs/ukpga_20150030_en.pdf.

Osterwalder, A., & Pigneur, Y. (2010). *Business model generation: A handbook for visionaries, game changers, and challengers.* John Wiley & Sons.

Peter, A. C., & Smith, C. S. (2011). The shift needed for sustainability. *The Learning Organization*, *18*(1), 73–86.

Porter, M., & Kramer, M. R. (2011, January-February). Creating Shared Value. How to reinvent capitalism - and unleash a wave of innovation and growth. *Harvard Business Review*.

Predenville, S., & Bocken, N. (2017). Sustainable business models through service design. *Procedia Manufacturing*, *8*, 292–299.

Ratajczak, M. (2017). Spór o rolę państwa w gospodarce. *Ruch Prawniczy, Ekonomiczny i Socjologiczny*, *2017*(1), 5–23.

Richardson, J. (2008). The business model: An integrative framework for strategy execution. *Strategic Change*, *17*, 133–144.

Schaltegger, S., Hansen, E. G., & Lüdeke-Freund, F. (2016). Business models for sustainability: Origins, present research, and future avenues. *Organization & Environment*, *29*(I), 3–10. https://doi.org/10.1177/1086026615599806.

Simons, L., & Nijhof, A. (2021). *Changing the game. Sustainable market transformation strategies to understand and tackle the big and complex sustainability challenges of our generation*. Routledge.

Sustainable Markets. Business, environment, society. (n.d). HiSoUR.com. https://www.hisour.com/sustainable-markets-40523.

Śliwińska, M. (2021). Fair Trade movement and market development for decent work and economic growth. In W. Leal Filho, A. M. Azul, L. Brandli, A. Lange Salvia, & T. Wall (Eds.), *Decent work and economic growth. Encyclopedia of the UN sustainable development goals*. Springer. https://doi.org/10.1007/978-3-319-95867-5_71.

Teece, D. J. (2010). Business models, business, strategy, and innovation. *Long Range Planning*, *43*(2/3), 172–194.

The International Fair Trade Charter. (2018, September 25). https://www.fair-trade.website/the-charter-1.

Tony's Chocolonely annual fair report. (2019/2020). https://tonyschocolonely.com/int/en/annual-fair-reports/annual-fair-report-2019–2020.

Tony's Chocolonely [1]. https://tonyschocolonely.com/int/en.

Tony's Chocolonely [2]. https://tonyschocolonely.com/int/en/our-story/our-mission.

Tony's Chocolonely [3]. https://tonyschocolonely.com/int/en/other-stuff/frequently-asked-questions.

Traidecraft Exchange. (2020). *Achieving supply chain transparency. A principles-to-practice guide for ethical businesses*. https://traidcraftexchange.org/transparency-guide.

Tukker, A. (2004). Eight types of product-service system: Eight ways to sustainability? Experiences from SusProNet. *Business Strategy and the Environment*, *13*(4), 246–260.

van Bommel, K. (2018). Managing tensions in sustainable business models: Exploring instrumental and integrative strategies. *Journal of Cleaner Production*, *196*, 829–841.

van der Stelt, J. (2009). *Since 59. 50 Jaar Fair Trade Original*. Fair Trade Original.

Vos, R. O. (2007). Defining sustainability: A conceptual orientation. *Journal of Chemical Technology and Biotechnology*, *82*(4), 334–339.

Warnick, J. (2020, January). *5 things to know about Starbucks new environmental sustainability commitment.* https://stories.starbucks.com/stories/2020/5-things-to-know-about-starbucks-new-environmental-sustainability-commitment.

WHO. (2019, July 15). *World hunger is still not going down after three years and obesity is still growing – UN report.* https://www.who.int/news/item/15-07-2019-world-hunger-is-still-not-going-down-after-three-years-and-obesity-is-still-growing-un-report.

Wells, P., & Seitz, M. (2005). Business models and closed-loop supply chains: A typology. *Supply Chain Management: An International Journal*, *10*(4), 249–251.

Zott, C., Amit, R., & Massa, L. (2011). The business model: Recent developments and future research. *Journal of Management*, *37*(4), 1019–1042.

3 Digital Megatrends and the Management Barriers They Form

Grzegorz Sobiecki

Introduction and Research Concept

Although a trend is a well-known concept, it is necessary for the purposes of this chapter to define its origins, stages of development, and possible analytical applications. This is even more important in the case of a megatrend, or more specifically, a digital megatrend. According to Schulman (2007, p. 1), the term "trend" in its present meaning "was formally christened in 1901, when the British statistician R.H. Hooker used it to describe the linear pattern traced by what would now be called a moving average: 'The curve or line representing the successive instantaneous averages I propose to call the trend'". The authorship of the term "megatrend" is attributed to John Naisbitt, who first used it in his 1982 work *Megatrends: Ten New Directions Transforming Our Lives*. He redefined the concept in 1990, describing megatrends as significant and permanent economic, social, political, and technological changes that are slow to form; however, once in place, they have an impact on all areas of life for some time, and consequently, on the future of the entire world (Gajewski et al., 2015, p. 15). With the advent of digital technologies, particularly the extensive application of artificial intelligence (AI) since 2010 (see Table 3.2), a new term was coined: technological/digital megatrends. These more modern versions "are based on disruptive innovations, i.e. new products, services, or business models that are initially addressed to (targeted at) small, seemingly unprofitable client segments, only to grow and expand across the entire market" (Gajewski et al., 2015, p. 17).

As indicated by a study employing the SALSA[1] methodology to verify the scope of peer-reviewed articles published between 2010 and 2018, the concept of megatrends has been used in research for "analyzing the impact of fundamental economic and social changes in three main areas: foresight studies of selected industries, analyses of existing and anticipated changes in management and business practices, and other socio-economic topics" (Malik & Jankowska, 2018, p. 209). This chapter focuses on business practices, covering considerable challenges faced by

DOI: 10.4324/9781003204343-3

company managers. In these contexts, destructive digital megatrends are amplified by the scale and impact of AI-based solutions. Therefore, one of the tasks is to prepare managers for two management options: (1) to actively and pre-emptively allow megatrends within their business, or (2) to respond to the competitive threat from those companies that have recognized the business opportunities associated with digital megatrends. The analysis of existing research shows that managers seem hesitant to take action because of the depiction of megatrends within scientific discourse. The problem is twofold: first, researchers tend to focus on the description of trends, leaving the task of figuring out the practical applications and possible management barriers to business; second, the "digital" context is frequently neglected in the discussion of trends. This inspires the following question: What management barriers do these problems generate in terms of systemic and methodical actions readily available, even in the face of high-impact megatrends requiring a prompt response? Unfortunately, there seems to be a gap in this area of research. Indeed, with the literature mostly limited to discussing the nature of trends, thus far there has been little exploration of the emerging barriers. To fill this gap, a research model is proposed that has been developed as a combination of two extant business models. The first, represented by Drucker (2010), consists of three dimensions: "Managing Business, Managing Managers, and Managing Employees". They may be characterized as three levels of management: the strategic level answers the question of what is to be achieved; the operational level answers the question of what is to be done; and the delivery level answers the question of how it is to be achieved. The second school is represented by Johnson et al. (2008, p. 5), whose business model consists of four dimensions: Customer Value Proposition (CVP), Profit Formula, Key Resources, and Key Processes. The research field includes a study of management barriers caused by trends in terms of their positioning in a 12-box grid representative of both business models (see Table 3.1). The research gap is addressed based on a trend analysis outlined by the American researcher Rohit Bhargava (2020), who identifies 10 "megatrends" with 75 further sub-trends as their phases in the period of 2011–2019. In light of the above, the research hypothesis proposes that there may be a relationship between the nature of the trend and the positioning of the barriers in Table 3.1.

An empirical approach, specifically inductive reasoning, has been adopted in the study. The chapter has the following structure: the digital component of the potential management barriers emerging from the ten megatrends is discussed in the section Trends Identified for the Pre-technology Era. The section Digital Megatrends in the 2000s and the Corresponding Management Barriers explores how the barriers related to each of the ten megatrends are distributed in Table 3.1. The section Pattern Mapping of Management Barriers Across All Megatrends

Table 3.1 The research model

		Business Model: I–IV *I. CVP*	*II. Profit Formula*	*III. Key Resources*	*IV. Key Processes*
		Customer Value Proposition (CVP), which is the genuine reason for the customer to buy the product or service.	The mechanism based on which the added value for the company is produced.	Resources necessary to ensure a profitable delivery of the CVP. They might include:	Processes that make the profitable delivery of the CVP repeatable and scalable. They might include:
Business Model: A–C	**A.Managing Employees**	**Offering that:** • Is defined not only by the CVP, but also by how it is sold	**Cost structure:** • Direct costs • Indirect costs	**Resources like:** • People • Equipment	**Norms:** • Opportunity size needed for investment • Approach to customers and channels
	B. Managing Managers	**Offering that:** • Satisfies the problem or meets the need • Is not defined only by what is sold	**Cost structure:** • How costs are allocated • Includes cost of key assets • Economies of scale	**Resources like:** • Technology, products • Information • Channels	**Rules & Metrics:** • Margin requirements for investments • Credit terms • Lead times • Supplier terms
	C. Managing Business	**Things to be done for the target consumer:** • To solve an important problem • To fulfill an important need • To address the target consumer	**Revenue model:** • How much money can be made: price x volume • Volume can be thought of in terms of market size • Purchase frequency • Ancillary sales	**Resources like:** • Partnerships • Alliances • Brand	**Processes:** • Design and product development • Sourcing and manufacturing • Marketing • Hiring and training • IT

Source: Based on: Sobiecki (2020), Drucker (2010), and Johnson et al. (2008, p. 5)

captures the patterns of the previously identified management barriers, and finally, conclusions and solutions for the barriers are presented in the section Solutions for Key Barriers: The Analytics Translator.

Trends Identified for the Pre-technology Era

The emergence of pre-technological trends had a significant impact on the 2001–2019 megatrends identified by Bhargava (2020). Infrastructural trends, such as miniaturization and computing power, network systems, sensor networks, and big data, ultimately leading to the emergence of AI, are illustrated in Table 3.2. They can be inscribed in four morphing waves of technological progress (Arthur, 2017, pp. 1–7), approximately reflecting the following periods: the 1970s–1980s, the 1990s–2000s, since 2010, and since 2015. The morphing waves, along with the corresponding trends, have continued to provide companies with a constantly evolving opportunity to build a competitive advantage. This process has been facilitated by reduced Internet traffic costs and increasing access speeds. For example, in 2008 and 2020 the revenues for global mobile data were estimated at USD 177 billion and USD 578 billion, respectively, with traffic increasing from 37 to 35,054 petabytes per month (Greenberg et al., 2017, p. 11). Traffic has grown dramatically since 2015, which aligns with the commercial use of AI (see Table 3.2). A rapid increase in the number of mobile devices has also improved data accessibility. The global population and the number of mobile devices were expected to reach, respectively, 7.8 billion and 26.3 billion in 2020 compared with 6.3 billion and 0.5 billion in 2010 (Cisco and United Nations, cited in: Greenberg et al., 2017, p. 10). The third and fourth waves of technological progress have resulted in cheaper and better access to mobile traffic, allowing technology to expand on a commercial scale. These phenomena have contributed to a transition of trends from offline in the pre-technology era to online in modern times. Table 3.2 offers a graphical representation of the respective stages of technological progress. It includes the concepts discussed further during the analysis of megatrends in the section Digital Megatrends in the 2000s and the Corresponding Management Barriers.

Digital Megatrends in the 2000s and the Corresponding Management Barriers

The unfolding analysis covers the digital megatrends of 2011–2019, discussed by Bhargava in his book *Non-Obvious Megatrends: How to See What Others Miss and Predict the Future* (2020). As already indicated in the section Introduction and Research Concept, his work identifies 10 megatrends with a further 75 sub-trends as their respective phases (see Table 3.3).

Table 3.2 Historical waves of technological progress

Morphing technological waves	1970s–1980s **I. First morphing** (Arthur, 2017)	**1990s–2000s** **II. Second morphing** (Arthur, 2017)	**Since 2010 (approx.)** **III. Third morphing** (Arthur, 2017)	**Since 2015 (approx.)** **IV. Fourth morphing and OMO** (Arthur, 2017)
	I. Miniaturization and computing power			
		II. Network systems		
			III. Sensor networks & big data. Integrated networks	
				IV. OMO Sapiens* (Lee, 2018)
Technological capabilities	**Miniaturization and computing power**	**Network systems**	**Associative intelligence outside the human mind**	**Technological unemployment**
	Integrated circuits	Commercial use of the Internet	Cheap and ubiquitous sensors	Offshoring/outsourcing has historically brought the transfer of workplaces to another physical economy and the reduction of workplaces that have not returned.
	Miniaturization	Telephone and optical lines	Wireless sensor networks (WSNs)	
		Internet-based services	Recognition of objects, faces, and voices	
		Cloud – external computing power	Large amounts of data generated by all of the above	The current transfer of workplaces takes place from the physical economy to the virtual economy – a new economy based on intangible assets. These places will not return.
		Network-based collaboration	Data used for modeling	
Applications	Computer-aided designing	Contemporary network – globalization	Development of smart-algorithm applications	The elimination of human workplaces by replacing them with AI.
	Computer-aided macro-economical forecasts	Remote monitoring of suppliers	Associative algorithms	
		Outsourcing	Voice and face recognition	A symbiosis of AI and humans in a number of workplaces that require the use of "Cognitive Labor" (Lee, 2018, p. 155).
		Global use of remote, cheap labor	Bots, e.g. chatbots	

Source: Developed by the author in the form of a table based on: Sobiecki (2020) and Arthur (2017, pp. 1–7). * OMO (Offline-Merge-Online) – the morphing of physical and virtual worlds; OMO Sapiens – a person representative of the OMO world (Lee, 2018, p. 117)

Table 3.3 Timeline of the ten megatrends identified in 2011–2019

	10 megatrends (Bhargava, 2020)	*Year or Decade* 70s	80s	90s	00s	10	11	12	13	14	15	16	17	18	19
1	Amplified Identity										X X	X X	X X		X
2	Evolution Ungendernity, p. 92								X			X	X	X	X
3	Instant Knowledge, p. 102								X X	X				X	
4	Evolution of Revivalism, p. 112								X+'17			X	X	X	X X
5	Human Mode, p. 123						X X	X		X X + '15 + '17		X+'18		X X	X
6	Attention Wealth, p. 137						X	X	X+18	X	X		X	X	X X
7	Purposeful Profit, p. 148								X		X		X	X	X
8	Data Abundance, p. 160							X		X	X	X		X	
9	Protective Tech, p. 171										X+18	X	X+19 X		
10	Flux Commerce, p. 182								X	X	X+18	X	X		X X
	Total mentions						3	3	7	7	8	8	11	12	11
Technology morphing waves (Arthur, 2017, pp. 1–7)	I. First wave	Miniaturization and computing power													
	II. Second wave			Network systems											
	III. Third wave					Sensor networks & big data. Integrated networks									
	IV. Fourth wave								Emergence of AI						
Lee, p. 117	OMO Sapiens wave											OMO Sapiens (Lee, 2018)			

Source: Developed by the author based on Arthur (2017, pp. 1–7) and Bhargava (2020, pp. 80, 92, 102, 112, 123, 137, 148, 160, 171, 182)

The four morphing waves introduced in Table 3.2 also feature in the lower part of Table 3.3. The aim is to illustrate how the phases of the megatrends identified by Bhargava (2020) (presented in the upper part of Table 3.3) can be shaped by the morphing waves of technological progress. In this section, each of the ten megatrends is subjected to a two-stage analysis: first, types of management barriers corresponding to a given trend are defined in relation to 12 fields of the research model; second, the management barriers are allocated to the respective fields within the research model (Table 3.1).

Trend No. 1: Amplified Identity

Amplified Identity is defined as a shift toward individuality and the means to control our stories on the Internet to make sure that our online identities are the ultimate expression of who we are (Bhargava, 2020, p. 80). This trend emerged at the intersection of two phenomena (Table 3.4)[2]: the individualistic need of Internet users to express themselves as they would like to be perceived and the availability of technological tools created in response to this need (e.g. smartphones with high-quality cameras, facial recognition, fast-speed Internet, access to cloud operations), developed as a result of technical solutions established during morphing phases I–IV. The Amplified Identity trend can cause barriers for companies that are technologically unprepared to meet their customer needs in this area. Due to their strategic nature, management barriers corresponding to this trend fall into field C.I of Table 3.1. They affect companies that are incapable of including AI-supported tools in their CVP formula and thus cannot meet their users' expectations regarding modern self-expression.

Trend No. 2: Evolution Ungendernity

Bhargava uses the term "Evolution Ungendernity" in order to highlight this megatrend's transgression beyond users' gender. He argues that when gender is no longer a priority issue, opportunities open up for buyers willing to reinvent themselves. The markets reserved for previously gender-specific products can now appeal to diverse audiences (Bhargava, 2020, p. 92). Although initially (2013–2017) it focused primarily on women, the trend has gradually shifted towards greater diversity in terms of gender in general, offering uniform products for diverse users. The participation of diversity-driven communities in this trend has largely been facilitated by the Internet; however, traditional social frameworks have also begun to fade away in the physical world. The management barriers arising from this trend affect companies that insist on a less diverse or inclusion-oriented way of thinking with regard to their customers as opposed to their competitors. The consequences of

Table 3.4 The amplified identity trend and its phases of development in 2011–2019

The Trend Name and Its Phases of Development in 2010–2019	*Year*								
	11	*12*	*13*	*14*	*15*	*16*	*17*	*18*	*19*
Trend 1. AMPLIFIED IDENTITY 1 Shift toward individuality and the means to control our stories. 2 Our online identities have become the ultimate expression of who we are (Bhargava, p.80).									
1. **SELFIE CONFIDENCE** The ability to share a carefully crafted online personality allows people to use their social content, such as selfies, to build their own confidence.					X				
2. **EVERYDAY STARDOM** The growth of personalization leads more consumers to expect that everyday interactions will be transferred into celebrity-type experiences.					X				
3. **PERSONALITY MAPPING** As the behavioral measurement tools map the details of our personalities, brands start using such data to bring like-minded people together to engage in unique experiences.						X			
4. **MAINSTREAM MULTICULTURALISM** After years of being minimized, multicultural citizens find widespread acceptance through a growing integration of diverse ideas and people in entertainment, products, and politics.						X			
5. **AUTHENTIC FAMESEEKERS** A new generation of creators is born: authentic fame seekers who turn to social media to establish their brands, build an audience, and become the next big thing.							X		
6. **OUTRAGEOUS OUTSIDERS** There is a rise in outsiders with an increasing willingness to say or do things we might describe as outrageous simply to capture attention.							X		
7. **SIDE QUIRKS** As the global shift toward individualism continues, people of all ages embrace what makes them unique, follow their passions, are able to establish side businesses, and increasingly appreciate quirky differences in one another.							X		X

Technology morphing phases 1970–2020, (Arthur 2017, pp. 1–7)	70	80	90	00	11	12	13	14	15	16	17	18	19
I. First wave					Miniaturization and computing power								
II. Second wave							Network systems						
III. Third wave					Sensor networks & Big Data. Integrated networks								
IV. Fourth wave									Emergence of AI				
OMO Sapiens (Lee, 2018, p. 117)										OMO Sapiens			

Source: Developed by the author based on Arthur (2017, pp. 1–7) and Bhargava (2020, p. 80)

this approach may be twofold. First, such enterprises can lose the strategic momentum in the development of their unique CVP by not tapping into product offer opportunities created by the megatrend (field C.I of Table 3.1). Such management barriers are a result of inertia and persistence in producing only gender-profiled goods. Second, companies may suffer from lower profitability (field A.II of Table 3.1) as the effectiveness of teams following traditional gender-specific norms is reduced compared with companies that promote diversity and inclusion in the workplace.

Trend No. 3: Instant Knowledge

According to Bhargava (2020), this is a trend that raises multiple concerns. As the cost of education rises, the perceived value of on-demand learning, both from experts and amateurs, also grows (p. 102). This forms a generation thirsty for fast-access surface knowledge that replaces deep knowledge and wisdom. In light of this, can the products and services produced by this generation be trusted and considered safe? Three types of management barriers can be identified in connection with this megatrend. First, customers can use Internet-based tools to verify company communication against the opinions of experts. This allows them to highlight any inconsistencies with the potential to cause difficulties with regard to customers' awareness, even if the communication is well designed. This barrier falls into field C.I of Table 3.1. Second, a company may wrongly target its communication flow, missing the steps and places where customers are present and are able to see or hear the information. This is particularly the case with the "OMO Sapiens" world, where a company continues to communicate offline (e.g. through TV advertising), whereas customers prefer to consult YouTube experts or online blogs. This barrier falls into the category of processes, i.e. field C.IV of Table 3.1. Third, a company may be systemically incapable of developing its awareness regarding ineffective communication. This happens when company employees and other resources are not focused on perusing and comprehending the feedback from the OMO world posted in response to a company's actions. In the meantime, their competitors equip their products with sensors to collect and send feedback on the extent to which the purpose of the CVP has been achieved (Johnson et al., 2008, p. 5). These two barriers fall into fields A.III and B.III of Table 3.1, respectively.

Trend No. 4: Evolution of Revivalism

Bhargava describes this megatrend as a desire to revert to simpler times as a coping mechanism in a rapidly changing world; people are equally interested in reviving the past as they are in preserving it, which includes the use of technology to retain artisanal products, simpler technologies, and historic brands (Bhargava, 2020, p. 112). The management barriers identified for this megatrend have both sociological and technological roots, and as such can be placed in field C.I of Table 3.1. In sociological terms, a barrier arises from the fact that, as is the case with every trend, revivalism also attracts a significant group of users belonging to the same market for a specific product. These individuals are looking for a cozy, familiar, and stable mental asylum – a refuge from excessive and overtly aggressive multi-channel marketing of products and new experiences (the OMO world, as described by Lee, 2018, p. 117). Such a shelter is represented by historically sentimental brands and products with which these brands are identified. From the point of view of technology, two types of management barriers can be identified. First, there are those faced by start-ups and new companies (field C.IV of Table 3.1), whose consumers never had the opportunity to develop a "historical-nostalgic" bond with their brand, as there was no prior "history" to legitimize it. Moreover, certain products, e.g. smartphones, will always be perceived as belonging to the high-tech world, regardless of their physical appearance. On the one hand, the downgrading of such products would pose a challenge for producers as, ultimately, their competitive advantage depends on technological progress; on the other hand, it would be desirable for the elimination of barriers to market entry governed by the revivalism trend. The downgrading of such products is unlikely to occur in a standard manner at the level of product design, development, marketing, or production. Producers are not willing to abandon their well-established processes because then they would have to invest in new ones.

The second type of technology-related barriers are those that affect companies, which have been able to secure an emotional bond by selling products offline under traditional brands. The dynamics of this approach was particularly visible during the 2015–2019 period, i.e. during the morphing waves of big data and AI (Arthur, 2017, pp. 1–7). This means that, having neither the resources nor people necessary to capture the technological aspect of this trend, traditional "offline" companies may encounter barriers falling into fields A.III and B.III of Table 3.1. These companies will most likely struggle with their CVP (field A.I in Table 3.1), as they need to prepare an offering that satisfies customer needs defined not only by *what* is sold but also *how* it is sold (Johnson et al., 2008, p. 5). The paradox of the "how" is that such enterprises must preserve their "traditional" image while staying up to date with electronic channels of communication and sales.

Trend No. 5: Human Mode

Bhargava connects the Human Mode trend with the spread of automation and its primary side effect: people's willingness to pay extra for human contact. Companies use technology to mimic human-like contact through robots, avatars, and virtual reality (VR). The latter in particular offers an opportunity to satisfy users' need for human-like interactions by means of cheap technological solutions. However, this carries a risk that genuine human contacts could become an unattainable luxury available only to a few (Bhargava, 2020, p. 123). Analyzing the dynamics of this trend, four periods can be differentiated: (1) the "Human Mode as Marketing Approach" (2011–2012), during which efforts were invested in enhancing the images of brands by adding components such as social capital, humanity, and employee history to the discourse; (2) the "Low-Cost Human Mode", (2013–2018), during which social media platforms were identified as ready-made solutions to make individuals and companies appear more human-like for their users; (3) the "Advanced Human Mode" (2014–2017), during which brands tapped into the social aspects of this megatrend – sharing experiences and personal qualities with a particular focus on personality quirks and intentional imperfections – to add authenticity to their products; and (4) the "AI vs. Personal Human Mode" (2018–2019), during which users were divided into those served by automated, AI-based, and inexpensive bots and those who value services provided by people (Bhargava, 2020, p. 123).

The first group of management barriers related to this trend belongs in fields A.III, B.III, and C.III of Table 3.1. Price difference is one of the consequences of the market split into two segments: mainstream users, who rely on affordable human-like AI-based interfaces, and premium users, who pay more for human interactions and services provided by people. Unable to integrate their brands into the "affordable" segment, companies offering premium (expensive) human-operated interfaces need to deal with a management barrier identified in field C.III of Table 3.1. Another barrier they face is related to costs. The cost structure of their competitors largely relies on automated interfaces and AI-based algorithms. This poses an obstacle for premium businesses, identified in field B.III of Table 3.1, as their rivals from the cheaper mainstream segment maintain the entry barrier by cutting operational costs and using predominantly AI-based interfaces that require only a handful of employees (field A.III in Table 3.1).

The market polarization into the premium and mainstream segments gives rise to another group of management barriers. Given the social component of the Human Mode trend (the longing for personal contact), the market segmentation produces emotional tensions in the "affordable" segment, as a result of which this segment is perceived as dehumanized. The commoditization of brands owned by mainstream companies puts pressure on their pricing policies; this creates a profitable growth management barrier, as identified in field A.I of Table 3.1, where what matters is not only *what* is sold (products and services) but also *how* it is sold ("dehumanized" brands) (Johnson et al., 2008, p. 5).

Trend No. 6: Attention Wealth

In an information economy, buyer attention has become a currency. Brands, the media, and politicians can monetize only by capturing our attention (Bhargava, 2020, p. 134). Information noise pushes us toward "trusted curators of information" who can help us make sense of it all. The never-ending battle for attention provides leverage to technologies capable of producing artificial avatars and fabricating deep fakes. By realizing how much wealth our attention represents, we can decide who deserves it and who does not (Bhargava, 2020, p. 134). Analysis of the dynamics of this trend clarifies that there are two distinct periods: (1) "Attention Wealth: The Battle for Attention to Retail" (2011–2015), oriented on experiences delivered by retail to attract customers' attention and the use of the internet by brands to maintain this attention through the "seamless integration of offline with online" (Bhargava, 2020, p. 137) – at this stage digital tools were not yet in wide-spread use; and (2) "Attention Wealth: Beyond Retail" (2016–2019), where retail was reinforced with social media in order to exploit emotions (e.g. anger)and sell fantasies. These aggressive manipulations, further exacerbated by the constant noise produced by massive streams of data, undermine public trust, and contribute to the erosion of truth.

Taking this into account, the key management barrier lies in the paradox of a need to attract attention contrasted with the rejection of the information noise and massive streams of untruthful messages constantly attacking our senses. Solving this paradox requires finding a balance between the form (narrative, story-telling) and the intensity of communication so as not to lose credibility. For companies whose brands do not carry an emotional component, attempts to attract attention by tapping into emotions may be perceived as artificial and lacking credibility. This barrier corresponds with field C.III of Table 3.1. Furthermore, for companies whose expertise does not originate from the digital/online world, the key barriers to business development will fall into: (1) field C.IV due to the poor design of communications responsible for merging offline with online; and (2) field B.IV due to an incorrectly defined combination of key performance indicators (KPIs) for measuring the return on investment (ROI) in communication activities (online/offline mix model).

Trend No. 7: Purposeful Profit

While avoiding overtly promotional activities, in the past companies would use the so-called "cause-related soft-branding" to support initiatives that appeared to be aligned with their core values[3] (Bhargava, 2020, p. 148). Today's customers make informed choices while employees seek jobs in firms interested in the greater good. Therefore, companies must earn trust through positive business models, an ethical approach to employees, charitable actions, corporate social responsibility (CSR) in supply chains, and a daily pursuit of the greater good on a par with profit (Bhargava, 2020, p. 148). Analyzing the dynamics of this megatrend, two phases may be suggested: (1) "Classic Branding" (2011–2015), with sub trends built on "classic" and "logical" cause-and-effect branding; and (2) "Digital Acceleration" (2017–2019), with consumers turning to trends that have a purpose and employees looking for meaningful jobs. Given that there is a clear expectation of immediate results within both groups, the trend has accelerated with the use of online platforms and AI-based systems.

The key barrier associated with this megatrend falls into field C.I of Table 3.1. Finding a purpose for a brand is equal to changing its CVP in order to satisfy customers' expectations of "purposeful profit". This barrier produces three distinct challenges. Firstly, a brand will not be considered credible if its practices or products are not recognized as purposeful. Such brands may need to redefine their CVP; otherwise, their development will be at risk. Secondly, when a company's CVP is perceived as meeting the practical need without serving the greater good, adding a purpose to eliminate this deficit will neither be a quick process nor a natural course of action for the company in question. Thirdly, for a brand to be seen as making "socially responsible choices" (Bhargava, 2020, p. 148), it will again be necessary to modify the CVP.

Trend No. 8: Data Abundance

While producing increasing amounts of data on social media and smart devices, consumers demand more control, intellectual property rights, safety, and incentives to share (Bhargava, 2020, p. 160). The huge quantities of data have created issues for companies as they have had to implement machine-learning systems and algorithms to sort the data and suggest automated insights and actions (Bhargava, 2020, p. 160). In an analysis of the dynamics of this megatrend during the 2011–2019 period, it is important to explore how data have influenced consumer behavior, how consumers have influenced business, and finally, how business can respond. The following two periods may be identified:(1) "Data Surge" (2011–2014), a period of intense data collection during which its usefulness was studied and businesses focused on issues related to privacy and data protection; and (2) "Data Extraction" (2015–2019), a period when data origin emerged as a new component of data segmentation. During this latter period, data began to be produced not only by companies or as Open Data but also through wearable technologies such as smart watches ("small data"). These three sources create a data overload that is difficult to manage and hinders any efforts to meet the demands of consumers regarding actual control over data. Consequently, companies seek structural support in the form of AI technology. The mechanisms leading to information overload, which intensified particularly in the second period (2015–2019), have created three types of management barriers falling into fields C.I, C.IV, and B.III of Table 3.1. Firstly, rather than simply focusing on data retrieval and monetization, companies should adapt their CVP to the phenomena identified within this megatrend. As a source of data themselves, consumers demand a share of the benefits provided by data processing. If this is to be achieved, such benefits must be meticulously designed. Companies have therefore been forced to rethink their CVP so that they can decide which data and for what purpose could flow back to customers. Implementation of this decision constitutes a management barrier located in field C.I of Table 3.1. Secondly, if data-related processes only allow for one-way data inflow (from the environment to the company), they have to be redesigned. Without an appropriate two-way data management process (whereby the data also flows to customers), users cannot become beneficiaries of what is processed. Companies must therefore overcome the management barrier identified in field C.IV of Table 3.1. Thirdly, lack of proper technology hinders data filtering, storing, and processing in AI systems. Gaps in the field of data management resources ensuring user participation in data processing benefits constitute a barrier classified in field B.III of Table 3.1.

Trend No. 9: Protective Tech

AI-based systems are already supporting or about to support key aspects of human life such as monitoring our health to alert us to diseases, tracking our finances to suggest modifications, predicting our arrival to turn the lights on, security (drones), or filling out tax forms. For these and even more sophisticated real-time predictions to be possible, complex and highly sophisticated systems and algorithms are being developed. These developments prompt a fundamental question: Where is the line between the 24/7 tracking and the requirement not to compromise our privacy and individual liberties (Bhargava, 2020, p. 171) The dynamics of this megatrend shows how technology has become a vital part of customers' lives without them noticing it. Step by step, data processing systems are not only monitoring our activities but have also become capable of suggesting certain actions or even take them for us. Functions enabling predictive behavior analytics are becoming invisible to us to the extent that we stop realizing that AI is doing something on our behalf. Protective Tech is a very recent trend that emerged and evolved during the 2015–2019 period (Table 3.3). Its development is a result of the fourth technological morphing, whereby AI-powered support systems have gradually been embedded in our everyday life.

Management barriers corresponding to this trend can be identified at three levels of the CVP business model. Firstly, a company may not have the right processes to monetize the data in a manner consistent with this megatrend, i.e. using AI systems to act on customers' behalf. Arising at the strategic level and falling into field C.IV of Table 3.1, this barrier has the potential to affect not only low-tech but also digitally native companies, even those with an appropriately defined CVP. Secondly, another barrier emerges at the operational level (field B.IV of Table 3.1) as managers must be capable of deciding to invest in modern technologies if AI-supported processes are to be introduced at all. Thirdly, there is the executive level, with a barrier identified in field A.IV of Table 3.1, where company employees directly involved in capturing novel investment opportunities lack the necessary skills. In addition, further barriers can be anticipated in Column III of Table 3.1 (Key Resources). To benefit from the economic potential of this megatrend, a company must be technologically advanced and have a highly skilled workforce: without the former, it faces a barrier within field B.III of Table 3.1; without the latter, a barrier in field A.III.

Trend No. 10: Flux Commerce

Boundaries that were once clear between industries are eroding as the latter begin to blur with each other (Bhargava, 2020, p. 182). Business models have shifted from products sold to product subscriptions or products offered as services, partly because distribution models tend to eliminate middlemen. Companies must accept and learn to play by this new and rapidly evolving rule that everything is changing: how customers buy and sell, how much they are willing to pay, whether they buy or rent, etc. (Bhargava, 2020, p. 182). When it comes to the dynamics of this megatrend, two periods – both related to the emergence of Big Data and AI (the lower part of Figure 3.1) – are evident: (1) "Product-Oriented Change" (2013–2015), during which business focused on changing and improving the product itself, i.e. changing an element in the business model –companies started offering the option to rent or subscribe to a product instead of buying it, reaching out to local users, and engaging in partnerships with former competitors; and (2) "Industry Blending" (2016–2019), during which the boundaries between industries and business approaches became blurred with innovation "driven" by incubation, recognition, or a desperate search for a new competitive advantage. With boundaries blurring between classic industries, changes arise both within and across business models. Therefore, the primary barrier corresponding to this trend lies in the question of whether a company understands change and can play the game by modifying its business model (innovation) rather than creating a new product (invention). In Table 3.1, this barrier cuts across all fields in Columns IV and I.

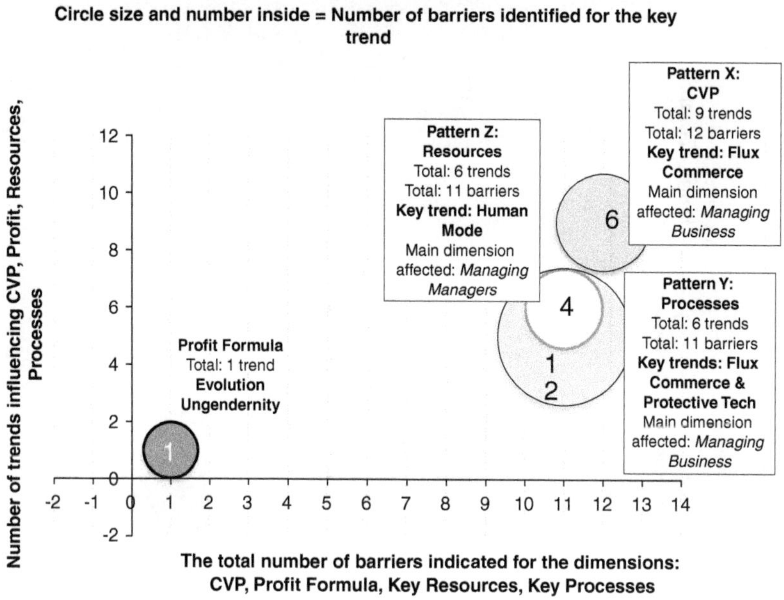

Figure 3.1 Patterns X, Y, and Z identified for management barriers across trends.

Pattern Mapping of Management Barriers Across All Megatrends

All observations regarding management barriers identified for the ten megatrends discussed in the section Digital Megatrends in the 2000s and the Corresponding Management Barriers are mapped in Table 3.5. The structure of Table 3.5 corresponds to the 12 fields present within the research model outlined in Table 3.1, reflecting the 12 dimensions of the business model, i.e. CVP, Profit Formula, Key Resources, and Key Processes, as indicated by Johnson et al. (2008, p. 5), and Managing Employees, Managing Managers, and Managing Business, as suggested by Drucker (2010).

Table 3.5 specifies the number of management barriers for each of the 12 fields. In addition, the numbers of management barriers are summarized. The total number of identified barriers (35) is presented in the final row of the table. The number of barriers for each of the four dimensions in business model I–IV is indicated in the penultimate row. The number of management barriers for each of the three dimensions in business model A–C is shown in the last column. Finally, the penultimate column specifies the number of management barriers for each megatrend separately.

Based on the analysis of Table 3.5, several management barrier patterns can be identified. These are presented in Figure 3.1. The patterns

Table 3.5 Management barriers mapped across trends

Scores – Research Model Results			*Business Model: I–IV*				*Scores: A–C*	
Pages in Bhargava, 2020	*Trend Names by Bhargava, 2020*	*BM A-C*	*I. CVP*	*II. Profit Formula*	*III. Key Resources*	*IV. Key Processes*	*Trends*	*Total*
80	Amplified Identity	**A. Managing Employees**					0	10
92	Evolution Ungendernity			1			1	
102	Instant Knowledge				1		1	
112	Evolution of Revivalism		1		1		2	
123	Human Mode		1		1		2	
137	Attention Wealth						0	
148	Purposeful Profit						0	
160	Data Abundance						0	
171	Protective Tech				1	1	2	
182	Flux Commerce		1			1	2	
80	Amplified Identity	**B. Managing Managers**					0	9
92	Evolution Ungendernity						0	
102	Instant Knowledge				1		1	
112	Evolutional Revival				1		1	
123	Human Mode				1		1	
137	Attention Wealth					1	1	
148	Purposeful Profit						0	
160	Data Abundance				1		1	
171	Protective Tech				1	1	2	
182	Flux Commerce		1			1	2	

80	Amplified Identity	**C. Managing Business**	1				1	16
92	Evolution Ungendernity		1				1	
102	Instant Knowledge		1			1	2	
112	Evolutional Revival		1			1	2	
123	Human Mode				1		1	
137	Attention Wealth				1	1	2	
148	Purposeful Profit		1				1	
160	Data Abundance		1			1	2	
171	Protective Tech		1			1	2	
182	Flux Commerce		1			1	2	
			Summary scores					
80	Amplified Identity	**Total Business Model: A–C and I–IV**	1				1	**35 = Total scores of BM A-C and those of the trends**
92	Evolution Ungendernity		1	1			2	
102	Instant Knowledge		1		2	1	4	
112	Evolutional Revival		2		2	1	5	
123	Human Mode		1		3		4	
137	Attention Wealth				1	2	3	
148	Purposeful Profit		1				1	
160	Data Abundance		1		1	1	3	
171	Protective Tech		1		2	3	6	
182	Flux Commerce		3			3	6	
	Total Scores of Business Model I. – IV.		12	1	11	11		
	Total scores				35			

Source: Developed by the author based on Bhargava (2020, pp. 80, 92, 102, 112, 123, 137, 148, 160, 171, 182)

are discussed throughout the remainder of this section, considering the previous conclusions regarding management barrier types. Profit Formula has been excluded from further discussion due to its relatively low importance in relation to the study objectives (only one barrier was recognized within this dimension; see Figure 3.1).

Pattern X: Customer Value Proposition vs. Flux Commerce

Pattern X could be characterized as follows:

1. Pattern X dominates in the CVP dimension, concentrating a total of 12 out of 35 management barriers identified in the section Digital Megatrends in the 2000s and the Corresponding Management Barriers (see the final row in Table 3.5).
2. Management barriers within Pattern X appear to be triggered by nine out of the ten megatrends, which indicates a relatively widespread penetration of the CVP dimension throughout all possible trend options.
3. Flux Commerce emerges as the key trend within this pattern; six management barriers have been identified for it across the research model, three of which lie solely within the CVP dimension. Given this concentration of barriers, it seems justified to focus the further discussion on how Flux Commerce influences the CVP within Pattern X.

The factors of management barriers concentrated specifically within Pattern X are determined by Flux Commerce, i.e. a trend that has blurred the boundaries between classic industries. Therefore, introducing innovation into a company's business model and blurring the boundaries across business models (Managing Business) are critical for the CVP. Since customer acquisition relies on these factors, any future development for a company incapable of such innovations is likely to become extremely challenging. In light of these observations and the trend analysis in the section Digital Megatrends in the 2000s and the Corresponding Management Barriers, the following two key management barriers can be identified within Pattern X:

- The first barrier is the lack of ability to innovate with regard to the business model (innovation) rather than improve the product (invention).
- Given the trend acceleration with the emergence of big data and AI-supported systems, the second barrier is the lack of digital skills in algorithm design.

Pattern Y: Key Processes vs. Flux Commerce and Protective Tech

Pattern Y could be characterized as follows:

1. Pattern Y dominates in the dimension of Key Processes, concentrating a total of 11 out of 35 management barriers.
2. Management barriers within Pattern Y appear to be triggered by six of the ten megatrends.
3. Two of these trends – Flux Commerce and Protective Tech – emerge as the key trends within this pattern. Three management barriers have been identified for each option across the research model, three of which lie solely within the Key Processes dimension. Given this concentration of barriers, it seems justified to focus the further discussion on how Flux Commerce and Protective Tech influence Key Processes within Pattern Y.

The management barrier factors concentrated specifically within Pattern Y are determined by Flux Commerce (already discussed with respect to the CVP dimension within Pattern X) and Protective Tech, i.e. a trend characterized by AI taking action on behalf of people as well as users' concerns regarding a thin line between the 24/7 tracking and a breach of privacy. Since customer relations and, consequently, customer loyalty rely on these factors (Managing Business), a company incapable of addressing them will find difficulties with any further development. In light of these observations and the analysis of both trends in the section Digital Megatrends in the 2000s and the Corresponding Management Barriers, the following two key management barriers can be identified within Pattern Y:

- The first barrier is the lack of processes providing for data management to a degree that would allow the use of AI-supported systems in the development of the CVP in predictive and prescriptive applications.
- The second barrier may result from the lack of resources, such as technology for the protection of customer privacy.

Pattern Z: Key Resources vs. Human Mode

Pattern Z could be characterized as follows:

1. Pattern Z dominates in the dimension of Key Resources, concentrating a total of 11 out of 35 management barriers.
2. Management barriers within Pattern Z appear to be triggered by six of the ten megatrends.
3. Human Mode emerges as the key trend within this pattern, with four management barriers identified for it across the entire research

model. Only three of these lie solely within the Key Resources dimension. Given this concentration of barriers, it seems justified to focus the further discussion on how Human Mode influences Key Resources within Pattern Z.

The factors of management barriers concentrated specifically within Pattern Z are determined by Human Mode, i.e. a trend that has introduced processes resulting in the gradual replacement of people in customer service roles with human-like avatars/bots and the subsequent division of customers into two segments: a premium category of customers who are willing to incur the additional cost of being served by people, and a much larger mainstream category of customers served by inexpensive avatars. The latter approach causes tension among customers as, although mainstream users also long for contact with people, this option is no longer financially viable for them. These factors have an effect on customer relations, and if a company proves incapable of addressing them (Managing Managers), it will encounter an obstacle to its further development. In light of these observations and the trend analysis in the section Digital Megatrends in the 2000s and the Corresponding Management Barriers, the following two key management barriers can be identified within Pattern Z:

- The first barrier is encountered by companies operating in the premium "human contacts" segment, which cannot position their CVP in the "affordable" avatar-based segment due to cost structure.
- The second barrier results from the market polarization, which can lead to a loss of "the point of differentiation built on empathy" (Bhargava, 2020, p. 123) by companies operating in the affordable segment.

Solutions for Key Barriers: The Analytics Translator

The proposed scheme of conduct aimed at addressing the barriers outlined in the previous section consists of three elements – the business model, technology and data management, and the human factor/skills – and is presented in Figure 3.2 as a strategy for business model transformation (developed based on Dewhurst & Willmott, 2014, pp. 2–3). The diagram focuses on the need to build an effective data management process linked with a company's business model. Such a data management process encompasses a sequence of steps: Step A – focusing on data extraction; Step B – processing data in order to find characteristic patterns/data sets (machine learning); Step C – delivery of data patterns to organizational cells in a manner that makes them available not only within a specific cell but also beyond (Elements 1 and 2 in Figure 3.2); Step D – using patterns/data sets to manage the respective elements of the

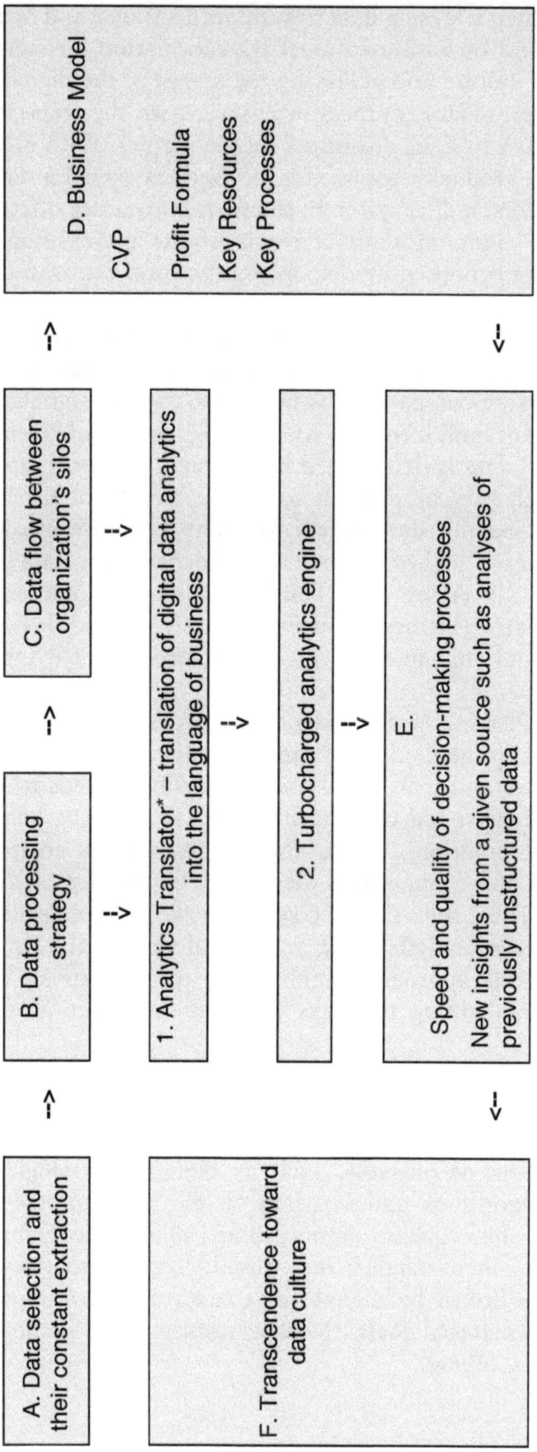

Figure 3.2 The data management strategy for business model transformation

business model; Step E – using data to support decisions; and finally, Step F – the final effect of business model transformation, i.e. withdrawal from the current culture and achieving the status of the digital culture/ data culture. The model is cyclical in nature, with the respective steps progressing from A to F, as illustrated by the arrows. With every cycle, the organization gradually transcends beyond its own limitations towards better understanding of the business opportunities offered by digitization. These limitations are a result of the pre-existing culture; however, with the proposed model, an organization can transcend to a new culture.

The process shown in Figure 3.2 enables a shift toward data culture (Step E). One can speak of data culture when an organization features several skills. First, a company must be able to capture signals from the market (an element built into Step A). This skill is crucial given that the type of extracted data is determined by strategic purposes (an element of Step B), which may be difficult to define in light of the excess of incoming data. Second, data extraction may be more effective if a company operates a highly efficient ("turbocharged") data analytics center (Element 2 in Figure 3.2). Third, a company should employ an Analytics Translator (Element 1 in Figure 3.2), whose job is to make sure that the data management process focuses on solving critical business problems.

According to Fleming et al. (2018, p. 5), an Analytics Translator is "someone on the business side who can help leaders identify high-impact analytics use cases and then 'translate' the business needs to data scientists, data engineers, and other tech experts so they can build an actionable analytics solution". These authors also suggest creating other positions within the organization dedicated to the digitally oriented business model. These roles should combine business management skills, data processing/data analysis skills, and digital skills. Table 3.6 offers a visualization of this approach, emphasizing the role of an Analytics Translator by highlighting the links between this function and other resources.

Fleming et al. (2018) also emphasize the need for a thoughtful approach to building resources. Based on the analysis of Table 3.6, today's business leaders should have in-depth knowledge regarding not only the operational aspects of business, such as digital technologies or the adaptation of algorithms and statistics to the needs of the business model, but also the requisite organizational skills to overcome management barriers. In particular, they should be able to reconcile the human resources driven by digital goals (data analytics, online) with those focused on material goals (the aspect of the business model based on tangible assets, offline).

Table 3.6 Key resources and their interdependence in addressing barriers

The Analytics Translator as a Solution for Management Barriers

		Interdependence of resources in addressing management barriers			
Skill name	**SKILLS**	I. Business + Analytical skills	II. Analytical + Technology skills	III. Technology + Business skills	**Skill description**
Business leaders	**A. BUSINESS SKILLS**	1			Lead analytics transformation across organization
Delivery managers		1			Deliver data and analytics driven insights and interface with end users
Analytics translators		1			***Ensure analytics solve critical business problems***
Visualization analysts					
Workflow integrators					
Data scientists					
Data engineers					
Data architects					
Business leaders	**B. ANALYTICAL SKILLS**				
Delivery managers					
Analytics translators			1		Ensure analytics solve critical business problem
Visualization analysts			1		Visualize data and build reports and dashboards

(*Continued*)

Table 3.6 (Continued)

The Analytics Translator as a Solution for Management Barriers

Workflow integrators		1		Build interactive decision-support tools and implement solution
Data scientists		1		***Develop statistical models and algorithms***
Data engineers				
Data architects				
Business leaders	**C. TECHNOLOGY SKILLS**		1	***Lead analytics transformation across organization***
Delivery managers				
Analytics translators				
Visualization analysts				
Workflow integrators				
Data scientists			1	Develop statistical models and algorithms
Data engineers			1	Collect, engineer, structure, and analyze data
Data architects			1	Ensure quality and consistency of data both in the present and future, design data flows

Source: Adapted from Fleming et al. (2018, p. 5). Exhibit 3

Summary and the 2030 Perspective

The findings presented in this chapter fill the research gap regarding the impact of the digital age trends on management barriers. Research started with defining the management barriers based on the holistic analysis of ten megatrends from 2011 to 2019, conducted with the use of the proposed research model (Table 3.1). The identified barriers were categorized and mapped as shown in Table 3.5. This allowed us to recognize three patterns for the barriers that were found to have the most inhibitory effect on business.

Based on this diagnosis, a solution was suggested: a dedicated approach to remove the said barriers through a well-designed data management process (Table 3.5). This process consists of the constant extraction of selected data, which are then processed by AI-supported systems. The obtained results can be used to continue feeding the business model with decisions supported by machine learning. To ensure the effectiveness and sustainability of the entire system, a new key resource is proposed – the Analytics Translator, i.e. a person with skills originating from business but trained by data scientists and visualization analytics specialists to act as a bridge between business and data (Table 3.6). Naturally, the study is not without flaws. One of them lies within the approach adopted to compile the list of barriers and map them, as shown in Table 3.5. During this process, the author did not employ an analytical approach other than his own educated judgment, based solely on over 30 years of experience in various management positions; therefore, it is possible that the resultant bias may have affected the final categorization.

Given that this chapter deals explicitly with management barriers, managers make up the primary target group of this study. The second target group is scientific researchers who can use the results presented here to continue research in three directions. First, the findings of this chapter can be verified by comparing the identified three patterns of management barriers against existing research. Second, this study offers no insight into the social aspects of the barriers. Moreover, at the time when the work on this article was coming to an end, research on the impact of the SARS-CoV-2/Covid-19 pandemic on the discussed trends and barriers was still rather scarce. Consequently, selected conclusions (if not all) will require verification in the coming years. As a final point, the ideas presented in this chapter can be used as educational material for students graduating in management, strategy, marketing, and technology faculties.

It would be extremely difficult to predict the future of the market forces currently at play or the emergence of future trends affecting business. Therefore, it seems safer to place a discussion about the possible sustainability or future changes in the scope of the diagnosed management barriers in a more universal perspective, e.g. a customer-behavior-based demand response model. The juxtaposition of this model with three most significant barrier generators among all megatrends, i.e. Flux Commerce, Protective Tech, and Human Mode, would in all likelihood lead to some useful conclusions regarding the durability of the barriers.

According to Edelman and Singer (2015), we can already see consumer behaviors influenced by the third technological wave (since 2010; see Table 3.3). The authors argue that "brands (...) not only react to customers as they make purchasing decisions but also actively shape those decision journeys"; the widespread use of AI-based systems allows these companies to actually act for the consumer, i.e. "design and continuously optimize decision journeys" (Edelman & Singer, 2015, p. 1).

The three megatrends, diagnosed in the section Pattern Mapping of Management Barriers Across All Megatrends as leading in creating management barriers, seem to be applicable to this perspective of operation where companies actively drive consumer behavior themselves rather than being driven by it. This approach includes several components, such as: automation (all megatrends), proactive personalization (Flux Commerce), contextual interaction (Human Mode), and innovation with regard to the consumer decision process (Protective Tech) (based on Edelman & Singer, 2015, p. 3). In light of the findings regarding the progress of technological waves, it seems that further strengthening of this approach may be expected. Therefore, it is concluded that the management barriers related to the discussed megatrends deeply intertwined with continued technological progress may remain valid for the next decade or so, insofar as companies will either be able to implement the proposed solutions to attract customers or the solutions themselves will become barriers to further development. All in all, given the current state of affairs in the area of management barriers, a division is likely to continue with two groups of firms emerging: large companies with digital solutions well embedded in their business models and companies that will continually struggle to preserve their traditional business models until they manage to digitize them.

Notes

1 SALSA is a method of systematic literature review: S – Search (define searching string and types of database), AL – Appraisal (pre-defined literature inclusion and exclusion), S – Synthesis (extract and categorize the data), and A – Analysis (narrate the results and finally reach conclusions) (Mengist et al., 2019).
2 Figures identical to Table 3.4 can be requested directly from the author for each trend discussed in Section 3. Although used for discovering the barriers, they are not included in this section due to space limitations.
3 Cause Related Marketing (CRM) is a mutually beneficial collaboration between a for-profit business and a non-profit organization entered into to promote the sales of the former and the cause represented by the latter.

References

Arthur, B. W. (2017, October). Where is the economy taking technology?. *McKinsey Quarterly*. Retrieved December 29, 2018, from https://www.mckinsey.com/business-functions/mckinsey-analytics/our-insights/where-is-technology-taking-the-economy.

Bhargava, R. (2020). *Non-obvious megatrends. How to see what others miss and predict the future*. Idea press Publishing.

Dewhurst, M., & Willmott, P. (2014, September). Manager and machine: The new leadership equation. *McKinsey Quarterly*. Retrieved May 7, 2020, from https://www.mckinsey.com/~/media/McKinsey/Featured%20Insights/Leading%20in%20the%2021st%20Century/Manager%20and%20machine/Manager%20and%20machine%20The%20new%20leadership%20equation.ashx.

Drucker, P. F. (2010). *The practice of management (Kindle)*. Harper-Collins Publishers.

Edelman, D., & Singer, M. (2015, October). The new consumer journey. *McKinsey Digital*. Retrieved April 16, 2021, from https://www.mckinsey.com/business-functions/marketing-and-sales/our-insights/the-new-consumer-decision-journey.

Fleming, O., Fountaine, T., Henke, N., & Saleh, T. (2018). Ten red flags signaling your analytics program will fail. *McKinsey Quarterly*. Retrieved May 7, 2020, from https://www.mckinsey.com/business-functions/mckinsey-analytics/our-insights/ten-red-flags-signaling-your-analytics-program-will-fail#.

Gajewski, J., Paprocki, W., & Pieriegud, J. (Eds). (2015). *Megatrendy i ich wpływ na rozwój sektorów infrastrukturalnych* [Megatrends and Their Impact on the Development of Infrastructure Sectors]. Gdańsk: Instytut Badań nad Gospodarką Rynkową – Gdańska Akademia Bankowa. Retrieved on April 20, 2021, from https://depot.ceon.pl/bitstream/handle/123456789/11161/Pieriegud_Megatrendy_2015.pdf?sequence=1&isAllowed=y.

Greenberg, E., Hirt, M., & Smit, S. (2017, April). The global forces inspiring a new narrative of progress. *McKinsey Quarterly*. Retrieved on April 11, 2020, from https://www.mckinsey.com/~/media/McKinsey/Business%20Functions/Strategy%20and%20Corporate%20Finance/Our%20Insights/Strategy%20and%20corporate%20finance%20special%20collection/Final%20PDFs/McKinsey-Special-Collections_Trends-and-global-forces.ashx.

Johnson, M. W., Christensen, M. C., & Kagermann, H. (2008, December). Reinventing your business model. One secret to maintaining a thriving business is recognizing when it needs a fundamental change. *Harvard Business Review*, 5. Retrieved on April 5, 2020, from https://hbr.org/2008/12/reinventing-your-business-model.

Lee, K. F. (2018). *AI superpowers: China, silicon valley, and the new world order*. Houghton Mifflin Harcourt Publishing Company.

Malik, R., & Jankowska, A. (2018). Megatrends and their use in economic analyses of contemporary challenges in the world economy. *Research Papers of Wrocław University of Economics, 523*. https://doi.org/10.15611/pn.2018.523.18.

Mengist, W., Soromessa, T., & Legese, G. (2019). Method for conducting systematic literature review and meta-analysis for environmental science research. http://dx.doi.org/10.1016/j.scitotenv.2019.134581.

Naisbitt, J. (1982). *Megatrends. Ten new directions transforming our lives.* Warner Books.

Sobiecki, G. (2020). Wyzwania dla przywództwa w dobie postępującej sztucznej inteligencji. [The Challenges of the leadership in an age of progressive artificial intelligence.] In R. Śliwiński (Ed.), *Strategiczne zarządzanie przedsiębiorstwem międzynarodowym* [*Strategic Management of International Enterprise*] (pp. 78–107). Difin SA.

Schulman, S. (2007, 21st September). Trend in trends. *Wall Street Journal.* Retrieved on April 5, 2020, from https://www.wsj.com/articles/SB119034805175835008.

Part II

Consumer World

4 Understanding Consumer-Perceived Value in Augmented Reality – Implications for Marketing Activities

Małgorzata Bartosik-Purgat and Milena Ratajczak-Mrozek

Introduction

New technologies and their systematic development radically change markets and the way that companies and individual consumers operate (Nagel et al., 2018; Pesonen & Horster, 2012). The development of new technologies allows consumers to satisfy their desires by providing them with new and interesting solutions (Pesonen & Horster, 2012). Pine and Gilmore (2014, p. 24) highlight "fusing digital technology with reality" among five value-creating opportunities that are likely to drive further progress. This "fusing [of] digital technology with reality" is reflected in the relatively new technological breakthrough of augmented reality (AR). In AR, images from the physical and real world, recorded by a camera, are synchronized with computer graphics and three-dimensional (3D) animations (Azuma, 1997; Correia Loureiro et al., 2020). This is done to have a sense of unity of the two spheres, the real and the digital. Unlike virtual reality, which immerses recipients in 3D simulation and detaches them from the physical world, AR seamlessly connects these two parallel spheres (Javornik, 2016; Poushneh & Vasquez-Parraga, 2017). The results of some studies indicate that the interaction between the consumer and AR systems contributes to consumers' highly assessed usage (e.g. Correia Loureiro et al., 2020; Neuhofer et al., 2013), and thus the AR becomes an attractive technology for the marketing activities of companies, who can diversify their offer, create additional services, or strengthen the sales process, especially online sales. AR also allows for the development of products that stand out from others on the market (Ghobakhloo & Fathi, 2019). As a result, the application of AR technology in product or service offerings creates high potential value for consumers.

Although much of the up-to-date research addresses "value" and "value creation", there is still no single, coherent understanding of these concepts. This is linked with the fact that, as emphasized by Vargo and Lusch (2006, p. 44), "experience and perception are essential to value determination", which means that value is determined subjectively and

DOI: 10.4324/9781003204343-4

can be understood in a variety of ways. Recent research on value is increasingly breaking the traditional economic and financial perspective of value (e.g. Chen & Dubinsky, 2003; Woodall, 2003; Zeithaml, 1988) in favor of adopting a psychological and sociological perspective (e.g. Butz & Goodstein, 1996; Holbrook, 2006). This has led to the proliferation of approaches and concepts related to value. At the same time, due to the focus on psychological and sociological aspects, value has become a very important concept in the area of the marketing activities of companies.

The application of AR technology in product or service offerings creates potential value for consumers (Caboni & Hagberg, 2019; Jiang et al., 2019; Turner & Welch, 2019), which in turn affects the marketing activities of companies. However, there is a lack of comprehensive and review studies devoted to the impact of AR on the marketing activities of companies going beyond the example of one industry. AR offers new possibilities of promoting, selling, and customizing products; however, to the best of our knowledge, most of the research (with the exception of Grzegorczyk et al., 2019) is limited to one industry or business activity, such as tourism and hospitality (e.g. Moro et al., 2019; Wei, 2019) or design (e.g. Hartless et al., 2020; Nee et al., 2012). Moreover, we are convinced that there is a need to take into consideration consumer perceptions of value to indicate AR's potential significance for marketing activities. By focusing on consumer-perceived value, we can ascertain more detailed implications for the needed shape of marketing activities focused on application of the AR technology. This should also expand theoretical knowledge regarding the determinants influencing the AR technology application in marketing activities. This is especially difficult as there is also no unanimity regarding the types of value resulting from AR technologies.

In reference to the considerations above, the purpose of this chapter is to examine the types of value perceived by consumers interacting with AR and thus to identify how the application of AR technology affects consumer-perceived value and thus the marketing activities of companies. Specific research questions (RQs) of the chapter include:

RQ1. How are the main types of consumer-perceived value resulting from AR defined and systematized in research on marketing?

RQ2. How does the application of AR translate into value perceived by consumers, and how does this affect the marketing activities of companies?

For this purpose, we identify the main areas of analysis in the current business and management literature devoted to the problem of value and AR. Nineteen papers from 2008 to 2019 were included for the analysis, which aimed at synthesizing and comparing evidence about consumer-perceived value resulting from AR and indicating the effects for companies' marketing activities linked with AR.

Our study contributes to the literature in two ways. First, it systematizes knowledge about the main types of consumer-perceived value resulting from the application of AR technology. Second, we conceptualize the influence of AR on companies' marketing activities achieved thanks to the different values perceived by consumers. In this way, we shift away from the focus in studies devoted to marketing activities and AR application, from general marketing effects to the importance of consumer-perceived value achieved thanks to AR technology and its implementation in companies' marketing activities. It is especially important as, to date, scant attention has been paid to "how value is formed via usage of immersive technologies" (Nussipova et al., 2019, p. 484). We propose a framework of the main types of value perceived by the consumers in the context of AR and their implementation in companies' marketing activities. From this, it is subsequently possible to identify future research directions.

The chapter is structured as follows: in the following section, we present the main assumptions regarding the concept of customer-perceived value and its types, as well as the main features of AR. Next, the method and results of the literature review are described. In the discussion, we return to the above-formulated research questions, indicating the main challenges regarding the value resulting from the application of the AR. Conclusions and implications are then forwarded, and finally, study limitations and suggestions for future research are outlined.

Literature Background

Consumer-Perceived Value

The concept of consumer-perceived value has evolved. However up to date research may be, there are difficulties associated with the description and measurement value, which is caused by the complexity, dynamism, and subjectivity of this concept (Sanchez-Fernandez & Iniesta-Bonillo, 2007). Consumer value is the result that the consumer wants to get from a consumption situation (Ha & Jang, 2013). Drucker (1959) claimed that wealth is generated for companies and owners, and value is created for consumers. Since then, there has been no agreement as to the interpretation of the concept of value in business and marketing literature. The main streams of research on value creation focus on its (1) monetary materialistic interpretation, (2) emotional interpretation, and (3) product attributes interpretation.

The first stream of research on value underlines the relation between costs incurred and benefits obtained. Anderson et al. (1993) indicate that value for the consumer is expressed in money and refers to a set of benefits that the consumer receives at a certain price. The consumer compares the benefits that he can get with the costs incurred (e.g. Chen & Dubinsky, 2003; Woodall, 2003; Zeithaml, 1988), which results in perceived value (or no value at all). Zeithaml (1988) emphasizes that value, as an exchange between costs and benefits, is individual and subjective. It can be perceived by consumers differently depending on the individual perceptions and needs.

A different view of value is taken in research that draws attention to emotional interpretation. This research links consumer value with the emotional aspects of relationships created between consumer and producer or service provider (e.g. Butz & Goodstein, 1996; Holbrook, 2006). Emotions arising as a result of product or technology usage can be shifted into attitudes and consumer behavior (e.g. purchasing or re-purchasing). The formation of relationships between consumer and producer or service provider is related to the process of value co-creation. Kotler et al. (2010) underline the significance of consumers' involvement in the process of identifying, creating, and offering value. This collaboration can increase the pleasure a consumer receives from consumption (positive emotions and, as a result, hedonistic value).

The third stream of research interprets the value as dependent on product attributes as well as the image and reputation of the company (e.g. Kaplan & Norton, 2001). This research also includes the utility the consumers achieve from using the product – their functional or physical performance and quality (Baker et al., 2002; Papista & Krystallis, 2012; Perrea et al., 2017). This way of interpretation is also suggested by Woodruff (1997, p. 142), who introduced consumer value as "a consumer's perceived preference for and evaluation of those product attributes, attribute performances, and consequences arising from use that facilitate (or block) achieving the customer's goals and purposes in use situations". Value not only corresponds to the attributes of the product but also arises in the process of distribution, acquisition, and communication between the company and the consumer. In line with this research is the product development model according to consumers' values, as suggested by Cagan and Vogel (2002), who underline the importance of utility, convenience (understood as ease of use), and ability to meet emotional needs. In turn, Vargo and Lusch (2011, 2017) moved from the traditional concept of creating consumer value focused on the product (goods-dominant logic) to services. In their opinion, the basis of services-dominant logic is consumer values and experience.

Augmented Reality in Product and Service Offerings

AR technology consists of generating virtual information in real time using electronic devices. It enables the formation of real phenomena as well as virtual 3D objects that can be used in real time (Azuma et al., 2001; Caboni & Hagberg, 2019). AR does not create a new, fully virtual 3D world, but rather supplements the real world with new images and information transmitted virtually (Azuma, 1997). Wei (2019, p. 540) underlines that "AR technology stresses the ability to present virtual information that is superimposed on the actual world view without compromising it". Likewise, Porter and Heppelmann (2017, p. 47) identify AR as "a set of technologies that superimposes digital data and images on the physical world". Caboni and Hagberg (2019) emphasize three general elements of AR technology, i.e. technology-augmented content (e.g. pictures, text, video, objects), context-augmented real environment, and augmented experience. The last element is related to the application of AR in products, allowing consumers to interact "with a virtual element in real time and physical space by enhancing their perception" (Caboni & Hagberg, 2019, p. 1130).

Products or services with the use of AR provide interactive and highly personalized new offers where traditional, real elements merge with digital technologies (Caboni & Hagberg, 2019). Because of the possible personalization (adaptation to individual needs and usage) and convenience of use, the use of AR technologies allows consumers to interact more profoundly with products or services (Javornik, 2016; Scholz & Smith, 2016).

McNamara (2016) indicates that AR not only allows support of the real world with virtual information to increase consumer understanding but also to increase consumer satisfaction. Products and services that apply AR deepen the consumer's experience and provide new stimuli related to the use of technological innovations, e.g. trying on clothes, glasses, and other accessories in online shops or checking the furniture arrangement in the consumer's room while browsing products in an online furniture store (Feng & Xie, 2018; Scholz & Smith, 2016). To achieve this effect, consumers often use mobile applications to satisfy their expectations, personalization, and comfort (Flavián et al., 2019; Scholz & Smith, 2016; Watson et al., 2018).

Method

The method used in the chapter is a systematic literature review, "with the goal being to have a firm foundation for advancing knowledge and facilitating theory development" (Snyder, 2019, p. 333). By comparing findings and perspectives of different authors and their empirical research, a literature review delivers information about unanswered questions and conclusions with wider and detailed results that no single study has covered to date (Snyder, 2019). A systematic literature review is generally conducted to synthesize and compare evidence on a particular topic and to evaluate the state of knowledge existing about this topic (in this case, AR and value creation) (Higgins & Green, 2019; Snyder, 2019). This review is also used to identify gaps in research, scientific discussion, research planning, or theory development (Snyder, 2019).

The systematic review analysis of key papers in the area of business and management included content analysis in terms of value creation and AR. Following the methodology of a systematic literature review, the search procedure adopted included three steps, namely (see Figure 4.1): (1) selection of the primary database, (2) selection of key words, and finally (3) selection of inclusion and elimination criteria (Snyder, 2019). The steps were used to ensure a thorough selection of the analyzed literature.

In the first step of the systematic literature review, the Scopus database of bibliometric entries was selected for analysis. It is the largest abstract and citation database of peer-reviewed literature, and its indexes cover many global publishers, including, among others, Elsevier, Wiley, Emerald, Taylor & Francis, Sage, and InderScience Publishing. As part of the query in step 2 of the analysis, the search key words "augmented reality" and "value" were used (Law et al., 2014; Wei, 2019) where indicated in the title and/or abstract and/or key words of the papers. Such a limitation was used to ensure that both main terms – AR and value – constitute an integral part of the papers concerned. This search limitation resulted in 1,090 records of papers published in the period 2008–2019 (earlier publications are usually conference papers that were excluded from the analysis presented in the paper).

In the next step, the search was narrowed down by limiting the area of publication to the "business and management" category (in fact reflecting papers devoted to management and marketing problems) and only to peer-reviewed papers (as opposed to conference papers, reviews, etc.). These inclusion criteria resulted in shortening the list of bibliographic records to 56. Next, a preliminary review of abstracts excluded papers in which the term "value" referred only to the definition of the formal Abstract section of the papers ("originality/value of the paper"). It resulted in another narrowing down of the list to 37 articles that have been thoroughly analyzed. After detailed analysis, only those papers that were intentionally devoted to the analysis of value in AR were included. Thus, the next exclusion criteria covered the use of the term "value" only as a synonym of very broadly and generally understood positive outcomes, its use as a price (the value of goods sold), or if value referred to the terms used in statistical analysis (e.g. t value, null value). Finally, 19 papers from 2008 to 2019 were included for the analysis. Next, the papers selected in the last part of the process were read in detail, highlighting the most important text that provided any information related to the topic of interest (especially AR and value) (Wei, 2019). The text analysis included highlighting the relevant parts of text, assigning key

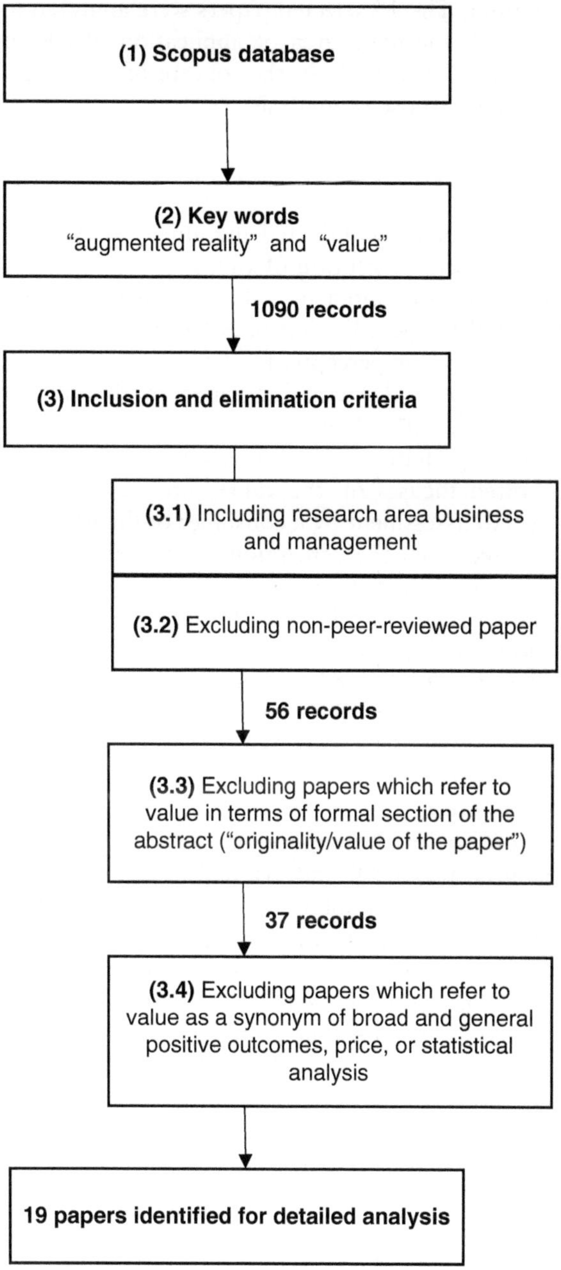

Figure 4.1 Process of the papers' selection for the literature review.

words to them, categorizing them in terms of various types of values, and comparing their research input. The 19 selected papers were analyzed in terms of (compare Table 4.1): the main area of application of AR to create value; the main purpose of the analysis; the concept of value; and the definition of value for the purpose of analysis.

Results

Table 4.1 presents the results of the conducted literature review concerning the application of AR and perception of value.

The analysis of the literature presented in Table 4.1 highlights the main areas of research related to the adoption of AR in the marketing activities of companies and the value perception.

The research devoted to value and AR is dominated by the area of sales and retail (e.g. Hilken et al., 2017; Plotkina & Saurel, 2019) as well as tourism and hospitality (e.g. Jiang et al., 2019; Lau et al., 2019). Therefore, this research often focuses on the value perceived by consumers defined as "the overall assessment by a consumer of the utility of a service or product evaluated from the perception of what is received (get factors) and what is given (input factors)" (Lau et al., 2019, p. 1009). AR is a potentially beneficial technology for online (e.g. Kang, 2014) and traditional shopping (e.g. Poncin & Mimoun, 2014) alike. The analysis of value in the area of sales and retail addresses the problem of value provided by the adoption of AR for both consumers and retailers (e.g. Dacko, 2017; Hilken et al., 2017), as the value perceived by consumers should transfer into sales increases and financial profits of retailers introducing AR solutions.

Research in the area of tourism and hospitality focuses on the utility of services or products (Jiang et al., 2019) and visitors' experiences that may change due to the adoption of AR solutions (e.g. Lau et al., 2019; Tom Dieck & Jung, 2017). This is due to the fact that the tourism industry is service-oriented and "in the current environment most of the value in the economy is created through services rather than manufacturing and services generally require that customers and firms co-create value" (Buhalis et al., 2019, p. 498). The problem of value co-creation is also addressed in the third area of research on AR and value, namely design, taking as an example the co-design experience in the mixed-reality context (Turner & Welch, 2019) and the co-creation experience for the interior design (Kymäläinen, 2013). Such value co-creation is associated with the benefits received by consumers when they are engaged in the product's or service's creation.

No single, uniform view emerges of the specific typology of value used in the analyzed research concerning AR technologies applied in different business areas. Based on the analysis of the presented literature, it is possible to identify four main streams of research on value definition and

Table 4.1 Results of the literature review concerning application of AR and consumer perception of value

Source	*Main Area of Research*	*Aim of the Analysis*	*The Adopted Definition and Types of the Value*	*Method of the Analysis*
Caboni and Hagberg, 2019	Retail	"to review augmented reality (AR) within retailing by identifying, outlining and discussing definitions of AR, applications of AR that are relevant for retailers, and the value AR provides for retailers and consumers"	• Value perceived by consumers and retailers • Value understood as benefits for consumers (interaction, experience, engagement, information entertainment and creativity, satisfaction) and retailers (advertising, experience, attracting, sales, environment, brand awareness and customer loyalty, information)	Literature review
Grzegorczyk et al., 2019	General	"to assess if AR is attractive to consumers and in which areas it can create the most value (…) to identify the most useful areas of AR applications, as well as factors influencing AR's attractiveness"	• Value perceived by consumers • Value understood as benefits for consumers	Case study
Plotkina and Saurel, 2019	Retail	"the impacts of the m-commerce interfaces on perceived hedonic value (perceived enjoyment) and utilitarian value (perceived convenience in examining the product, perceived ease of use, and perceived usefulness) and assesses	• Value perceived by consumers • Hedonic value (enjoyment) and utilitarian value (convenience, ease of use, and usefulness) in the purchase process	Experiment

(*Continued*)

Table 4.1 (Continued)

Source	*Main Area of Research*	*Aim of the Analysis*	*The Adopted Definition and Types of the Value*	*Method of the Analysis*
		how these values mediate the impact of the m-commerce interfaces on the attitude toward the shopping technology and purchase intention"		
Buhalis et al., 2019	Tourism/ Hospitality	"to explore critical technological advancements using a value co-creation lens to provide insights into service innovations that impact ecosystems"	• Value co-creation	Theoretical/ Conceptual
Jiang et al., 2019	Tourism/ Hospitality	"to examine how perceived value and technology acceptance are related to visitors' preference for AR experiences, specifically in the context of a national park visit"	• Value perceived by consumers • Perceived value studied from rational, emotional, economic, and experiential perspectives	Quantitative/ Survey
Turner and Welch, 2019	Design	"to define a mixed reality toolkit and explore its potential influence on the consumer's perception of value"	• Value perceived by consumers • Relational value for consumers (understood as relational benefit and "the means by which the user experiences the co-design process") • Consumers' perceived value of the co-design experience • Value co-creation	Theoretical/ Conceptual
Lau et al., 2019	Tourism/ Hospitality	"to develop conference stakeholders' adoption intention of the AR app	• Value perceived by consumers • Perceived value defined as "the overall assessment by a consumer	Quantitative/ Survey

		for conferences using the value-based adoption model (VAM)”	on the utility of a service or product evaluated from the perception of what is received (get factors) and what is given (input factors)”. • Adoption of value-based adoption model (Kim et al., 2007) – “the technology adoption intention of individuals is the result of perceived value evaluated by the cognitive trade-off between benefits (“get” factors) and sacrifice (“input” factors) associated with technology use. The perceived benefits items included usefulness and enjoyment, while the perceived sacrifice features are technicality and perceived fee”.	
Nussipova et al., 2019	Design	“to contribute a framework that explains how value is formed during the usage of immersive technologies in industrial contexts”	• Activity-centric view of value – “ the value formation through physical and emotional activities enabled by deploying immersive technology”. Value seen as a process “consisting of a number of value-forming activities”. • Value as a result of experiences (formed through an actor’s physical and mental activities during use of immersive technologies and	Case study

(*Continued*)

Table 4.1 (Continued)

Source	*Main Area of Research*	*Aim of the Analysis*	*The Adopted Definition and Types of the Value*	*Method of the Analysis*
			socially constructed through the actor's experiences)	
Hilken et al., 2017	Retail	"how the deployment of AR can transform online shopping into a value added service experience"	• Value perceived by consumers • Customers' utilitarian and hedonic value of the online service experience, "where the former captures the performance-related effectiveness and the latter the experiential enjoyment provided in a service experience."	Experiment
Dacko, 2017	Retail	"to describe and discover how, why and to what extent mobile augmented reality (MAR) apps contribute to smart retail settings by creating additional value to customers as well as benefiting retailers"	• Value perceived by consumers • Experiential value – adoption of Mathwick et al.'s (2001) typology of experiential value, including an extrinsic-active value, an extrinsic-reactive value (the value of service excellence), an intrinsic-active value (value in "playfulness" or value associated with the intrinsic enjoyment of shopping) and intrinsic-reactive value (associated with the visual appeal of a retail offer and/or its entertainment appeal)	Quantitative/ Survey
				Case study

Tom Dieck and Jung, 2017	Tourism/ Hospitality	"to explore the perceived value of the implementation of AR within the museum context using a stakeholder approach"	• Value perceived by the stakeholders • A number of perspectives on perceived value: ecological, social, emotional, economic and functional value, epistemic value, environmental, historical, cultural, tourist value	
Jung and Tom Dieck, 2017	Tourism/ Hospitality	"to propose a value co-creation framework through examining the opportunities of implementing augmented reality, virtual reality and 3D printing into the visitor experience at cultural heritage places"	• Value perceived by consumers • Value co-creation (between firm and a customer)	Case study
de San Eugenio Vela et al., 2017	Tourism/ Hospitality	"to propose an initial, exploratory and tentative theoretical construct related to the current consumption of landscape as a key symbolic and physical element in territorial representation and evocation, and for the deployment of place branding strategy"	• Value of a landscape	Theoretical
Poncin and Mimoun, 2014	Retail	"the effects of using two technologies in a physical toy store (magic mirror with augmented reality, interactive game terminals) on holistic perceptions of store atmospherics, affective reactions,and perceived	• Value perceived by consumers • Perceived shopping values • Experiential value	Experiment

(*Continued*)

Table 4.1 (Continued)

Source	*Main Area of Research*	*Aim of the Analysis*	*The Adopted Definition and Types of the Value*	*Method of the Analysis*
		shopping values, which should have consequences for satisfaction and patronage intentions"		
Kang, 2014	Retail	"to examine: whether monetary, convenience, emotional, and social values were related to utilitarian and hedonic performance expectancies, which were then related to usage intention of augmented reality and motion capture (ARMC) e-shopping via a webcam and whether ego involvement and cognitive effort moderated the links between performance expectancies and usage intention"	• Value perceived by consumers • Customer value defined as "a customer's perceived preference for and evaluation of those product attributes, attribute performance, and consequences arising from use that facilitate achieving the customer's goals and purposes in use situations" (Woodruff, 1997, p. 27) • Content-related customer perceived values (i.e. emotional, social, convenience, and monetary values) – Based on Prospect Theory and the Value-Attitude-Behavior hierarchy consumer decision model.	Quantitative analysis
Yaoyuneyong et al., 2014	Retail	"how consumers will use these new technologies and how virtual dressing rooms (VDR) will impact consumer attitudes and purchase intentions"	• Entertainment value referring to the extent to which a media format is fun for users	Theoretical/ Conceptual

Huang and Hsu Liu, 2014	Retail	"to examine the extent to which presence, media richness, and narrative experiences yield the highest experiential value in augmented-reality interactive technology"	• Value perceived by consumers • Experiential value	Quantitative analysis
Kymäläinen, 2013	Design	"to construct a science-fiction prototype 'Dreamnesting'. The prototype presents a new service enterprise that engages a user–customer deeply in the co-creation experience and introduces a new technology platform for the interior design task: augmented reality (AR) technology in an intelligent service environment"	• Value co-creation (between firm and customer)	Other (science-fiction prototype)
Maad et al., 2008	Finances	"to discuss the horizon of emerging digital media technologies in electronic financial trading with reference to a novel application drawing expertise from two important fields of study, namely: digital media (video and image) processing and augmented reality"	• The added value understood as additional benefits of the AR	Case study/ experiment

value typology related to the adoption of AR, including: (1) more general understanding of value as benefits, (2) division into hedonic and utilitarian value, (3) focus on experiential value, and (4) highlighting different, additional perspectives of perceived value (in addition to hedonic, utilitarian, and experiential perspectives).

Within the first identified stream of research on value, the concept is understood as the benefits obtained by consumers (Grzegorczyk et al., 2019; Maad et al., 2008) or consumers and retailers alike (Caboni & Hagberg, 2019). Grzegorczyk et al. (2019, p. 1258) emphasize that general values of AR technology for consumers can be considered as the ability to "observe and analyze things and perform difficult tasks (...), control multiple factors (e.g. aviation, automotive), speed up the process of decision-making (e.g. in medicine, architecture, education and aviation), etc." Such a broad understanding of value is related to the definition of perceived value as a result of a comparison of what is received and what is given (Lau et al., 2019).

A relatively common typology of values in research on the adoption of AR includes the division into hedonic and utilitarian value (e.g. Hilken et al., 2017; Plotkina & Saurel, 2019). Hedonic value is associated with the enjoyment and pleasure the consumer gets when using products or services including AR technology. The hedonic value is very often connected with entertainment and the positive emotions that consumers receive with that usage. It is understood as "enjoyment provided in a service experience" (Hilken et al., 2017, p. 889) and also defined as entertainment value referring to the extent to which something "is fun for users" (Yaoyuneyong et al., 2014, p. 287). Utilitarian value reflects the value in use, the desire to achieve convenience, and ease of use thanks to the adoption of the AR, usability, and "performance-related effectiveness" (Hilken et al., 2017, p. 889).

The next stream of research focuses on experiential value, which is an effect of experience associated with the positive effects for consumers resulting from AR technology (Dacko, 2017; Huang & Hsu Liu, 2014; Nussipova et al., 2019; Poncin & Mimoun, 2014). Nussipova et al. (2019) underline that experiential value is seen as a process "consisting of a number of value-forming activities and their resulting experiences (...) formed through an actor's physical and mental activities during use of immersive technologies (...), and socially constructed through the actor's experiences". Huang and Hsu Liu (2014, p. 90) refer to AR technologies in the shopping behavior of consumers and underline that an AR shopping experience can deliver "a reactive experiential value such as aesthetics and service excellence". Such results are in line with other current research on AR, which underlines that when looking for satisfaction consumers nowadays search for new experiences (Han et al., 2018). This is a situation when instead of just specific products or services, consumers want emotions, experiences, and desires, which these products should provide.

Additional perspectives of perceived value resulting from the adoption of AR are presented in the up-to-date research. These include the division into i) emotional, social, convenience, and monetary values (Kang, 2014); ii) rational, emotional, economic, and experiential perspectives (Jiang et al., 2019); and iii) ecological, social, emotional, economic, functional, epistemic, environmental, historical, cultural, and tourist perspectives (Tom Dieck & Jung, 2017). We can perceive emotional value (Jiang et al., 2019; Kang, 2014; Tom Dieck & Jung, 2017) as similar to the hedonic value cited above. In turn, convenience (Kang, 2014) and functional (Tom Dieck & Jung, 2017) values may be identified as a utilitarian value. From the above-mentioned additional perspectives of perceived value resulting from the adoption of AR, it is possible to especially pinpoint social value (Kang, 2014; Tom Dieck & Jung, 2017) and monetary (Kang, 2014) or economic values (Jiang et al., 2019; Tom Dieck & Jung, 2017). However, these values did not receive much attention in the research devoted to the adoption of AR in business and management literature.

Discussion

We are convinced that in order to indicate AR's significance for marketing activities there is a need to focus on consumers' perception of value. Based on the literature review, we present a framework of the main types of value perceived by the consumers facing AR and their implementation in companies' marketing activities (see Figure 4.2). In other words, knowledge about consumers' perceived values according to AR technology can be used by companies to implement the marketing activities delivering particular values.

The application of AR impacts both the product or service and the process of the consumer's use of the product or service. For example, immersive technologies in industrial contexts (Nussipova et al., 2019) change the main features of the products offered, which reflects the change of a product adopting AR. In turn, deployment of AR during online shopping (Dacko, 2017; Hilken et al., 2017) exemplifies the consumer's AR-enabled use of service. These two processes, that is: (i) the consumer's use of a product or service that adopts AR, and (ii) the consumer's AR-enabled use of a product or service, lead to specific types of values perceived by consumers. Based on the conducted analysis, we identify four main types of value resulting from the application of AR technologies and the value perceived by consumers. These include: (1) utilitarian (convenience, functional) value, (2) hedonic (emotional, entertainment) value, (3) value co-creation, and the most important (4) experiential value. Utilitarian value is the value that consumers achieve from the use of the product (Hilken et al., 2017; Plotkina & Saurel,

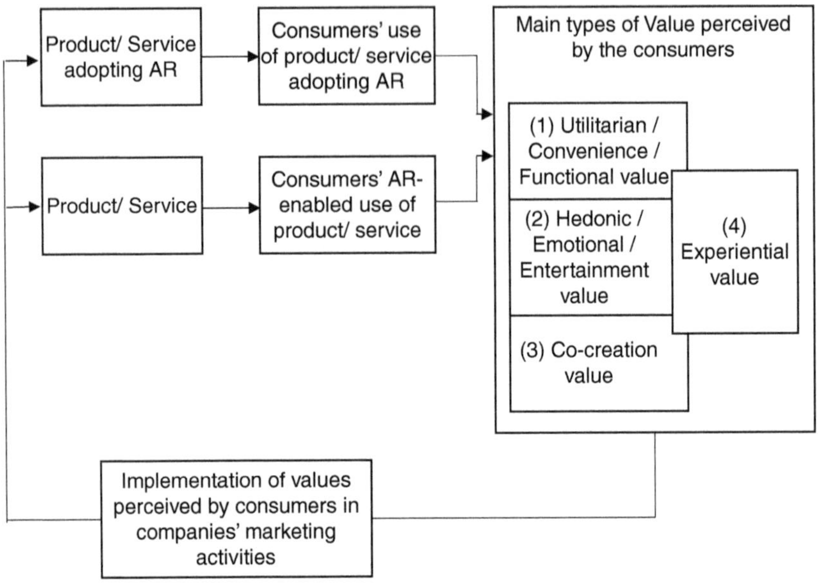

Figure 4.2 Main types of value perceived by the consumers in the context of AR and their implementation in companies' marketing activities.

2019), whereas hedonic value reflects positive emotional engagement and entertainment (Hilken et al., 2017; Yaoyuneyong et al., 2014). The third type of value addresses consumers' participation in the production or service processes and emotional relationship formation between consumers and producers (value co-creation) (Buhalis et al., 2019; Jung & Tom Dieck, 2017; Kymäläinen, 2013). It should be underlined that the three types of values mentioned and perceived by the consumers who interact with AR are not completely new or different compared to the values resulting from the product or service offered without AR use. However, in the case of the adoption of AR, a special importance of experiential value emerges. The AR application brings consumers new sensations and experiences that can and should be perceived as key values (Dacko, 2017; Huang & Hsu Liu, 2014; Nussipova et al., 2019; Poncin & Mimoun, 2014). The conceptualization of experiential value comes from the studies of Mathwick et al. (2001, p. 2002) and was quickly adopted in research on the retail industry (e.g. Dacko, 2017; Huang & Hsu Liu, 2014). Mathwick et al. (2001, 2002) introduce and test a scale of experiential value in relation to an experience-based value concept. In their definition, an experiential value is "a perceived, relativistic preference for product attributes or service performances arising from interaction within a consumption setting that facilitates or blocks achievement of customer goals or purposes" (Mathwick et al., 2002, p. 53). In other words, the authors state that the basis of customer value is their experiential perception (Mathwick et al., 2001). The experiential value of consumers can be perceived as a result of their indirect or direct contact with the product during the consumption process. This is the reason why experiential value is especially important in AR, because this technology offers such contact between a consumer and a product. Consumers can recognize and experience a product's features even in a virtual situation. Dacko (2017) emphasizes that AR is able to influence consumer engagement, and elsewhere Poncin and Mimoun (2014, p. 852) concluded that AR technologies deliver new shopping experiences to consumers because they "reduce boundaries between classical in-store atmospherics and e-atmospherics and yield important insight".

We argue that the experiences and experiential value may be underpinned by an exceptional utilitarian value, positive emotional engagement (that is, hedonic value), or a value co-creation process resulting in a new product or service. Thus, we agree with Nussipova et al. (2019, p. 485), who see the value "as a process – not only as an outcome – consisting of a number of value-forming activities and their resulting experiences". There are studies in the context of AR application that underline the importance of utilitarian and hedonic value for consumers' experiences (Grzegorczyk et al., 2019; Plotkina & Saurel, 2019). When analyzing factors positively and negatively influencing consumers' adoption of, or attitudes towards, AR, Grzegorczyk et al. (2019) claim that both hedonic and utilitarian aspects of the user experience are important for AR's adoption. In turn, Plotkina and Saurel (2019, p. 362) state that "researchers should investigate how to deliver utilitarian and hedonic value to consumers and create rich shopping experiences with retailing mobile applications". Interestingly, though, none of the research on values and AR includes the importance of value co-creation along with the utilitarian and hedonic value for experiential value. Nowadays, most consumers want to experience the product first before buying it, which also constitutes the basis of experience marketing development activities. AR technology delivers such a possibility.

The achievement of particular types of value can be differentiated both by industry and the characteristics of its consumers (potential buyers). For example, the tourism and hospitality industry focuses on the hedonistic, emotional, and co-creation values achieved thanks to AR (e.g. Buhalis et al., 2019; Jiang et al., 2019; Jung & Tom Dieck, 2017), whereas design underlines the importance of the ability to participate in the product's creation (e.g. Kymäläinen, 2013; Turner & Welch, 2019). The retail industry focuses on utilitarian values associated with the convenience and ease of use (e.g. Hilken et al., 2017; Plotkina & Saurel, 2019) and experiential values that deliver previously unknown sensations and experiences to consumers (Dacko, 2017; Huang & Hsu Liu, 2014; Nussipova et al., 2019; Poncin & Mimoun, 2014).

From the marketing point of view, it is important to analyze how the application of AR translates into value perceived by consumers and how this affects the marketing activities of companies. The highest perceived experiential value (underpinned by hedonic, utilitarian, and co-creation value) resulting from AR application influences consumer engagement in purchasing decisions (Huang & Hsu Liu, 2014) and consequently influences companies' sales (Caboni & Hagberg, 2019; Hilken et al., 2017). That may be achieved especially in the retail sector because AR technologies are usually used in cross-channel marketing strategies, thanks to the increasing availability of products by, e.g. interactive terminals, smartphone applications, etc. (Caboni & Hagberg, 2019; Poncin & Mimoun, 2014). For example, Poncin and Mimoun (2014, p. 852) point out that "magic mirror with AR offers strong positive benefits in terms of satisfaction and patronage intentions", which is related to the experiential value perceived by consumers.

In addition to increased sales, companies may achieve other positive marketing effects resulting from the adoption of AR and emphasis on the values perceived by consumers in these marketing activities. These other marketing effects may be classified into three groups: (i) creation of positive attitude of consumers towards companies and brand (e.g. good company's image and recognition in the market); (ii) consumer loyalty; and (iii) communication between consumer and company. If consumers perceive high experiential values underpinned by hedonic, utilitarian, and co-creation values, these translate into their positive attitude towards the company and brand (Caboni & Hagberg, 2019) and increased recognition of the company and brand in the market (Xu et al., 2019; Yaoyuneyong et al., 2014). Caboni and Hagberg (2019) indicate that one of the main goals that can be achieved by retailers in their advertising and marketing strategy, thanks to the use of AR, is increased brand awareness and consumer loyalty. Similarly, findings of the research conducted by Yaoyuneyong et al. (2014, p. 283) show that AR technology used in virtual dressing rooms has a positive effect on consumer self-confidence and consumer–brand relationships during online shopping. Moreover, the adoption of AR improves communication between producers and consumers (Dacko, 2017; Xu et al., 2019) because companies are better able to converse with consumers using AR and receive quick feedback. Similarly, communication (marketing communication) of that type on company's activities should be used to inform consumers about the type of values that can be achieved through the AR application.

Conclusions

Theoretical Contribution

Our study systematizes knowledge about the main types of values perceived by consumers using AR technology. This contribution is directly linked with the biggest challenge in the study, caused by the discrepancy of up-to-date research on consumers' perceived values. We underline that the experiential value is underpinned by hedonic, utilitarian, and co-creation values, although simultaneous occurrence of all three values listed is not necessary for the creation of experiential value. Experiential value considers positive emotions and the positive engagement of consumers.

Our second contribution lies in the conceptualization of the influence of AR on companies' marketing activities achieved thanks to the different values perceived by consumers. We underline that there is a need to take consumer-perceived value into consideration to indicate AR's significance for marketing activities. This task was especially difficult because of no unanimity regarding the types of value resulting from AR technologies. We propose a framework of main types of value perceived by consumers in the context of AR and their implementation in companies' marketing activities. We suggest that there are three main groups of effects related to AR application in the company: (1) building the company's image and recognition among consumers, (2) building consumers' loyalty, and (3) communication.

Practical Implications

Our research has practical implications as well. The results show the diversity of consumers' perceived values resulting from the application of AR technology. Focusing on values may help companies to be more competitive in the market and fulfill consumers' needs. These values should be kept in mind when introducing AR technology into products, services, or their offering processes and can form the basis for product and service customization. Moreover, the identified values should be emphasized in the communication strategies of companies. Firms using AR technologies should learn the detailed characteristics, needs, and attitudes of their potential buyers of technological innovation in the form of AR. These determinants may influence the values perceived by the consumers; therefore, their inclusion should translate into highly adapted marketing strategies. Companies should undertake marketing activities in the form of communication strategies to create the best impressions and experiences among consumers who use the products or services applying AR technologies.

The challenge associated with the application of AR technology results from the potential limitations in terms of AR implementation. Potential problems related to the application of AR technology should be considered and usually have their source in companies' financial (financial resources needed for the development of new technologies), technological (access to new technologies), and personal (attitude and ability to create and use new technologies) resources (Järvinen et al., 2012).

The costs and technological know-how of AR application (both for companies and consumers) are some of the reasons for modest AR use in marketing activities. However, the use of AR technology can increase during and after the Covid-19 pandemic. AR is helpful in searching, recognizing, matching, or trying on products without leaving home. It is especially important as current research states that for a long time, consumers will prefer buying products online rather than going shopping in crowded shopping malls (Kissler et al., 2020). The Covid-19 pandemic will impact not only AR technology use in retail, but also in education and tourism. Consumers' isolation, restrictions, and fear about coming into contact with crowds makes consumers eager to visit e.g. museums or tourist sites virtually and with AR technology use. Elsewhere, online teaching and learning will force the use of AR technology in order to teach students at a higher quality level.

Limitations and Future Research

We need to address a few limitations of our study, which at the same time set the direction for future research. We considered only positive effects for companies' marketing activities and consumer-perceived value associated with the application of AR technology. Although AR may translate into value perceived by consumers, this may not always be the case. The application of AR technology may lead to consumers' resistance or even negative emotions. Therefore, further studies should analyze, in detail, different factors that influence the actual appearance of consumers' perceived highly positive value. Such factors may include consumers' characteristics (e.g. age, gender) as well as industry-related factors. The latter is important as the perception of AR depends on whether consumers want to, for example, visit museums or tourist sites or shop online. These determinants could be interesting variables to be measured in the future in terms of the values perceived when consumers are faced with AR technology. Thus, the proposed conceptual framework needs to be empirically verified among companies from different industries.

Moreover, future studies should focus on the key features of AR technology and their application that are important to the creation of experiential value, regardless of the industry analyzed. Such studies need to focus on the psychological aspects of human behavior. It is also advisable to continue the research on the detailed interrelations between the key identified types of value – hedonic, utilitarian, co-creation, and experiential value. A key question arises: how exactly do the identified values strengthen (or weaken) each other's occurrence, and to what extent is the creation of experiential value possible without the occurrence of other values – hedonic, utilitarian, and co-creation value?

These proposals for future research related to AR technology use in marketing strategies, are especially significant when it comes to the coronavirus pandemic. AR technology will be used to co-create value not only in the case of tourism – the industry most affected and paralyzed by the Covid-19 pandemic (e.g. AR can be used to visit museums around the world online) but also in other industries such as fashion (e.g. AR for trying on clothes, shoes, and accessories online), education and training (AR as a new tool in online education), medicine (AR as a tool for examining the internal parts of the body), and aviation (AR as a tool for navigation). These are the key trends until approximately the end of this decade (around 2030) in the development of AR, important for the life of each consumer and the development of companies. To increase the use of this technology by consumers, it will be necessary to miniaturize the equipment used for AR and make it more affordable. An indispensable element of AR implementation in companies will probably be the purchase of individual equipment, such as glasses, tablets, and smartphones with appropriate applications. When introduced correctly, AR may help companies to increase their competitiveness for a long time.

The development of new technologies will continue, due to the advancement of technological progress, constant market competition, and the increase of consumers' higher needs from the needs hierarchy (e.g. need for development, creativity). Therefore, it is necessary to continue researching the values delivered by the application of AR technology.

Acknowledgments

Authors would like to acknowledge that this research was conducted with financial support from scientific grant no. 2015/17/B/HS4/00309 of National Science Centre, Poland.

References

Anderson, J. C., Jain, D. C., & Chintagunta, P. K. (1993). Customer value assessment in business markets: A stage-of-practice study. *Journal of Business to Business Marketing*, *1*(1), 3–29.

Azuma, R. T. (1997). A survey of augmented reality. *Presence*, *6*(4), 355–385.

Azuma, R. T., Baillot, Y., Behringer, R., Feiner, S., Julier, S., & Macintyre, B. (2001). Recent advances in augmented reality. *IEEE Computer Graphics and Applications*, *21*(6), 34–47.

Baker, J., Parasuraman, A., Grewal, D., & Voss, G. B. (2002). The influence of multiple store environment cues on perceived merchandise value and patronage intentions. *Journal of Marketing*, *66*(2), 120–141.

Buhalis, D., Harwood, T., Bogicevic, V., Viglia, G., Beldona, S., & Hofacker, C. (2019). Technological disruptions in services: Lessons from tourism and hospitality. *Journal of Service Management*, *30*(4), 484–506. https://doi.org/10.1108/JOSM-12-2018-0398.

Butz, H. E., & Goodstein, L. D. (1996). Measuring customer value: Gaining the advantage. *Organizational Dynamics*, *24*, 63–77.

Caboni, F., & Hagberg, J. (2019). Augmented reality in retailing: A review of features, applications and value. *International Journal of Retail & Distribution Management*, *47*(11), 1125–1140. https://doi.org/10.1108/IJRDM-12-2018-0263.

Cagan, J., & Vogel, C. M. (2002). *Creating breakthrough products: Innovation from product planning to program approval*. Prentice Hall.

Chen, Z., & Dubinsky, A. J. (2003). A conceptual model of perceived customer value in e-commerce: A preliminary investigation. *Psychology and Marketing*, *20*(4), 323–347.

Correia Loureiro, S. M., Guerreiro, J., & Ali, F. (2020). 20 years of research on virtual reality and augmented reality in tourism context: A text-mining approach. *Tourism Management*, 77. https://doi.org/10.1016/j.tourman.2019.104028.

Dacko, S. G. (2017). Enabling smart retail settings via mobile augmented reality shopping apps. *Technological Forecasting and Social Change*, *124*, 243–256.

de San Eugenio Vela, J., Nogué, J., & Govers, R. (2017). Visual landscape as a key element of place branding. *Journal of Place Management and Development*, *10*(1), 23–44. https://doi.org/10.1108/JPMD-09-2016-0060.

Drucker, P. F. (1959). *The practice of management*. Harper.

Feng, Y., & Xie, Q. (2018). Measuring the content characteristics of videos featuring augmented reality advertising campaigns. *Journal of Research in Interactive Marketing*, *12*(4), 489–508.

Flavián, C., Ibáñez-Sánchez, S., & Orús, C. (2019). The impact of virtual, augmented and mixed reality technologies on the customer experience. *Journal of Business Research*, *100*, 547–560.

Ghobakhloo, M., & Fathi, M. (2019). Corporate survival in Industry 4.0 era: The enabling role of lean-digitized manufacturing. *Journal of Manufacturing Technology Management*, *31*(1), 1–30. https://doi.org/10.1108/JMTM-11-2018-0417.

Grzegorczyk, T., Sliwinski, R., & Kaczmarek, J. (2019). Attractiveness of augmented reality to consumers. *Technology Analysis and Strategic Management*, *31*(11), 1257–1269. https://doi.org/10.1080/09537325.2019.1603368.

Ha, J., & Jang, S. (2013). Attributes, consequences, and consumer values: A means-end chain approach across restaurant segments. *International Journal of Contemporary Hospitality Management*, *25*(3), 383–409. https://doi.org/10.1108/09596111311311035.

Han, D.-I., Tom Dieck, M. C., & Jung, T. (2018). User experience model for augmented reality applications in urban heritage tourism. *Journal of Heritage Tourism*, *13*(1), 46–61.

Hartless, J. F., Ayer, S. K., London, J. S., & Wu, W. (2020). Comparison of building design assessment behaviors of novices in augmented-and virtual-reality environments. *Journal of Architectural Engineering*, *26*(2). https://doi.org/10.1061/(ASCE)AE.1943-5568.0000396.

Higgins, J., & Green, S. (Eds.). (2019). *Cochrane handbook for systematic reviews of interventions*. Wiley Blackwell Publishing.

Hilken, T., de Ruyter, K., Chylinski, M., Mahr, D., & Keeling, D. I. (2017). Augmenting the eye of the beholder: Exploring the strategic potential of augmented reality to enhance online service experiences. *Journal of the Academy of Marketing Science*, *45*(6), 884–905. https://doi.org/10.1007/s11747-017-0541-x.

Holbrook, M. B. (2006). Consumption experience, customer value, and subjective personal introspection: An illustrative photographic essay. *Journal of Business Research*, *59*(6), 714–725.

Huang, T.-L., & Hsu Liu, F. (2014). Formation of augmented-reality interactive technology's persuasive effects from the perspective of experiential value. *Internet Research*, *24*(1), 82–109.

Javornik, A. (2016).Augmented reality: Research agenda for studying the impact of its media characteristics on consumer behavior. *Journal of Retailing and Consumer Services*, *30*, 252–261.

Järvinen, J., Töllinen, A., Karjaluoto, H., & Jayawardhena, C. (2012). Digital and social media marketing usage in B2B industrial sector. *Marketing Management Journal*, *22*(2), 102–117.

Jiang, S., Scott, N., & Tao, L. (2019). Antecedents of augmented reality experiences: Potential tourists to Shangri-La Potatso National Park, China. *Asia Pacific Journal of Tourism Research*, *24*(10), 1034–1045. https://doi.org/10.1080/10941665.2019.1653949.

Jung, T. H., & Tom Dieck, M. C. (2017). Augmented reality, virtual reality and 3D printing for the co-creation of value for the visitor experience at cultural heritage places. *Journal of Place Management and Development*, *10*(2), 140–151. https://doi.org/10.1108/JPMD-07-2016-0045.

Kang, J. Y. M. (2014). Augmented reality and motion capture apparel e-shopping values and usage intention. *International Journal of Clothing Science and Technology*, *26*(6), 486–499. https://doi.org/10.1108/IJCST-05-2013-0055.

Kaplan, R. S., & Norton, D. P. (2001). Transforming the balanced scorecard from performance measurement to strategic management. *Accounting Horizons*, *15*(1), 87–104.

Kim, H.-W., Chan, H. C., & Gupta, S. (2007). Value-based adoption of mobile internet: An empirical investigation. *Decision Support Systems*, *43*(1), 111–126.

Kissler, S. M., Tedijanto, C., Goldstein, E., Grad, Y. H., & Lipstich, M. (2020). Projecting the transmission dynamics of SARS-CoV-2 through the postpandemic period. *Science*, *368*(6493), 860–868. https://doi.org/10.1126/scienceabb5793.

Kotler, Ph., Kartajaya, H., & Setiawan, I. (2010). *Marketing 3.0: From products to customers to the human spirit*. John Wiley & Sons Inc.

Kymäläinen, T. (2013). Dreamnesting – Co-created future vision of an intelligent interior design experience. *Futures*, *50*, 74–85. https://doi.org/10.1016/j.futures.2013.03.013.

Lau, C. K. H., Chui, C. F. R., & Au, N. (2019). Examination of the adoption of augmented reality: A VAM approach. *Asia Pacific Journal of Tourism Research*, *24*(10), 1005–1020. https://doi.org/10.1080/10941665.2019.1655076.

Law, R., Buhalis, D., & Cobanoglu, C. (2014). Progress on information and communication technologies in hospitality and tourism. *International Journal of Contemporary Hospitality Management*, *26*(5), 727–750.

Maad, S., Garbaya, S., & Bouakaz, S. (2008). From virtual to augmented reality in financial trading: A CYBERII application. *Journal of Enterprise Information Management*, *21*(1), 71–80.

Mathwick, C., Malhotra, N., & Rigdon, E. (2001). Experiential value: Conceptualization, measurement and application in the catalog and Internet shopping environment. *Journal of Retailing*, *77*(1), 39–56.

Mathwick, C., Malhotra, N., & Rigdon, E. (2002). The effect of dynamic retail experiences on experiential perceptions of value: An internet and catalog comparison. *Journal of Retailing*, *78*(1), 51–61.

McNamara, A. (2016). *Eye-tracking and mobile augmented reality*. In Proceedings of AR and VR Conference: Perspectives on Business Realities, 27th of April 2016, edited by M. C. Tom Dieck, & T. Jung, 14–17. Institute of Technology.

Moro, R. P., Ramos, P., & Esmerado, J. (2019). Analysing recent augmented and virtual reality developments in tourism. *Journal of Hospitality and Tourism Technology*, *10*(4), 571–586.

Nagel, D. M., Jr, Cronin, J. J., & Utecht, R. L. (2018). Consumption or prosumption? A question of resources. *Journal of Services Marketing*, *32*(6), 739–754.

Nee, A. Y. C., Ong, S. K., Chryssolouris, G., & Mourtzis, D. (2012). Augmented reality applications in design and manufacturing. *CIRP Annals – Manufacturing Technology*, *61*(2), 657–679.

Neuhofer B., Buhalis D., & Ladkin A. (2013). A typology of technology-enhanced tourism experiences. *International Journal of Tourism Research*, *16*(4), 340–350.

Nussipova, G., Nordin, F., & Sörhammar, D. (2019). Value formation with immersive technologies: An activity perspective. *Journal of Business & Industrial Marketing*, *35*(3), 483–494. https://doi.org/10.1108/jbim-12-2018-0407.

Papista, E., & Krystallis, A. (2012). Investigating the types of value and cost of green brands: A conceptual framework. *Journal of Business Ethics*, *115*(1),75–92.

Perrea, T., Krystallis, A., Engelgreen, C., & Chrysochou, P. (2017). Much too new to eat it? Customer value and its impact on consumer-product relationship in the context of novel food products. *Journal of Product & Brand Management*, *26*(6), 616–630. https://doi.org/10.1108/JPBM-09-2015-0984.

Pesonen, J., & Horster, E. (2012). Near field communication technology in tourism. *Tourism Management Perspectives*, *4*, 11–18.

Plotkina, D., & Saurel, H. (2019). Me or just like me? The role of virtual try-on and physical appearance in apparel M-retailing. *Journal of Retailing and Consumer Services*, *51*, 362–377. https://doi.org/10.1016/j.jretconser.2019.07.002.

Pine II, B. J., & Gilmore, J. H. (2014). A leader's guide to innovation in the experience economy. *Strategy & Leadership*, *42*(1), 24–29. https://doi.org/10.1108/SL-09-2013-0073.

Poncin, I., & Mimoun, B. (2014). The impact of "e-atmospherics" on physical stores. *Journal of Retailing and Consumer Services*, *21*(5), 851–859. https://doi.org/10.1016/j.jretconser.2014.02.013.

Porter, M. E., & Heppelmann, J. E. (2017). Why every organization needs an augmented reality strategy. *Harvard Business Review*, *95*(6), 46–57.

Poushneh, A., & Vasquez-Parraga, A. Z. (2017). Discernible impact of augmented reality on retail customer's experience, satisfaction and willingness to buy. *Journal of Retailing and Consumer Services*, *34*, 229–234.

Sanchez-Fernandez, R., & Iniesta-Bonillo, M. A. (2007). The concept of perceived value: A systematic review of the research. *Marketing Theory*, *7*(4), 427–451.

Scholz, J., & Smith, A. N. (2016). Augmented reality: Designing immersive experiences that maximize consumer engagement. *Business Horizon*, *59*(2), 149–161.

Snyder, H. (2019). Literature review as a research methodology: An overview and guidelines. *Journal of Business Research*, *104*, 333–339.

Tom Dieck, M. C., & Jung, T. H. (2017). Value of augmented reality at cultural heritage sites: A stakeholder approach. *Journal of Destination Marketing and Management*, 6(2), 110–117. https://doi.org/10.1016/j.jdmm.2017.03.002.

Turner, F., & Welch, I. (2019). The mixed reality toolkit as the next step in the mass customization co-design experience. *International Journal of Industrial Engineering and Management*, *10*(2), 191–199. https://doi.org/10.24867/ijiem-2019-2-239.

Vargo, S. L., & Lusch, R. F. (2017). Service-dominant logic 2025. *International Journal of Research in Marketing*, *34*(1), 46–67. https://doi.org/10.1016/j.ijresmar.2016.11.001.

Vargo, S. L., & Lusch, R. F. (2011). It's all B2B...and beyond: Toward a systems perspective of the market. *Industrial Marketing Management*, *40*(2), 181–187. https://doi.org/10.1016/j.indmarman.2010.06.026.

Vargo, S. L., & Lusch, R. F. (2006). Service-dominant logic: What it is, what it is not, what it might be. In R. F. Lusch, & S. L. Vargo (Eds.), *The service-dominant logic of marketing: Dialog, debate and directions* (pp. 43–56). M.E. Sharpe Inc.

Watson, A., Alexander, B., & Salavati, L. (2018). The impact of experiential augmented reality applications on fashion purchase intention. *International Journal of Retail & Distribution Management*. https://doi.org/10.1108/IJRDM-06-2017-0117.

Wei, W. (2019). Research progress on virtual reality (VR) and augmented reality (AR) in tourism and hospitality. A critical review of publications from 2000 to 2018. *Journal of Hospitality and Tourism Technology*, *10*(4), 539–570. https://doi.org/10.1108/JHTT-04-2018-0030.

Woodall, T. (2003). Conceptualising 'Value for the Customer': An attributional, structural and dispositional analysis. *Academy of Marketing Science Review*, *12*, 1–42.

Woodruff, R. B. (1997). Customer value: The next source for competitive advantage. *Journal of the Academy of Marketing Science*, *25*(2), 139–153.

Xu, L., Zhang, L., Cui, N., & Yang, Z. (2019). How and when AR technology affects product attitude. *Asia Pacific Journal of Marketing and Logistics*, *32*(6), 1226–1241. https://doi.org/10.1108/APJML-03-2019-0221.

Yaoyuneyong, G., Foster, J. K., & Flynn, L. R. (2014). Factors impacting the efficacy of augmented reality virtual dressing room technology as a tool for online visual merchandising. *Journal of Global Fashion Marketing*, *5*(4), 283–296. https://doi.org/10.1080/20932685.2014.926129.

Zeithaml, V. A. (1988). Consumer perceptions of price, quality and value: A means-end model and synthesis of evidence. *Journal of Marketing*, *52*(3), 2–22. https://doi.org/10.1177/002224298805200302.

5 Consumer Resistance to the Internet of Things: A Privacy Perspective

Grzegorczyk Tomasz

Introduction

One of the latest revolutionary technological advances that implements the three characteristics of Web 4.0 – ubiquity, identity, and connectivity – is the Internet of Things (IoT) (de Boer et al., 2019). It may allow the creation of a "smart world", where communication between multiple devices and people is omnipresent (Lu et al., 2018). This idea is very attractive to academics, entrepreneurs, and consumers. The IoT could give birth to countless "smart" services and products, disrupting existing business models, companies, and products, as well as consumers' lifestyles (Klein et al., 2017).

Although the IoT is gaining popularity with consumers, and companies are dynamically expanding its capabilities, it still has not become a mass technology. In order to do so, the IoT needs to overcome the challenges lying ahead – and technological ones might not be the greatest. Due to a huge amount of data generated and gathered by IoT devices, consumers deem them to be tools that can invade their privacy. Consumers are often reluctant to adopt this technology, and they are the ones who "vote" with their wallets and decide if the vision of "smart world" will come true. "For companies, lack of user acceptance of new technology has long been a painful obstacle in the technological innovation process" (Kim & Kim 2016). The concern for privacy has become one of the major inhibitors to the adoption and acceptance of technological innovations in general (Mani & Chouk, 2019). In the case of the IoT, privacy and trust-related issues have already delayed the based smart-meter rollouts (Hoenkamp et al., 2011). Research on privacy concerns related to the IoT is still at an early stage (MC-19-2). Therefore, the aim of this chapter is to identify the influence of consumer privacy concerns on resistance to the IoT and to identify the processes that guide such influence.

Research Method

The research method is a scoping literature review. The purpose of a scoping review is to "provide an overview of the available research

DOI: 10.4324/9781003204343-5

evidence without producing a summary answer to a discrete research question" (Sucharew & Macaluso, 2019). Scoping reviews are useful for answering broad questions, especially in terms of issues that are still under-researched or at an early stage of research.

Internet of Things

In 2025, the number of IoT devices is supposed to reach 75.44 billion, which is an increase of 146% from 2020 (Oshana & Kraeling, 2019). While there is no commonly accepted definition of the IoT (Whitmore et al., 2015), Van Deursen and Mossberger (2018) consider the IoT to be "systems that (1) contain ubiquitous 'everyday' objects that are accessible through the Internet and equipped with sensing, storing, and processing capabilities that allow these objects to understand their environments; (2) contain identifying and networking capabilities that allow them to communicate information about themselves; (3) involve object-object, object-person, and person-person communication; and (4) make autonomous decisions". Collectively, the above-mentioned IoT features are changing the nature of Internet use. The IoT is possible thanks to the dynamic development of communication technology, sensing devices, machine learning, and big data processing techniques (Atzori et al., 2014; Pauleen & Wang, 2017).

The capabilities of devices using the IoT can be grouped into four areas: monitoring, control, optimization, and autonomy (Porter & Heppelmann, 2015). Each subsequent function builds on the previous one. According to Touzani et al. (2018), four types of IoT products may be distinguished: (1) devices that follow simple orders (e.g. connected coffee makers); (2) objects that provide access to information (e.g. applications with QR codes); (3) objects that collect and analyze data and provide consumers with reports (e.g. smartwatches), and can even set challenges (e.g. connected forks); and (4) objects that can act autonomously (e.g. intelligent cars) [4]. Weinberg et al. (2015) classify IoT devices by their applications: wearables (e.g. smartwatches), home automation (e.g. connected light and temperature control), smart cities (e.g. smart traffic control), healthcare (e.g. remote health monitoring), smart manufacturing (e.g. flow optimization), and automotive (e.g. telemetry).

Internet of Things' Disruptive Nature

IoT products and services are re-shaping views on consumer value creation, how companies compete, and the boundaries of competition itself. Business models will be challenged, and new services initiated (Lu et al., 2018; Shin, 2014; Wunderlich et al., 2013). These shifts will have an effect on almost every industry (Porter & Heppelmann, 2015). The IoT has the potential to reinterpret the way businesses gather data and reshape many aspects of strategy, management, marketing, human resources, product development accounting, auditing, distribution, and other areas (Porter & Heppelmann, 2015).

This third wave of information technology revolution not only will create improvements in product capability and performance but will also radically improve companies' ability to meet business and human needs (Porter & Heppelmann, 2015). Chouk and Mani (2019) give an example of a smart thermostat connected to the Internet that can monitor the home and gather warnings from the heating and cooling systems. With time, it can study the habits of consumers and adjust the temperature by itself. IoT-based products and services may make consumers' lives easier by allowing them to access services anytime, anywhere, and through any device (Chouk & Mani, 2019).

Why Consumer Resistance to the Internet of Things Matters

It is the consumers who pay for a novel product and service; thus, they determine the success or failure of a new venture (Krotov, 2017). Therefore, it is crucial for high-tech companies' success to create products that meet the expectations of consumers and are accepted by them (Im and Workman, 2004; Kline & Rosenberg, 1986, p. 278; Viardot, 2004, pp. 5–6). This is a demanding challenge, as technologically advanced products often evoke conflicting feelings (Mick & Fournier, 1998), because they often are characterized by especially positive (e.g. relative advantage) and negative features (e.g. multidimensional risk), which are the basis of ambivalent attitudes. Hence, their acceptance and purchase are not obvious.

In order to meet these challenges, in line with the marketing orientation of the company, companies should study the determinants of consumers' decisions and cooperate with consumers from the early stages of developing an innovative product (Mohr et al., 2010). In turn, obtaining information on factors affecting willingness to use innovative products allows businesses to introduce changes at the product development stage, as well as make subsequent improvements, not to mention take the opportunity to formulate an appropriate communication strategy.

The literature studying factors determining the success of innovative products and services among consumers can be divided into two main paradigms (Chouk & Mani, 2019; Laukkanen, 2016). The first notion aims to understand the factors of technology acceptance (or adoption) and is generally based on Rogers' Theory of Diffusion of Innovation (2003), the Theory of Reasoned Action (Fishbein & Ajzen, 1975), or planned behavior (Ajzen, 1991) and technology acceptance models (e.g. the Unified Theory of Acceptance and Use of Technology created by

Venkatesh et al., 2003). In comparison, the second literature notion is concentrated on the acceptance barriers that trigger resistance to innovation (Kleijnen et al., 2009; Ram & Sheth, 1989). The marketing literature perceives consumer resistance to innovation as a negative attitude to innovative products and services (Heidenreich & Spieth, 2013; Mani & Chouk, 2019; Ram, 1987; Ram & Sheth, 1989). Consumer resistance may take the form of rejecting the innovation, calling for boycotts, spreading negative word of mouth, or taking actions against companies (Mani & Chouk, 2018). Moreover, according to Kleijnen et al. (2009) and Szmigin and Foxall (1998), resistance manifests itself in three forms of consumer response: rejection (consumers may not accept the IoT product); postponement (consumers may not adopt IoT products because the circumstances are not suitable); or opposition (consumers may consider IoT products to be a threat and resist their adoption) (Mani & Chouk, 2019). Consumer resistance is one of the main causes of the market failure of novel products and services (Bagozzi & Lee, 1999; Ellen et al., 1991; Mani & Chouk, 2017). It is therefore vital for managers to understand the factors that may cause it. The concern for privacy has become one of the major inhibitors to the adoption and acceptance of technological innovations (Mani & Chouk, 2019).

What Is Consumer Privacy?

Privacy is usually defined as the individual's ability to control his or her personal information (Bélanger & Crossler, 2011; Lancelot-Miltgen et al., 2016; Mani & Chouk, 2019). Privacy has lately achieved the status of the central topic in the marketing and consumer behavior literature (Lancelot-Miltgen et al., 2016), especially literature that focuses on new technologies. According to a systematic literature review of literature from the user perspective (Lu et al., 2018), one of the main drivers of consumer resistance to the IoT are privacy concerns.

How Does the Internet of Things Threaten Privacy?

New technologies are often regarded as the greatest threat to an individual's privacy (Santanen, 2019). It is the result of the fact that companies gather huge amounts of information concerning consumers on the Internet, e.g. e-mail, clicks on a website, and social media content. There are multiple factors that drive this process, including increased processing power, portability and storage capacity of both consumer devices and companies' servers, as well as their decreasing cost (Santanen, 2019). As novel technologies generate policy vacuums, consumer concerns are often well justified.

Those issues are magnified when it comes to the IoT, where data play a pivotal role. "Without data, IoT does not exist" (Weinberg et al., 2015). Furthermore, the data that drive the IoT are in majority consumer related. The following processes are especially concerning when it comes users' privacy (Aleisa & Renaud, 2017; Hsu & Lin, 2016; Krotov, 2017; Mani & Chouk, 2019; Wiegard & Breitner, 2017):

a. (Big) data generation – due to the abundance of various interconnected IoT devices, they might use their sensors to track people's movement, location, behavior patterns, habits, preferences, needs, and body parameters, creating big data (Suppatvech et al., 2019). The issue is not only the huge amount of data being generated, but also it's very sensitive content (Wünderlich et al., 2015).
b. Data transmission – the process of data transmission between sensors, devices, and applications, as well as between companies, is difficult to control.
c. Data usage – there is a risk of malevolent data usage, e.g. surveillance without control.
d. Data anonymity – there is inadequate preservation of anonymity, which allows the identification (e.g. by name or address) of the consumer.
e. Data security risks – the IoT is susceptible to serious security threats by allowing intruders to control physical objects remotely. The automatic identification between products and services leads to novel security risks.

The issue of data security is especially significant due to the possible repercussions of a breach. While hacking into a bank account and stealing money is obviously serious, the risks associated with the diffusion of the IoT are grave. Imagine the scenario where an autonomous car is hacked and steered remotely by the hacker. Moreover, such car might analyze the consumer's driving style and provide insurers with the consumer's driving history (Mani & Chouk, 2017) – not necessarily a bad idea, which only shows the dilemmas involved in the protection of privacy. Another sensitive group of IoT products are healthcare wearables that measure and interact with users' body functions. Furthermore, burglars may use IoT devices' data to find a safe time to break into a user's home (Aleisa & Renaud, 2017).

Those risks seem even more real taking into account the results of a study that showed that 72 out of 82 consumer IoT devices shared data with third parties who were unrelated to the devices' producers and exposed information to eavesdroppers (Ren et al., 2019). However, ubiquitous IoT devices gathering data allow firms to deliver better and better personalized offers and services (Ostrom et al., 2015), not to mention other utilitarian and hedonic benefits.

Internet of Things and the Privacy Paradox

Privacy paradox is a phenomenon that was reported by research on Internet users (Barnes, 2006; Norberg et al., 2007). It is maintained that while consumers are usually concerned over their privacy, they fail to take adequate precautions or to refrain from disclosing information (Bandara et al., 2020). This would support the view that privacy-related decision making is irrational (Tsai et al., 2011). However, there are still doubts if this paradox really exists (Dienlin & Trepte, 2015) and if it applies to the IoT setting. The findings presented in the literature are mixed as some studies show that the privacy paradox does not exist in the context of the IoT, whereas others show the opposite.

For instance, in 2019 consumers from multiple countries were surveyed about the factors that influence their buying decisions concerning IoT devices (Internet Society, 2019). The findings show that 75% of people distrusted companies transferring the data, 63% found data collection by IoT devices "creepy", and 53% did not believe IoT devices would protect their privacy. Aleisa et al. (2020) confront such findings with other studies showing that consumers do not take proper care of protecting their privacy (e.g. Hsu & Lin, 2016). This would confirm the existence of the privacy paradox in the IoT context.

However, there are studies that show that consumers are not aware of the threat to privacy connected with IoT devices. For example, Burgess et al. (2019) showed that there exists an information asymmetry between industry and consumers around this issue, in particular in terms of understanding key issues such as personal data collection and use, consumer rights, and industry responsibilities. Consequently, if consumers are unaware of the issue at stake, they cannot act accordingly. Another – at least partial – explanation of the privacy paradox in regard to consumers' inaction are Zheng's et al. (2018) findings that consumers trust IoT device manufacturers to protect consumers' privacy, but are generally unaware of the possibility for machine learning algorithms to reveal sensitive information from this data.

Aleisa's et al. (2020) study shows that IoT users are reluctant to read privacy policies and consequently do not try to secure their private data. The authors explain this situation and the privacy paradox by splitting the consumers' privacy concerns into two components: automatic, intuitive concerns (in line with Kahneman's (2003) system 1 of fast thinking) and slow-thinking processes based on logic (system 2). Using system 1 rather than system 2 leads to the privacy paradox. The digital world in which the IoT users spend more and more time seems to favor system 1 thinking, which leads to preferring hedonistic and utilitarian benefits over long-term threats.

The Acceptance of Privacy Trade-offs Related to the Internet of Things

According to Weinberg et al. (2015), consumers will consider the balance between the conveniences offered by the IoT and the losses in privacy. This is based on the models of privacy calculus that imply that consumers' intention to disclose personal information depends on the result of such comparison (Dienlin & Metzger, 2016). Privacy calculus is a term similar to "privacy trade-offs", which means conditions under which consumers would "share personal information or permit surveillance in return for getting something of perceived value" (Rainie & Duggan, 2015). According to this theory, consumers aim to optimize their interests by minimizing the cons connected with data-sharing and maximizing the (utilitarian and hedonistic) pros. For example, in the case of the Internet, the privacy calculus includes perceived privacy risk, privacy concerns, personal Internet interest, and Internet trust (Distler et al., 2020).

The privacy calculus has been researched in various contexts. According to Distler et al. (2020), this model has since been used (and supported) in the context of mobile devices (Barth et al. 2019; Keith et al., 2013), social networks (Dienlin & Metzger, 2016; Krasnova et al., 2012), e-commerce (Luo et al., 2010), and location-based services (Sun et al., 2015).

Various factors have been found to impact the privacy calculus. For instance, in Wilson's et al. (2017) study of the acceptance model of IoT in-home voice assistants, the factor of perceived privacy was used as a variable moderating other relationships in the model. It turned out that the introduction of this variable results in a reduction of the significance of the variables motivating use (e.g. utilitarian and social benefits). While it clearly shows that perceived privacy risk is a concern for consumers and a barrier to using the IoT voice assistants, this method does not provide the answer whether consumers would refrain from buying and using such devices. Furthermore, Zheng et al. (2018) found that IoT users' opinions concerning who should have access to their smart home data depend on perceived benefit from entities that create, track, regulate, or manage IoT devices and their data. According to Goad et al. (2020), while people will be willing to pay more to address their privacy concerns in the IoT context, the valuations that consumers assign to privacy are low and determined by the personal benefit stemming from disclosing private data. Those benefits might depend on the type of IoT device or service. For instance, in terms of wearable healthcare devices, Li et al. (2016) found that users' perceived privacy risk is formed by health information sensitivity, personal innovativeness, legislative protection, and perceived prestige, whereas users' perceived benefit is determined by perceived informativeness and functional congruence.

Pridmore and Mols (2020) studied the practices of early adopters of in-home personal assistants (IPAs, e.g. Amazon Alexa, Apple's Siri) and showed that they actively seek to set boundaries to data gathering in their home setting. Some users put the device only in spaces that are regarded as less intimate and private, whereas others often physically mute the assistant. Moreover, while modern voice assistants can perform high-priority commands concerning personal account details and place orders on the Internet (Feng et al., 2017; McLean & Osei-Frimpong, 2019), users often are reluctant to use them in order to make payments due to privacy concerns. Such conclusions confirm the findings of Lau et al. (2018), who showed that IPA users have difficulty balancing the benefits of using new technologies and protecting their privacy.

Moreover, Rainie and Duggan (2015) studied the acceptance of privacy trade-offs in six different scenarios, one of which is focused on the IoT. The data collected by the studied device (smart thermostat) included basic activities in the house, e.g. the movement of inhabitants. The majority of participants accepted this device. As one respondent put it: "The security risks are not outweighed by the benefits". Similarly, Williams et al. (2017) found that price and functionality outweigh privacy, leading to the adoption of IoT devices or services in spite of having privacy concerns. They also showed that users of smart devices are more careless when it comes to using privacy protection tools than non-IoT users. Such findings confirm the existence of privacy calculus in the IoT context, and it seems that users generally choose using such devices, despite the privacy concerns. Furthermore, Yang created a model of smart home acceptance based on the Theory of Planned Behavior. While they found that security/privacy risk negatively affected attitude towards smart home appliances, it was not the main determinant.

Mani and Chouk (2019) proposed a model identifying privacy concerns as antecedents to resistance to IoT services. In accordance with previous studies (e.g. Hsu & Lin, 2016), they confirmed the positive relationship between perceived intrusion (the anxiety caused by the possibility of privacy violation) and negative consumer reaction to IoT innovation, measured as lower intention to use such products. The greatest antecedent of the resistance to IoT services was the unauthorized secondary use of personal information. Other impactful factors were the concern for privacy of information and perceived intrusion. All of the above-mentioned variables were significantly influenced by the "Big Brother effect" drawn from Orwell's dystopian novel. It is defined as "the perception by the individual of a world subject to monitoring and control by known or unknown, visible or invisible entities that possess specific and above-average technical powers" (Mani & Chouk, 2019). Therefore, the research confirms that the central variable explaining IoT consumer privacy concerns is connected to the notion that everything a person does may be recorded and stored. Similar results were presented by a study by Touzani et al. (2018), who identified consumer "skepticism" regarding good intentions of IoT providers in terms of privacy and surveillance. However, it needs to be taken into account that this research is based on participants' declarations and not actual consumer behavior. Consequently, the conclusion of a pivotal role of privacy concerns needs to be taken cautiously.

Methodologically sound research was undertaken by Aleisa et al. (2020), who studied actual IoT device (smart plug) users in Saudi Arabia. The participants' concerns increased, and trust in IoT devices lowered, after their awareness of actual privacy invasions was raised. However, a month after the experiment, those parameters regressed to pre-awareness levels. The participants generally preferred to continue using the device due to its convenience and other benefits, despite expressing their disapproval of the privacy intrusion. However, cultural aspects might have played a role in this study. Therefore, more such studies should be undertaken in different cultures.

Kim et al. (2019) showed that while the perceived benefit is positively associated with willingness to provide privacy information, perceived privacy risk has no significant effect on such willingness in the context of investigated IoT services in healthcare, smart transport, and smart home services. Consequently, this study contradicts the existence of the privacy calculus in consumer behavior.

Theoretical Contribution

The majority of the reviewed studies show that the privacy paradox is a phenomenon that applies to the IoT context. However, there still were studies that found that consumers were unaware of the risk that IoT devices and services pose to their privacy in terms of scope of the data being gathered, possible transmission of data between devices and its security, as well as the potential of machine learning algorithms to infer significant conclusions regarding consumers (e.g. Zheng et al., 2018).

It seems that the privacy calculus (or privacy trade-off) is a more useful paradigm for further studies, according to which consumers try to compare the (utilitarian and hedonistic) benefits (e.g. convenience) and losses in order to balance the outcome. In the case of the IoT, the majority of studies show that consumers are not willing to resign from using those devices. This trend may be strengthened as IoT devices and services become more ubiquitous, which will improve their convenience and usefulness even further (Pridmore & Mols, 2020). However, some consumers try to introduce measures that would limit the scope of the data the IoT devices may gather, e.g. by consciously refraining from making payments with the connected device. This shows that in terms of privacy calculus, the balance is not univocally tipped towards IoT use.

Despite the fact that the majority of studies use the approach of privacy calculus and they support its main idea that consumers try to balance the benefits and privacy concerns, not all studies support this perspective. Kim et al. (2019) showed that privacy concerns do not play a significant role in such decisions. Such disparity asks for explanation by further studies.

Studies that are rooted in the technology acceptance or resistance models seem to be prone to overlooking the privacy paradox and overexaggerate the privacy concern side of the privacy calculus. This is probably due to the fact that the majority of such research does not study actual IoT users, but rather introduces respondents to the IoT through a written description or a video and then lets them declare their preferences and potential actions.

While the majority of research is based on the declarations of respondents, there are already studies that focus on actual users of IoT devices (e.g. Aleisa et al., 2020). This method seems to be the best in verifying the privacy paradox and the disparity between consumers' declarations and their actions. However, caution should be taken as the current IoT users usually belong to the innovators and early adopters group in accordance with Roger's (2003) classification of innovation adopters (Pridmore & Mols, 2020). Therefore, their behavioral patterns might be different from the early and late majority, who will mostly adopt IoT devices in the future.

Practical Implications

Practical implications may be directed towards policy makers and IoT device manufacturers and service providers. In terms of policy, as the existence of the privacy paradox among IoT consumers is supported by the majority of research, it should be inferred that privacy awareness educational campaigns are not enough to persuade consumers to protect their privacy. A more effective measure might be the introduction of laws strengthening privacy protection and allowing state authorities to easily control IoT companies dealing with data. An interesting route was taken by Williams et al. (2019), who showed that encouraging consumers to play a specific game helped to raise their privacy awareness and – more importantly – encouraged protective behavior in the smartwatch context.

When it comes to implications for companies, the introduction of privacy protection measures still might be beneficial for them. It is crucial for firms to reinforce their brand reputation by introducing policies that guarantee transparent and careful handling of consumers' data. This may be aided by promotional and educational campaigns. Consumers value transparency in terms of potential use of their data (Goad et al., 2020). They might be more willing to accept data gathering if they know how and to what means it is used. Thus, it might not only be more ethical to openly inform consumers about such issues, but also more profitable. Moreover, as Mani and Chouk (2019) suggest firms should be able to acquire "privacy protection" labels in partnership with an independent organization, which would confirm a high standard of corporate data policy. Companies might also create corporate communication units aimed at strong social media presence in order to interact with consumers and respond to fake news.

This is especially important due to the fact that early adopters of the IoT seem to be more tech-savvy and privacy aware than the majority of potential future users (Pridmore & Mols, 2020). Consequently, strict consumer-oriented privacy policy might be crucial at the moment of "crossing the chasm" between early adopters and the early majority. It is possible that after initial adoption of the IoT, data-gathering practices will be easily accepted by the majority of users.

However, more and more consumer devices will become a part of the IoT and will gather data concerning consumers. Consequently, not only the amount of data gathered will rise, but also the type and quality. This will even further increase the role of big data analysis for the competitive advantage of companies. Along with this trend, consumer data awareness might also increase.

As noted by Kim et al. (2019), IoT service providers and device manufacturers should concentrate on underlining the value provided to consumers in return for their data. Consequently, consumer value should be the priority of IoT companies in terms of service and product design, as well as communication strategies.

Moreover, the majority of analyzed studies are biased towards Western culture. They often are written by European or American authors who study Western consumers, who might have a more strict approach to data sharing than other cultures. Such conclusions are partly confirmed by a study by Aleisa et al. (2020), undertaken in Saudi Arabia. Chinese companies Alibaba, Xiaomim, and Baidu offer IoT devices and services to Chinese citizens, who seem to have different attitudes towards data protection than Europeans (Pridmore & Mols, 2020). Therefore, global IoT companies might consider introducing different data gathering and handling policies depending on the region.

Barth et al. (2019) give an example of newest Android systems, where the permission to gather and use consumer's data is requested late – after already installing the application. This is based on heuristics that make users unwilling to uninstall the application due to their earlier engagement (choosing and installing the app). Consequently, moving the data policy acceptance to the end of the process of IoT service adoption might be a route IoT companies could take.

Firms also might measure the costs and profits from data gathering and tailor their data policy accordingly. Consumers' willingness to accept reduction in privacy was valued by them from USD $30.79 to as high as USD $139.62 per person, depending on the type of data provided (the cheapest being location data, and the most expensive being health data) (Goad et al., 2020). Consequently, companies might want to estimate how their consumers value various types of data in particular contexts and adjust their data gathering and handling practices with regard to the costs and profits connected with a particular type of data and particular type of consumer. Thus, segmentation of data and consumers might be advantageous.

Conclusions

The balance between securing consumers privacy and gathering data is very fragile, which constitutes a significant challenge for IoT companies. On the one hand, consumers declare they are reluctant to share their private information and use products and services that gather such data. On the other hand, the IoT revolution is data-driven, as the major benefits of this technology to consumers rely on consumer data.

As this review has showed, the majority of studies confirm the occurrence of the privacy paradox. The lack of unanimity that some studies show in this context (e.g. Burgess et al., 2019; Zheng et al., 2018) stems from the lack of consumers' awareness. Consequently, it is possible that if the respondents in those studies were aware of the IoT's threats to privacy, they would still choose to use it.

In order to deepen the knowledge concerning IoT privacy concerns of consumers, a privacy calculus perspective is advised. This study shows that while the majority of reviewed studies support the privacy calculus as the main process guiding consumer choices in the context of various IoT services and devices, there still are studies that provide us with different conclusions (e.g. Kim et al., 2019). Such disparity in results asks for further studies.

Future empirical research should focus on studying actual IoT users, e.g. by using observation as a research method rather than survey or interview. This may have a drawback of concentrating on a group of innovators who already have bought such devices and have different characteristics and preferences than the majority of future IoT users. However, it can be handled by studying a representative (e.g. in terms of socio-demographic traits) sample of consumers who are provided with IoT devices.

Although the existence of the privacy paradox in the IoT context is supported by the majority of studies, future research might focus on the privacy calculus and analyze which factors play the major role in the trade-offs, as well as their antecedents. Various IoT services and products should be taken into account. Moreover, as the number of empirical studies concerning the IoT in the privacy context rises, a systematic review of the literature could be helpful in organizing accumulated knowledge and providing us with novel, updated, and comprehensive findings. Researchers might also dwell on the emotional responses of consumers using IoT services and products and their impact on consumer acceptance of data sharing, based on similar research on online shops (Li et al., 2017). Another important research direction is the study of the impact of cultural differences on consumer attitudes towards IoT's threat to consumer privacy.

The main limitation of this literature review resides in its method, as it does not have a systematic character. Consequently, some studies might have been omitted, and no quantitative analysis has been conducted. This could lead to limited generalizability of the conclusions.

References

Ajzen, I. (1991). The theory of planned behavior. *Orgnizational Behavior and Human Decision Processes*, *50*, 179–211. https://doi.org/10.1016/0749-5978(91)90020-T

Aleisa, N., & Renaud, K. (2017). Privacy of the Internet of Things: A systematic literature review. *Proceedings of the 50th Hawaii International Conference on System Sciences*, *2017*, 5947–5956. https://doi.org/10.24251/hicss.2017.717

Aleisa, N., Renaud, K., & Bongiovanni, I. (2020). The privacy paradox applies to IoT devices too: A Saudi Arabian study. *Computers and Security*, *96*, 101897. https://doi.org/10.1016/j.cose.2020.101897

Atzori, L., Iera, A., & Morabito, G. (2014). From "smart objects" to "social objects": The next evolutionary step of the Internet of Things. *IEEE Communication Magazine*, *52*(1), 97–105.

Bagozzi, R. P., & Lee, K.-H. (1999). Consumer resistance to, and acceptance of, innovations. In E. J. Arnould, & L. M. Scott (Eds.), *Advances in consumer research* (Vol. 26, pp. 218–225). Association for Consumer Research.

Bandara, R., Fernando, M., & Akter, S. (2020). Explicating the privacy paradox: A qualitative inquiry of online shopping consumers. *Journal of Retailing and Consumer Services*, *52*(August 2019), 101947. https://doi.org/10.1016/j.jretconser.2019.101947

Barnes, S. B. (2006). A privacy paradox: Social networking in the United States. *First Monday*, *11*(9). https://doi.org/10.5210/fm.v11i9.1394.

Barth, S., de Jong, M. D. T., Junger, M., Hartel, P. H., & Roppelt, J. C. (2019). Putting the privacy paradox to the test: Online privacy and security behaviors among users with technical knowledge, privacy awareness, and financial resources. *Telematics and Informatics*, *41*(February 2019), 55–69. https://doi.org/10.1016/j.tele.2019.03.003

Bélanger, F., & Crossler, R. (2011). Privacy in the digital age: A review of information privacy research in information systems. *MIS Quarterly*, *35*(4), 1017–1041. https://doi.org/10.2307/41409971

Burgess, L. C., Skatova, A., Ma, S., McDonald, R., & Maple, C. (2019). The value of personal data in IoT: Industry perspectives on consumer conceptions of value. *IET Conference Publications*, *2019*(CP756). https://doi.org/10.1049/cp.2019.0150

de Boer, P. S., van Deursen, A. J. A. M., & van Rompay, T. J. L. (2019). Accepting the Internet-of-Things in our homes: The role of user skills. *Telematics and Informatics*, *36*(July 2018), 147–156. https://doi.org/10.1016/j.tele.2018.12.004

Chouk, I., & Mani, Z. (2019). Factors for and against resistance to smart services: Role of consumer lifestyle and ecosystem related variables. *Journal of Services Marketing*, 33(4), JSM-01-2018-0046. https://doi.org/10.1108/JSM-01-2018-0046

Dienlin, T., & Metzger, M. J. (2016). An extended privacy calculus model for SNSs: Analyzing self-disclosure and self-withdrawal in a representative U.S. Sample. *Journal of Computer-Mediated Communication*, *21*(5), 368–383. https://doi.org/10.1111/jcc4.12163

Dienlin, T., & Trepte, S. (2015). Is the privacy paradox a relic of the past? An in-depth analysis of privacy attitudes and privacy behaviors. *European Journal of Social Psychology*, *45*(3):285–297. https://doi.org/10.1002/ejsp.2049

Distler, V., Lallemand, C., & Koenig, V. (2020). How acceptable is this? How user experience factors can broaden our understanding of the acceptance of privacy trade-offs. *Computers in Human Behavior*, *106*(December 2019), 106227. https://doi.org/10.1016/j.chb.2019.106227

Ellen, P. S., Bearden, W. O., & Sharma, S. (1991). Resistance to technological innovations: An examination of the role of self-efficacy and performance satisfaction. *Journal of the Academy of Marketing Science*, *19*(4), 297–307. https://doi.org/10.1007/BF02726504

Feng, H., Fawaz, K., & Shin, K. S. (2017). Continuous authentication for voice assistants. *Proceedings of the 23rd Annual International Conference on Mobile Computing and Networking*, 343–355.

Fishbein, M. & Ajzen, I. (1975). *Belief, attitude, intention, and behavior: An introduction to theory and research*. Reading, MA: Addison-Wesley.

Goad, D., Collins, A. T., & Gal, U. (2020). Privacy and the Internet of Things–An experiment in discrete choice. *Information and Management*, *2018*, 103292. https://doi.org/10.1016/j.im.2020.103292

Heidenreich, S., & Spieth, P. (2013). Why innovations fail—The case of passive and active innovation resistance. *International Journal of Innovation Management*, 17(5), 1–42. https://doi.org/10.1142/S1363919613500217

Hoenkamp, R., Huitema, G. B., & de Moor van Vugt, A. J. C. (2011). The neglected consumer: The case of the smart meter rollout in the Netherlands. *Renewable Energy Law Policy Review*, *4*, 269–282.

Hsu, C. L., & Lin, J. C. C. (2016). An empirical examination of consumer adoption of Internet of Things services: Network externalities and concern for information privacy perspectives. *Computers in Human Behavior*, *62*, 516–527. https://doi.org/10.1016/j.chb.2016.04.023

Im, S., & Workman, J. P. (2004). Market orientation, creativity, and new product performance in high-technology firms. *Journal of Marketing*, *68*, 114–132. https://doi.org/10.1509/jmkg.68.2.114.2778

Internet Society. (2019). *The trust opportunity: Exploring consumers' attitudes to the internet of things*. Uploads/2019/05/CI_IS_Joint_Report-EN.pdf, Accessed 3 March 2020. https://www.internetsociety.org/wp-content/

Kahneman, D. (2003). A perspective on judgment and choice: Mapping bounded rationality. *American Psychologist*, *58*(9), 697–720.

Keith, M. J., Thompson, S. C., Hale, J., Lowry, P. B., & Greer, C. (2013). Information disclosure on mobile devices: Re-examining privacy calculus with actual user behavior. *International Journal of Human-Computer Studies*, *71*(12), 1163–1173. https://doi.org/10.1016/j.ijhcs.2013.08.016.

Kim, S. & Kim, S. (2016). A multi-criteria approach toward discovering killer IoT application in Korea. *Technological Forecasting and Social Change*, *102*, 143–155. https://doi.org/https://doi.org/10.1016/j.techfore.2015.05.007

Kim, D., Park, K., Park, Y., & Ahn, J. H. (2019). Willingness to provide personal information: Perspective of privacy calculus in IoT services. *Computers in Human Behavior*, *92*(October 2018), 273–281. https://doi.org/10.1016/j.chb.2018.11.022

Kleijnen, M., Lee, N., & Wetzels, M. (2009). An exploration of consumer resistance to innovation and its antecedents. *Journal of Economic Psychology*, *30*(3), 344–357. https://doi.org/10.1016/j.joep.2009.02.004

Klein, A., Pacheco, F., & Righi, R. (2017). On developing business models for internet of things-based products: Process and Challenges. *Journal of Information Systems and Technology Management*, *14*(3), 439–461. https://doi.org/10.4301/s1807-17752017000300009

Kline, S., & Rosenberg, N. (1986). *An overview of innovation*. In R. Landau, & N. Rosenberg (Eds.), *The positive sum strategy. Harnessing technology for economic growth*. National Academy Press.

Krasnova, H., Veltri, N. F., & Günther, O. (2012). Self-disclosure and privacy calculus on social networking sites: The role of culture: Intercultural dynamics of privacy calculus. *Business & Information Systems Engineering*, *4*(3), 127–135. https://doi.org/10.1007/s12599-012-0216-6

Krotov, V. (2017). The Internet of Things and new business opportunities. *Business Horizons*, *60*(6), 831–841. https://doi.org/10.1016/j.bushor.2017.07.009

Lancelot-Miltgen, C., Henseler, J., Gelhard, C., & Popovič, A. (2016). Introducing new products that affect consumer privacy: A mediation model. *Journal of Business Research*, *69*(10), 4659–4666.

Lau, J., Zimmerman, B., & Schaub, F. (2018). Alexa, are you listening? Privacy perceptions, concerns and privacy-seeking behaviors with smart speakers. *Proceedings of the ACM on Human-Computer Interaction*, 2(CSCW), 1–31.

Laukkanen, T. (2016), Consumer adoption versus rejection decisions in seemingly similar service innovations: The case of the internet and mobile banking. *Journal of Business Research*, *69*(7), 2432–2439. https://doi.org/10.1016/j.jbusres.2016.01.013

Li, H., Luo, X. (Robert) Zhang, J., & Xu, H. (2017). Resolving the privacy paradox: Toward a cognitive appraisal and emotion approach to online privacy behaviors. *Information and Management*, *54*(8), 1012–1022. https://doi.org/10.1016/j.im.2017.02.005

Li, H., Wu, J., Gao, Y., & Shi, Y. (2016). Examining individuals' adoption of healthcare wearable devices: An empirical study from privacy calculus perspective. *International Journal of Medical Informatics*, *88*(555), 8–17. https://doi.org/10.1016/j.ijmedinf.2015.12.010

Lu, Y., Papagiannidis, S., & Alamanos, E. (2018). Internet of things: A systematic review of the business literature from the user and organisational perspectives. *Technological Forecasting and Social Change*, *136*(2), 285–297. https://doi.org/10.1016/j.techfore.2018.01.022

Luo, X., Li, H., Zhang, J., & Shim, J. P. (2010). Examining multi-dimensional trust and multi-faceted risk in initial acceptance of emerging technologies: An empirical study of mobile banking services. *Decision Support Systems*, *49*(2), 222–234. https://doi.org/10.1016/j.dss.2010.02.008.

Mani, Z., & Chouk, I. (2017). Drivers of consumers' resistance to smart products. *Journal of Marketing Management*, *33*(1–2), 76–97. https://doi.org/10.1080/0267257X.2016.1245212

Mani, Z., & Chouk, I. (2018). Consumer resistance to innovation in services: Challenges and barriers in the Internet of things era. *Journal of Product Innovation Management*, *35*(5), 780–807. https://doi.org/10.1111/jpim.12463

Mani, Z., & Chouk, I. (2019). Impact of privacy concerns on resistance to smart services: Does the 'Big Brother effect' matter? *Journal of Marketing Management*, *35*(15–16), 1460–1479. https://doi.org/10.1080/0267257X.2019.1667856

Mazurek, G., & Małagocka, K. (2019). What if you ask and they say yes? Consumers' willingness to disclose personal data is stronger than you think. *Business Horizons*, *62*(6), 751–759. https://doi.org/10.1016/j.bushor.2019.07.008

McLean, G., & Osei-Frimpong, K. (2019). Hey Alexa... examine the variables influencing the use of artificial intelligent in-home voice assistants. *Computers in Human Behavior*, *99*(January), 28–37. https://doi.org/10.1016/j.chb.2019.05.009

Mick, D. G., & Fournier, S. (1998). Paradoxes of technology: Consumer cognizance, emotions, and coping strategies. *Journal of Consumer Research*, *25*(2), 123–143. https://doi.org/10.1086/209531.

Mohr, J., Sengupta, S., & Slater, S. (2010). *Marketing of high-technology products and innovations*. Pearson Education Inc.

Norberg P., Horne D. R., & Horne D. A. (2007). The privacy paradox: Personal information disclosure intentions versus behaviors. *Journal of Consumer Affairs*, *41*(1), 100–126.

Oshana, R., & Kraeling, M. (2019). *Software engineering for embedded systems: Methods, practical techniques, and applications*. Newnes.

Ostrom, A. L., Parasuraman, A., Bowen, D., Patrício, L., & Voss, C. (2015). Service research priorities in a rapidly changing context. *Journal of Service Research*, *18*(2), 127–159.

Pauleen, D. J. & Wang, W. Y. C. (2017). Does big data mean big knowledge? KM perspectives on big data and analytics. *Journal of Knowledge Management*, *21*(1), 1–6. https://doi.org/10.1108/JKM-08-2016-0339

Porter, M. E., & Heppelmann, J. E. (2015). How smart, connected products are transforming companies. *Harvard Business Review*, *93*(10), 96–114. 10.1017/CBO9781107415324.004

Pridmore, J., & Mols, A. (2020). Personal choices and situated data: Privacy negotiations and the acceptance of household Intelligent Personal Assistants. *Big Data and Society*, *7*(1). https://doi.org/10.1177/2053951719891748

Rainie, L., & Duggan, M. (2015). *Privacy and information sharing*. Pew Research Center.

Ram, S. (1987). A model of innovation resistance. *NA – Advances in Consumer Research*, *14*, 208–212.

Ram, S., & Sheth, J. N. (1989). Consumer resistance to innovations: The marketing problem and its solutions. *Journal of Consumer Marketing*, *6*(2), 5–14. https://doi.org/10.1108/EUM0000000002542

Rauschnabel, P. A., He, J., & Ro, Y. K. (2018). Antecedents to the adoption of augmented reality smart glasses: A closer look at privacy risks. *Journal of Business Research*, *92*(November), 374–384. https://doi.org/10.1016/j.jbusres.2018.08.008

Ren, J., Dubois, D. J., Choffnes, D., Mandalari, A. M., Kolcun, R., & Haddadi, H. (2019). Information exposure from consumer IOT devices: A multidimensional, network informed measurement approach. In: *Proceedings of the Internet Measurement Conference*, 267–279.

Rogers, E. M. (2003). *Diffusion of innovations*. The Free Press.

Santanen, E. (2019). The value of protecting privacy. *Business Horizons*, *62*(1), 5–14. https://doi.org/10.1016/j.bushor.2018.04.004

Shin, D. (2014). A socio-technical framework for internet-of-things design: A human-centered design for the internet of things. *Telematics and Informatics*, *31*, 519–531.

Sucharew, H., & Macaluso, M. (2019). Methods for research evidence synthesis: The scoping review approach. *Journal of Hospital Medicine*, *7*, 416–418. https://doi.org/10.12788/jhm.3248

Sun, Y., Wang, N., Shen, X. L., & Zhang, J. X. (2015). Location information disclosure in location-based social network services: Privacy calculus, benefit structure, and gender differences. *Computers in Human Behavior*, *52*, 278–292.

Suppatvech, C., Godsell, J., & Day, S. (2019). The roles of internet of things technology in enabling servitized business models: A systematic literature review. *Industrial Marketing Management*, *82*(August 2018), 70–86. https://doi.org/10.1016/j.indmarman.2019.02.016

Szmigin, I., & Foxall, G. (1998). Three forms of innovation resistance: The case of retail payment methods. *Technovation*, *18*(6–7), 459–468. https://doi.org/10.1016/S0166-4972(98)00030-3

Touzani, M., Charfi, A. A., Boistel, P., & Niort, M. C. (2018). Connecto ergo sum! an exploratory study of the motivations behind the usage of connected objects. *Information and Management*, *55*(4), 472–481. https://doi.org/10.1016/j.im.2017.11.002

Tsai, J. Y., Egelman, S., Cranor, L., & Acquisti, A. (2011). The effect of online privacy information on purchasing behavior: An experimental study. *Information Systems Research*, *22*(2), 254–268. https://doi.org/10.1287/isre.1090.0260

Van Deursen, A. J. A. M., & Mossberger, K. (2018). Any thing for anyone? A new digital divide in Internet-of-Things skills. *Policy & Internet*, *10*(2), 122–140. https://doi.org/10.1002/poi3.171

Venkatesh, V., Morris, M. G., Hall, M., Davis, G. B., & Davis, F. D. (2003). User acceptance of information technology: Toward a unified. *MIS Quarterly*, *27*(3), 425–478.

Viardot, E. (2004). *Successful marketing strategy for high-tech firms*. Artech House.

Weinberg, B. D., Milne, G. R., Andonova, Y. G., & Hajjat, F. M. (2015). Internet of Things: Convenience vs. privacy and secrecy. *Business Horizons*, *58*(6), 615–624. https://doi.org/10.1016/j.bushor.2015.06.005

Whitmore, A., Agarwal, A., & Da Xu, L. (2015). The Internet of Things—A survey of topics and trends. *Information Systems Frontiers*, *17*(2), 261–275. https://doi.org/10.1007/s10796-014-9489-2

Wiegard, R.-B., & Breitner, M. H. (2017). Smart services in healthcare: A risk-benefit-analysis of pay-as-you-live services from customer perspective in Germany. *Electronic Markets*, *29*(1), 107–123.

Williams, M., Nurse, J. R. C., & Creese, S. (2019). (Smart)Watch Out! Encouraging privacy-protective behavior through interactive games. *International Journal of Human Computer Studies*, *132*(July), 121–137. https://doi.org/10.1016/j.ijhcs.2019.07.012

Williams, M., Nurse, J. R. C., & Creese, S. (2017). "Privacy is the boring bit": User perceptions and behaviour in the Internet-of-Things. *Proceedings of the 15th International Conference on Privacy Security and Trust*. https://doi.org/10.1109/PST.2017.00029

Wilson, C., Hargreaves, T., & Hauxwell-Baldwin, R. (2017). Benefits and risks of smart home technologies. *Energy Policy*, *103*, 72–83. https://doi.org/10.1016/j.enpol.2016.12.047

Wünderlich, N. V., Heinonen, K., Ostrom, A. L., Patricio, L., Sousa, R., Voss, C., Lemmink, J. G. A. M. (2015). "Futurizing" Smart service: Implications for service researchers and managers. *Journal of Services Marketing*, 26(1), 442–447. https://doi.org/10.1108/JSM-01-2015-0040

Wunderlich, P., Kranz, J., Totzek, D., Veit, D., & Picot, A. (2013). The impact of endogenous motivations on adoption of IT-enabled services: The case of transformative services in the energy sector. *Journal of Service Research*, *16*(3), 356e371.

Yang, H., Lee, H., & Zo, H. (2017). User acceptance of smart home services: An extension of the theory of planned behavior. *Industrial Management and Data Systems*, *117*(1), 68–89. https://doi.org/10.1108/IMDS-01-2016-0017

Zheng, S., Apthorpe, N., Chetty, M., & Feamster, N. (2018). User perceptions of smart home IoT privacy. *Proceedings of the ACM on Human-Computer Interaction*, 2(CSCW). https://doi.org/10.1145/3274469

6 The Effects of Social Media Tools' Usage in International Marketing Communication – Corporation Perspective

Bartosik-Purgat Małgorzata, Staszków Michał, and Lemański Michał

Introduction

Communication is a process of sharing and exchanging information with others. Its interdisciplinary nature means that there is no single definition recognized and preferred by scientists. Hartman (2008) states that communication is a way of perceiving reality and understanding the world, as well as sharing with others. Griffin et al. (2015) write about communication as being between individuals who interact with each other through conversation, whereas Giddens (2009) refers to communication as interaction via the use of various mass media. Within business, the significance of communication comes from the importance of access to information: Whoever has information first, has an advantage in the market (Hollensen, 2014). Such information helps businesses to make faster and more accurate decisions and, from there, take specific actions.

Marketing communication is a form of communication between a company and the recipient, who is usually a potential buyer (Gabrielli & Balboni, 2010; Li, 2021). International marketing communication concerns a situation when participants in this process operate from different countries and cultures. The mainstreaming instruments of such communication (e.g. TV ads) allow companies to provide information to their clients using one-way messaging (Finne & Grönroos, 2017). The development of the Internet and digitalization has led to the appearance of new communication possibilities, both in national and international contexts (Bansal & Gupta, 2020). According to Katsikeas et al. (2019, p. 405), "new digitalized technologies have indeed revolutionized the way firms are conducting their business with buyers abroad, by providing significant help in searching for, targeting, serving and communicating with customers in any part of the world". These technologies allowed the development of two-way communication, which enabled not just companies but also clients to actively participate in this process (Bansal & Gupta, 2020; Li, 2021). Communication instruments provided by these technologies include, among others, social media (SM).

DOI: 10.4324/9781003204343-6

The variety and possibilities of SM services have made them very popular for use by both individuals and businesses around the world (Kemp, 2020). Thanks to them, customers are engaged in a dialog with producers about their offers and services. Moreover, these communication tools are now playing even more important roles during the Covid-19 pandemic, when direct access to international markets and customers is almost impossible.

Some research and scientific papers present the significance of SM in marketing communication, e.g. the role of SM in brand equity creation (Bruhn et al., 2012; Liu et al., 2019; Mukherjee, 2019; Simon & Tossan, 2018), the use of SM in the achievement of companies' competitive advantage (Kumar & Pansari, 2016), the advantage of SM for communication with young consumers (Duffett, 2017; Florenthal, 2019), SM's significance in business to business (B2B) communication (Gruner & Power, 2018; Zhang & Du, 2020), SM's use for customer involvement in product development (prosumer activities) (Bartosik-Purgat & Bednarz, 2021; Seran Potra & Izvercian, 2014), and the adoption diversity of SM in the cross-cultural marketplace (Alsaleh et al., 2019; Olaniran, 2018). However, the literature indicates that there remain few studies analyzing SM marketing communication's effects from an international and corporate perspective (e.g. Johnston et al., 2018; Okazaki & Taylor, 2013). A majority of this research presents the point of view of consumers who take into account SM messages in their purchasing decisions (see Bansal & Gupta, 2020; Duffett, 2017; Kushwaha et al., 2020; Morra et al., 2018; Mukherjee, 2019; Voramontri & Klieb, 2018). One of the latest papers presented by Katsikeas et al. (2019) explores the opportunities and challenges faced by companies in the new digital era concerning their international marketing strategy. However, it does not emphasize the outcomes of SM usage in marketing in the international marketplace (instead, the authors concentrate on a marketing mix strategy). The main contribution of this chapter and the research herein is to combine a corporate point of view and international dimension together and present the main effects of SM usage in international marketing communication from a business to consumer (B2C) company's perspective. The B2C market is strongly associated with SM use in communication between the company and the mass audience (Bartosik-Purgat, 2019). In turn, mass audiences include many individual consumers who are users of SM tools, such as Facebook, Instagram, or YouTube (Gruner & Power, 2018; Zhang & Du, 2020).

A literature study on the presented issues allowed us to form three research questions (RQs):

RQ 1. What kind of SM tools are used in different geographical regions by companies from the B2C market in marketing communication?

RQ 2. How do companies assess the features of SM tools in international marketing communication?

RQ 3. What effects do the use of SM tools bring for B2C companies in marketing communication with international consumers?

The main purpose of the study is twofold: first, to identify the frequency of SM tool usage in marketing communication on the international market, and second, to determine their features and effects from the B2C company's point of view. The research methods used in the study are threefold: a literature analysis, primary qualitative research, and quantitative research divided into three stages. First, pre-research was conducted in order to identify SM tool use by companies in international marketing communication as well as their features and outcomes they helped to achieve (qualitative: focus group interviews). Second, a pilot study was used in order to check the adequacy of the questionnaire (online individual interviews), and third, the main research was conducted in 205 production companies operating in Poland in the B2C market and doing business internationally (individual interviews).

The chapter consists of five parts. In the first part, the theoretical background and literature review are developed. Following this, the research methods, main results, and discussion are all presented in turn, before concluding with implications and limitations of the study and future research directions.

Theoretical Background and Literature Review

Marketing Communication Models

Traditional marketing communication is the situation when the sender is a company or other institutional entity (e.g. a university or a state administration unit) that wants to communicate a specific message to a mass audience. The recipients are usually both current customers and potential buyers of particular goods or services (Hollensen, 2014; Smith & Zook, 2016). Most often, the message is information necessary for a potential customer to make a purchasing decision (or other action). It can be information about a product or service; its characteristics, place, and conditions of purchase; its use; or benefits of the purchase, as well as catchy slogans to make the brand more memorable and recognizable among others available on the market (Danaher & Rossiter, 2011; Smith & Zook, 2016). These marketing communication goals are usually described as "direct" (Heinonen & Strandvik, 2005), but among the intermediate and long-term objectives one can distinguish an increase of economic indicators of companies (increase in sales volume, profit), an increase of company name and product recognition (also brand positioning), an increase of customer engagement and loyalty, improvement of company image, and finally strengthening of the business's dialog and relationship with the market and its actors (Balaji et al., 2016; Bansal & Gupta, 2020; Hänninen & Karjaluoto, 2017; Li, 2021; Smith & Zook, 2016).

As already mentioned above, the traditional marketing communication model presents a one-to-many situation, because communication is interpreted as an "act of transferring a message to others and making it understood in a meaningful way" (Andersen, 2001, p. 168). The sender may use various forms and means of communication, but this is usually the same message addressed to all potential buyers (Hänninen & Karjaluoto, 2017). This model of mass marketing communication presents an example of unilateral communication in which there is no feedback from the recipient of the message. The lack of the possibility of an answer is caused by the use of specific mass media, e.g. TV, radio, or outdoor advertising (Hoffman & Novak, 1996; Fawkes & Gregory, 2000; Finne & Grönroos, 2017). The customer takes the position of the message's recipient and is a passive actor in the communication process (Hänninen & Karjaluoto, 2017; Finne & Grönroos, 2017). A bilateral model of marketing communication – which includes the features of interpersonal communication, and at the same time reaching many recipients with the message (mass communication features) – can use media that will provide an opportunity for interaction, e.g. the recipient of the message can respond quickly and express their opinion (Andersen, 2001; Bansal & Gupta, 2020; Gabrielli & Balboni, 2010). Marketing communication in the online environment presents such an opportunity, offering a many-to-many situation where both buyers and sellers actively participate in the exchange of information, e.g. on websites, in SM, etc. (Bansal & Gupta, 2020; Porcu et al., 2017). This method of communication serves a better option for relationship and trust building (Balaji et al., 2016; Bartosik-Purgat, 2019; Hänninen & Karjaluoto, 2017). Andersen (2001) argues that traditional one-way communication, with an active sender and passive recipient, is outdated both in the literature and practice. Two-way communication is now possible via the Internet (Bartosik-Purgat, 2019; Danaher & Rossiter, 2011), and what is more, the consumer can also initiate the communication process. The dialog that is achieved in such communication processes can lead to better consumer understanding by the business.

Social Media in Marketing Communication

There are many ways of defining SM in the literature. Kaplan and Haenlein (2010) describe SM as a set of applications that are technically and ideologically based on the foundations of Web 2.0, allowing the creation and exchange of content among users. Kietzmann and Hermkens (2011) underline the use of online technologies by users to publish and exchange information with others. Many definitions emphasize the character and possibilities of SM that are related to connecting people into groups and exchanging information, knowledge, opinions, etc. (Bingham & Conner, 2015; Lee, 2014). Elsewhere, Williams et al. (2012) present SM as a mechanism that allows users to communicate with a large number of people around the world.

The utilization of SM tools in international marketing communication is mainly associated with their advantageous features, including (Bartosik-Purgat, 2019; Taiminen & Karjaluoto, 2015; Valos et al., 2016): large geographical coverage and the ability to reach many recipients quickly (most international SM platforms are available in a majority of countries); fast publication of information; the ability to strengthen the quality of customer service or conduct quick and low-cost customer research (users of SM); accessibility (SM tools are accessible to a large amount of the world's population); responsiveness (users can create posts reacting to information that appears in the media in a very short time); the possibility of two-way communication; and the possibility of gathering information about customers, their needs, interests, preferences, behaviors, and views through observations of their posts, comments, and affiliations to specific fan pages. According to Okazaki and Taylor (2013), SM differs from traditional media in three fundamental aspects. First, SM enables greater availability of information. Next, it makes it possible to move value production from a company to a consumer (it stems from increasing consumer activity). And finally, it changes the direction of influence and power of a consumer.

Companies can employ different types of SM tools in international marketing communication depending on the audience's features or goals they want to achieve. SM tools divide them into two basic groups, based on the number of recipients of a message (Bartosik-Purgat, 2019): (1) instant messengers, and (2) social networking sites.

Instant messengers are applications that allow quick content transfer between users, which can take the form of a written, verbal, video, and pictorial (images) message. The most popular instant messengers in the world are QQ, WeChat, and Line (mainly in Asian markets); Facebook Messenger; WhatsApp; Viber; Snapchat; as well as Skype. These instruments are most frequently used in communication between individual users (one-on-one), primarily by mobile devices, most notably smartphones. Because of the nature of instant messengers, they are not frequently used by companies in marketing communication.

Social networking sites transmit content to a greater number of users. Among others, these include (Bartosik-Purgat, 2019): blogs and microblogs (e.g. Twitter, Blip, Tumblr, Weibo); Internet forums and wikis (e.g. Wikipedia); media sharing (e.g. YouTube, Youku, Instagram, Periscope, Vimeo); social bookmarking (e.g. Reddit, Digg, Livejournal, Pinterest); social networks aimed at exchanging information or maintaining relationships with friends (e.g. Facebook, Google+, MySpace, Qzone, Renren – on Asian markets, VKontakte – on the Russian market); and social network platforms aimed at creating communities of professionals (professionally active people, e.g. LinkedIn, ResearchGate, Academia.edu, GoldenLine).

The newest report related to the use of SM around the world, *Digital Use Around the World in July 2020,* shows that the most popular (based on the number of active users) SM in the group of instant messengers are: WhatsApp, Facebook Messenger, and WeChat (Kemp, 2020). In the group of social networking sites, the world's most-used were Facebook, YouTube, and Instagram (Kemp, 2020). The characteristics of SM types influence the effect and character of communication. For example, Zhang et al. (2020, p. 364) indicated that Twitter and companies' tweets are "focused more on providing information and promoting action than on facilitating dialogue".

Although there is some research showing the usage of SM in marketing communication, it is usually concentrated on a single and particular market, and thus does not take into account the international dimension. For example, the literature study indicated some results partially related to the research questions and the main purpose of the paper. Moreover, a majority of the research presents the consumers' point of view (users of SM tools), not companies' (Duffett, 2017; Kaiser et al., 2020; Lee et al., 2011; Liu et al., 2019; Whiting & Williams, 2013), and to the best of authors' knowledge, the corporate perspective is presented very rarely. For example, Bruhn et al. (2012) conducted one of the first studies on this topic. They investigated the influence of brand communication on brand equity through SM in comparison to traditional communication. Their results show a strong influence of SM on a brand image, whereas traditional media impact brand awareness. In another study of Finnish small and medium-sized enterprises, Taiminen and Karjaluoto (2015) emphasized the positive effects of using SM in marketing communication. Among them, the most important are: cost savings; adaptation to changing consumer preferences and behaviors (and thus better acceptance of products and brands on the market); the speed of information transfer to potential buyers or business partners; influence on increasing customer awareness; better and more effective targeting of the message; improving (speed and quality) service; increasing sales, especially among regular customers (increasing loyalty through the media); and improving dialog with customers. A further paper by Majumdar and Bose (2019) explored the positive correlation between Twitter's application and a company's value. They proved that usage of Twitter impacts the market value of the company. Li et al. (2013) investigated the connection between the Twitter profile of the company and its reputation. Prokofieva (2015) indicated that corporate Twitter accounts their tweets (information transferred in them) may lead to better recognition of the company and influence investors. Some of the latest research presented by Li (2021) shows that companies should focus on improving community reputation in a virtual sphere to achieve good sales results, while also taking care of product quality and building a relationship with customers.

Despite the many benefits of including SM in marketing communication strategies, Valos et al. (2016) indicated some limitations. They are mainly related to the reduction of control over communication activities. It is extremely difficult to "control" when negative opinions and posts directed at a specific company or its brands appear (although it must be noted that the paper focuses mainly on the positive effects that may be achieved by SM tool usage in international marketing communication). Therefore, new professions and positions are often created in organizations and institutions that use SM, where people are responsible for monitoring and promptly responding to specific posts from users. Kaplan and Haenlein (2010) add that the use of SM in marketing communication requires a new way of communication between individuals within companies.

The literature study's results supported the formulation of the following hypotheses concerning the research questions:

H1. The most widespread SM tool used by companies from the B2C market in marketing communication, regardless of geographic region, is Facebook (RQ 1).

H2. Cost saving is the most significant feature of SM tool usage in international marketing communication (RQ 2).

H3. The highest impact of usage of SM tools in international marketing communication is related to brand recognition (RQ3).

Method

Research Process and Methods

A deductive methodological approach was used, first, to identify the most internationally widespread SM tools used by companies in marketing communication and, second, to identify the features of SM and the outcomes achieved thanks to SM tool usage (Babbie, 2014). This methodological approach is associated with the literature review, which is supported in hypotheses' formulation (Craig & Douglas, 2005).

The researched group consisted of production companies from the B2C market based in Poland, which operate internationally (in different geographical regions: Europe, Asia, North and South Americas, Africa, and Australia). That group of companies was used because they offer products to individual consumers and communicate with them in marketing strategies. A triangulation of research methods was used in order to achieve the main research goals; this means that both qualitative and quantitative methods were employed. The research procedure consisted of the following steps: (1) pre-research was conducted in order to identify the SM tools used by companies in international marketing communication, as well as their features and the outcomes achieved (qualitative: focus groups interviews); (2) a pilot study was applied in order to check the adequacy of the questionnaire (online individual interviews); and (3) the main research was conducted in 205 production companies operating in Poland on the B2C market and doing business internationally (individual interviews).

The pre-research study (focus group interviews) invited managers (one manager represented one company) responsible for the companies' international strategies – both export and marketing. Two focus interviews, each with six managers (the first with export and the second with marketing specialists), were conducted in order to find out: what kind of SM tools they use in international marketing communication, what the most important features are, and what kinds of effects they achieve by using SM tools in international marketing communication. This information was used to prepare a preliminary version of the questionnaire that was tested during a pilot study – online individual interviews (with the same managers who took part in the pre-research). The main purpose of the pilot study was to check the adequacy and intelligibility of the preliminary version of the questionnaire. After the pilot study, a final version of the questionnaire was produced to be used in the main study. In the main study, individual interviews were employed using a standardized questionnaire. The same selection criteria were used for companies in all steps of the research procedure. The research instrument used in the main study was a questionnaire, mainly with closed questions. The pre-research was conducted at the end of 2017, the pilot study was carried out in the middle of 2018, and the main study was conducted in late 2018 and early 2019, with managers responsible for international marketing and export strategies.

Sampling Method

The selection of companies and managers for the pre- and pilot research was purposive as each had to meet the selection criteria and give consent to participate in the study. However, in the main study, the companies were sampled, employing a random sampling method. The sampling frame of the researched population was a database developed by Kompass (a reliable database of companies available in Poland). There were around 10,000 companies indicated that met the criteria of sampling: production companies, B2C, both Polish and foreign capital, selling their products abroad and communicating with consumers internationally. The sample size was determined by using a level of confidence of 95%, 0.5 of fraction size, and the maximum permissible error was 5%. To obtain an acceptable sample size, first, a calculator sample: www.calculator.net was used, and second, the Cochran Formula for Sample Size Calculation in Smaller Populations was employed. Both methods for sample size creation calculated that approximately 370 entities needed to be researched. Against this background, 370 companies from the 10,000 list were randomly drawn. Then, authors of the paper contacted (using the telephone or e-mail) the 370 selected companies and tried to establish who the appropriate person (manager) in the company was to take part in the main study and invite them for the interview. Finally, only 205 managers (representing 205 companies) agreed to participate.

Sample Characteristics

The managers who participated in the study represented production companies operating abroad, in different geographical regions, namely: Europe, Asia, North and South Americas, Africa, and Australia. Almost all companies (97.7%) that took part in the main research internationalize their strategies on European markets. The second most common geographical region where companies run business is Asia (almost 30%), followed by North America (25%). The fewest number of companies are present in Africa and Australia (6% in both regions).

The companies were differentiated in terms of country of origin. Namely, 57.5% of this group belonged to the group of foreign companies (with the predominance using foreign capital), and 42.5% used mostly Polish capital. Both foreign and Polish companies that took part in the research were located in Poland.

Results

Managers participating in the pre-research assisted in creating a list of SM tools, as well as their features and outcomes. For the first point, Facebook, YouTube, Instagram, and Twitter were indicated as the main SM tools used to have contact with international customers. Managers also pointed out that there are some markets where communication through international SM is limited, e.g. some Asian markets. That is why a category of local social media (LSM) was added to the list of SM tools. Managers emphasized that their companies mainly have profiles and run adverts on SM. In the second part, managers assessed the most significant (subjective opinion) advantages/features of international communication through SM tools. These were: low costs of communication, wide access to consumers, ability to reach consumers quickly and get quick feedback from consumers, and ease of use. In the third part, managers indicated the outcomes their companies obtain through SM tool usage in international marketing communication. They underlined, among others: increasing product sales; improving the image of the company and its products; increasing recognition of the company's brand; keeping customers and increasing their loyalty; learning about consumer preferences; providing reliable information about offers; providing information about activities in which the company is involved (e.g. corporate social responsibility or public relations); and allowing consumers to participate in the development of a product for a given market (e.g. taste tests or packaging design).

Referring to RQ1, the SM tools used by companies in marketing communication mainly focus on SM profile management and advertising spots. The pre-research study identified the SM tools most frequently used by respondents in international marketing communication. In the main study, they were evaluated based on the frequency of use in particular markets (on a scale of 1 to 5, where *5 – very often; 4 – often; 3 – sometimes; 2 – rarely; 1 – very rarely*). The researched companies highlighted the highest frequency of usage concerning Facebook in all indicated geographical regions (Table 6.1). YouTube, Instagram, or Twitter, as well as LSM, were rated a little lower. However, it should be emphasized that the highest percentage of indications and frequency of using LSM for mass communication with the relevant segment of buyers were achieved in the Asian market. This is certainly related to the popularity of local media in this geographical area and restrictions concerning international media (Bartosik-Purgat, 2019). Taking into account these findings, it should be indicated that the H1: *The most widespread SM tool used by companies from the B2C market in marketing communication, regardless of the geographic region, is Facebook*, is supported.

Concerning RQ2, the researched companies were asked to assess the characteristics of SM tools used in international marketing communication according to their significance. These features were identified during the pre-research. In the main study, the respondents were asked to indicate the degree of compliance, related to identified characteristics, with the statements (on a scale of *5 – very significant feature; 4 – significant feature; 3 – it is hard to say; 2 – insignificant feature; 1 – very insignificant feature*) that are presented in Table 6.2.

Generalizing the results, Facebook achieved the highest ranks according to all presented features, and LSM, the lowest. Taking into account the averages attained from all SM tools in relation to particular characteristics, the respondents evaluated "easy to use" with the highest score (4.2) concerning the significance in international marketing communication. This was followed by cost savings (4.137), providing wide access to consumers (4.084), and allowing the company to reach consumers quickly (4.076). Providing quick feedback to consumers was

Table 6.1 Social media (SM) tools used by companies in international marketing communication in relation to geographical regions

SM Tools in International Marketing Communication	*Geographical Regions*	*% of Total Respondents*	*Average Freque-ncy*	*Coefficient of Variation*
Facebook (profile, advertising)	North America	10.18	3.76	38.2
	South and Central America	3.59	3.75	39.6
	Europe	38.02	3.76	35.6
	Asia	9.58	3.22	53.4
	Australia and Oceania	2.40	3.25	53.9
	Africa	2.10	3.57	50.8
YouTube (advertising)	North America	8.98	3.00	51.8
	South and Central America	3.59	3.08	54.4
	Europe	23.95	2.79	57.0
	Asia	7.49	2.60	56.6
	Australia and Oceania	2.40	2.63	57.4
	Africa	2.40	3.25	48.7
Twitter (profile, advertising)	North America	5.99	2.15	69.6
	South and Central America	2.40	2.50	67.6
	Europe	20.66	2.51	67.2
	Asia	6.59	2.36	68.5
	Australia and Oceania	1.80	2.00	77.5
	Africa	1.80	2.67	61.2
Instagram (profile, advertising)	North America	6.59	2.91	59.0
	South and Central America	2.10	2.57	77.3
	Europe	20.66	2.62	62.1
	Asia	5.69	2.05	61.8
	Australia and Oceania	1.50	2.20	74.7
	Africa	1.20	1.25	40.0
Local social media (LSM) – profile, advertising	North America	5.69	2.00	76.4
	South and Central America	2.40	2.50	70.9
	Europe	22.75	2.68	63.3
	Asia	11.38	3.03	45.8
	Australia and Oceania	0.90	1.00	0.0
	Africa	1.50	1.40	63.9

Source: Adapted from Bartosik-Purgat (2019)

given the lowest score. Taking into consideration these findings, it should be indicated that the H2: *Cost saving is the most significant feature of SM tool usage in international marketing communication,* is not supported. However, it needs to be added that features associated with the cost savings were ranked only just below ease of use in relation to its significance in SM tool usage.

Table 6.2 Assessment of the characteristics of social media tools used by companies in international marketing communication

Characteristics SM Tools	*SM tools*	*% of Total Respondents*	*Average Assessment*	*Coefficient of Variation*
It is a cheap method of communication.	Facebook	34.43	4.59	16.0
	YouTube	17.37	4.09	26.4
	Twitter	14.07	4.00	30.8
	Instagram	14.97	4.14	28.0
	LSM	19.76	3.85	35.4
It provides wide access to consumers.	Facebook	34.13	4.54	17.2
	YouTube	17.37	4.28	23.1
	Twitter	14.07	3.96	27.9
	Instagram	14.67	3.88	29.1
	LSM	20.06	3.76	33.1
It allows us to reach consumers quickly.	Facebook	33.83	4.52	18.0
	YouTube	17.37	4.24	25.5
	Twitter	14.07	3.96	31.2
	Instagram	14.67	3.76	34.6
	LSM	20.36	3.90	33.5
It provides quick feedback.	Facebook	33.53	4.34	20.9
	YouTube	16.77	3.64	32.0
	Twitter	13.77	3.48	35.7
	Instagram	14.37	3.50	35.4
	LSM	17.37	3.60	34.8
It is easy to use.	Facebook	33.53	4.57	15.2
	YouTube	16.77	4.23	25.9
	Twitter	14.67	4.12	29.6
	Instagram	14.37	4.13	28.6
	LSM	18.86	3.95	31.0

Source: Adapted from Bartosik-Purgat (2019)

About RQ3, managers indicated the possible effect of SM tool application in international marketing communication on marketing strategies (on a scale of 5 to 1, where 5 – *very large impact, and 1 – low impact*). The general results (Table 6.3) show the relatively high (above average) impact of all SM tools on international marketing communication effects. The findings emphasize the highest significance of Facebook concerning the achievement of all particular marketing effects identified in the pre-research study.

Taking into account particular marketing effects, the highest score (an average from the ranks of all SM tools) was achieved in the case of increasing brand and company recognition (3.86), followed closely by providing information on activities in which the company is involved (3.85), providing reliable information about offers (3.716), and improving the image of the company and its products (3.634). Subsequent effects were keeping customers and their loyalty (3.436), learning about preferences (3.252), and participating in the development of new

Table 6.3 The influence of social media tools on the effects of international marketing communication

Effects of Using SM Tools in International Marketing Communication	*SM tools*	*% of Total Respondents*	*Average Assessment of Influence*	*Coefficient of Variation*
Increasing product sales directly	Facebook	32.34	3.68	32.6
	YouTube	16.17	3.11	41.3
	Twitter	12.87	2.86	50.9
	Instagram	12.87	2.56	53.5
	LSM	18.56	3.37	42.0
Improving the image of the company and its products	Facebook	32.63	4.21	23.3
	YouTube	16.17	3.69	33.7
	Twitter	12.87	3.51	42.3
	Instagram	12.87	3.16	48.8
	LSM	17.37	3.60	35.6
Increasing recognition of brand and products	Facebook	33.23	4.35	21.6
	YouTube	16.17	4.08	30.0
	Twitter	12.87	3.65	40.7
	Instagram	12.87	3.53	42.9
	LSM	17.66	3.69	36.3
Keeping customers and increasing their loyalty	Facebook	31.44	4.04	24.3
	YouTube	15.87	3.30	40.5
	Twitter	12.28	3.34	41.6
	Instagram	12.87	3.14	40.3
	LSM	16.47	3.36	38.1
Learning about consumer preferences	Facebook	31.74	4.02	28.9
	YouTube	15.87	3.11	42.1
	Twitter	12.87	2.95	52.7
	Instagram	12.87	2.79	49.2
	LSM	16.17	3.39	39.9
Providing reliable information about offers	Facebook	32.63	4.22	21.7
	YouTube	16.17	3.83	29.4
	Twitter	12.87	3.51	39.5
	Instagram	12.87	3.21	40.5
	LSM	17.07	3.81	32.3
Providing information on activities in which the company is involved (e.g. within corporate social responsibility or public relations)	Facebook	31.14	4.37	23.9
	YouTube	15.87	3.83	32.7
	Twitter	12.87	3.79	38.0
	Instagram	12.57	3.26	42.9
	LSM	15.87	4.00	31.4
The possibility for consumers to participate in the development of a product for a given market (e.g. taste contests or packaging design)	Facebook	29.64	3.99	34.6
	YouTube	14.97	2.86	54.3
	Twitter	11.98	3.03	51.0
	Instagram	11.98	2.65	52.4
	LSM	14.37	3.29	44.3

Source: Adapted from Bartosik-Purgat (2019)

products (prosumer activities) (3.164). The lowest score was achieved in relation to the direct impact of SM tool usage on sales increases (3.116), which is somewhat surprising given companies' goals are usually to increase revenue. The main reason for that may be associated with the word "directly", which could have led to managers not assessing it higher. Generally, a majority of the effects indirectly lead to an increase in sales over a longer time. Concluding the above considerations, it should be underlined that H3: *The highest impact of usage of SM tools in international marketing communication is related to brand recognition,* has been confirmed.

Discussion

The development of new media (including SM), continually increasing access to the Internet, and the need for internationalization in order to enter new markets all influence companies' decision to involve new tools in international communication between themselves and consumers (Kemp, 2020; Li, 2021). What is more, the preferences of consumers on SM usage, as well as their activities on these media and the general changes in communication, all impact the necessity for adaptations to marketing strategies of companies. When a company wants to be competitive in the international marketplace, it should develop marketing communication based on innovative solutions.

The paper focused on three aspects related to the research questions formulated in the first part of the research procedure, namely: application of SM tools in international marketing communication, assessing the features of SM tools in marketing communication, and assessing the impact of SM tools on the effects associated with the SM tool usage in international marketing communication.

The results presented in the paper show the great importance of SM in the international communication strategy. Similar findings were achieved in the project of Šerić (2017), where strong positive and significant relationships were identified between the social Web and integrated marketing communication. What is more, "national culture was found to exert a statistically significant moderating effect" in that relationship (Šerić, 2017, p. 646). The research findings related to the types of SM tools used by companies in international marketing communication confirm the results achieved by Kemp (2020), who found Facebook to be the most used SM tool in the world, with YouTube close behind. Kemp's report (2020) refers to individual users, whereas the data presented in this paper describe companies' SM tool usage. Lower scores were achieved in relation to Twitter and Instagram in the presented research, SM tools that were highly ranked in Kemp's report (2020). The specific companies and the messages provided to their customers may influence these platforms (Twitter and Instagram) being used to a smaller extent.

Zhang and Du (2020) compared messages presented in SM on B2B and B2C markets. They indicated that B2B companies usually use a more rational and less emotional style than B2C. Besides this, they present a lower degree of informativeness and perform better in interactivity and variety (Zhang & Du, 2020). Facebook and YouTube transfer such messages. On the other hand, Twitter is adequate for advertising. These findings are partially similar to the achievements of Zhang et al. (2020), who state that tweets sent by companies usually deliver information and do not allow a dialog to be conducted with customers. An interesting result was achieved concerning LSM, a category that was developed in the presented research, in Asia. Companies highlighted quite high (above average) usage of such media in Asian markets, which may be associated with the legal controls on the operation of "international" SM tools. This aspect has also been emphasized by other authors, e.g. Duan and Dholakia (2015) and Yu et al. (2019).

When it comes to features of SM tools used by companies in international marketing communication, some elements were highlighted and assessed more positively by managers. The ease and low cost to use the tools achieved the highest scores. These traits were also noted by the Finnish organizations examined by Taiminen and Karjaluoto (2015). Such features complement each other because usually when something is simple and easy to do, it does not require a large amount of money. These features and possibilities greatly influence the employment of SM tools in reaching and communicating with consumers from distant geographical regions (Okazaki & Taylor, 2013).

Underlying the impact of particular SM tools on the indicated effects of international marketing communication, it is necessary to indicate the great importance of these tools in this area. Their influence was highly rated with almost all possible effects. This is connected with many advantages that are attributed to the potential effects of SM (Bansal & Gupta, 2020; Finne & Grönroos, 2017; Taiminen & Karjaluoto, 2015). The findings indicate that the most important effect of SM tool usage in international marketing communication was brand recognition. Bruhn et al. (2012) have also indicated the importance of SM in the brand creation strategy of companies, although they did not consider an international dimension in their study. Also, Šerić (2017) underlined the role of SM, both in integrated marketing communication and brand equity. Brand recognition, as a purpose of SM employment in marketing strategy, has also been identified in research conducted by Simon and Tossan (2018), Mukherjee (2019), and Liu et al. (2019). The newest findings presented by Cheung et al. (2021) showed the significance of five social media marketing (SMM) elements, like entertainment, customization, interactivity, electronic-word-of-mouth (e-WOM), and trendiness, on consumers' intent to participate in value co-creation, on consumer–brand engagement and perceived brand value in turn. Value co-creation was strongly associated with entertainment, customization, and e-WOM. These predictors strengthen indirectly also consumer-brand engagement and perceived brand value (Cheung et al., 2021).

Conclusion

SM tools resulting from the development of the Internet and technology, directly and to a large extent, influence the means and ways of marketing communication between producers and consumers. SM's underlying attribute is a dialog and not a monolog, even in the international dimension. Their features enable fast exchange, collection, and analysis of information, as well as taking action.

The main contribution and originality of the paper is the linkage of three elements, namely marketing communication, SM, and the international marketplace. Existing research only takes into account particular issues individually or two of them (e.g. Okazaki & Taylor, 2013; Taiminen & Karjaluoto, 2015). The findings described in the paper may contribute to the model of two-way communication presented in the theoretical part. This contribution concerns, first, the communication tools which can be used (here, SM tools), and second, the effects that may be achieved thanks to the employment of these instruments. Such expected effects are sometimes the main purpose of SM tool application. It directly influences the recognition of companies and their brands in the international arena and offers indirect effects in the form of increased sales of products outside the domestic market.

The findings introduced in this paper have a two-fold applied character: implications for companies and implications for SM creators. First, the analyses and research results (literature, quantitative, and qualitative) can be a significant source of information for companies conducting (or intending to conduct) international marketing communication. Such firms can take an example from the experiences of the researched entities and employ those SM tools that are indicated by respondents in relation to particular geographical regions. Second, SM creators should take into account the most important effects for companies (managers) when developing new tools and applications that can be used in international marketing communication. The findings indicated that the most important features pertained to ease of use.

Taking into account the newest analysis provided by Zhao et al. (2021), "social networks and social media are both research hotspots within the discipline of marketing research". Moreover, the Covid-19 pandemic forced both individual consumers and producers to adapt new technologies in their daily settings. They were especially used in the process of communication. SM was one of the most useful tools for companies' communication with their potential consumers. The greater their importance, the farther the market was located. The prediction for the end of this decade (until approximately 2030) is the continuous development of SM tools and learning about the changes related to international consumers' preferences. One can predict the development of new solutions (e.g. new functions, applications) of such tools in terms of consumers' encouragement to use them. Sarin et al. (2021) indicate the necessity of mobile applications' development towards SM in the short future. The future of SM may be related to the development of the vlogosphere (instead of the blogosphere), where users will talk, watch, and listen instead of write and read. Such SM tools as Instagram, Pinterest, and TikTok will still be in development. Such behavior is usually observed among the youngest users of SM – generation Z. Nowadays, some of the SM platforms allow users to conduct live streams (in the form of "Stories" or live coverage). The popularity of such activities allows predicting the relentless growth in this aspect (Camilleri & Falzon, 2020; Koul et al., 2020; Sarin et al., 2021).

Conducting empirical studies and using primary methods is almost always associated with certain limitations. The sample size identified in the random procedure was larger than the final group examined. The reason for this was managers' refusal to participate in the study. Second, descriptive statistic measures were employed, but they were dictated by the research method, research instrument, and scales used in the questionnaire. Despite these calculations, the results are useful to achieve the main purpose of the study and answer the research question. Third, the results concern geographical regions, and studies conducted on single markets could provide more detailed information. Fourth, a deep exploration of individual aspects and an increased research group size could lead to more detailed results and areas of their application. However, any limitations are a challenge for further theoretical investigations and empirical studies.

Acknowledgments

The authors would like to acknowledge that this research was conducted with financial support from scientific grant no. 2015/17/B/HS4/00309 of National Science Centre, Poland.

References

Andersen, P. H. (2001). Relationship development and marketing communication: An integrative model. *Journal of Business & Industrial Marketing*, *16*(3), 167–182.

Alsaleh, D. A., Elliott, M. T. Fu, F. Q., & Thakur, R. (2019). Cross-cultural differences in the adoption of social media. *Journal of Research in Interactive Marketing*, *13*(1), 119–140. https://doi.org/10.1108/JRIM-10-2017-0092.

Babbie, E. (2014). *The basics of social research*. Wadsworth Cengage Learning.

Balaji, M. S., Roy, S. K., & Wei, K. K. (2016). Does relationship communication matter inB2C service relationships? *Journal of Services Marketing*, *30*(2), 186–200.

Bansal, R. S., & Gupta, V. (2020). The influence of social media on consumer purchase intention. *International Journal of Scientific and technology Research*, *9*(3), 3136–3142.

Bartosik-Purgat, M. (2019). *New media in the marketing communication of enterprises in the international market*. PWN Publ.

Bartosik-Purgat, M., & Bednarz, J. (2021). The usage of new media tools in prosumer activities – A corporate perspective. *Technology Analysis & Strategic Management*, *33*(4), 453–464. https://doi.org/10.1080/09537325.2020.1820475.

Bingham, T., & Conner, M. (2015). *The new social learning* (2nd ed.). Connect. Collaborate. Work, ATD Press.

Bruhn, M., Schoenmueller, V., & Schäfer, D. B. (2012). Are social media replacing traditional media in terms of brand equity creation? *Management Research Review*, *35*(9), 770–790. https://doi.org/10.1108/01409171211255948.

Camilleri, M. A., & Falzon, L. (2020). Understanding motivations to use online streaming services: Integrating the technology acceptance model (TAM) and the uses and gratifications theory (UGT). *Spanish Journal of Marketing - ESIC*, in print. https://doi.org/10.1108/SJME-04-2020-0074.

Cheung, M. L., Pires, G., Rosenberger III, P. J., Leung, W. K. S., & Chang, M. K. (2021). The role of social media elements in driving co-creation and engagement. *Asia Pacific Journal of Marketing and Logistics*, in print. https://doi.org/10.1108/APJML-03-2020-0176.

Craig, C. S., & Douglas, S. P. (2005). *International marketing research*. Wiley & Sons Ltd.

Danaher, P. J., & Rossiter J. R. (2011). Comparing perceptions of marketing communication channels. *European Journal of Marketing*, *45*(1/2), 6–42.

Duan, J. & Dholakia, N. (2015). The reshaping of Chinese consumer values in the social media era: Exploring the impact of Weibo. *Qualitative Market Research*, *18*(4), 409–426.

Duffett, R. G. (2017). Influence of social media marketing communications on young consumers' attitudes. *Young Consumers*, *18*(1), 19–39. https://doi.org/10.1108/YC-07-2016-00622.

Fawkes, J., & Gregory, A. (2000). Applying communication theories to the Internet. *Journal of Communication Management*, *5*(2), 109–124.

Finne, Å., & Grönroos, C. (2017). Communication-in-use: Customer-integrated marketing communication. *European Journal of Marketing*, *51*(3), 445–463.

Florenthal, B. (2019). Young consumers' motivational drivers of brand engagement behavior on social media sites. *Journal of Research in Interactive Marketing*, *13*(3), 351–391. https://doi.org/10.1108/JRIM-05-2018-0064.

Gabrielli, V., & Balboni, B. (2010). SME practice towards integrated marketing communications. *Marketing Intelligence & Planning*, *28*(3), 275–290.

Giddens, A. (2009). *Sociology* (6th ed.). Polity Press.

Griffin, E., Ledbetter, A., & Sparks, G. (2015). *A first look at communication theory* (9th ed.). McGraw-Hill Education.

Gruner, R. L., & Power, D. (2018). To integrate or not to integrate? Understanding B2B social media communications. *Online Information Review*, *42*(1), 73–92. https://doi.org/10.1108/OIR-04-2016-0116.

Hartman, J. (2008). *Wstęp do filozofii (Introduction to philosophy)*. PWN Publ.

Hänninen, N., & Karjaluoto, H. (2017). The effect of marketing communication on business relationship loyalty. *Marketing Intelligence & Planning*, *35*(4), 458–472.

Heinonen, K., & Strandvik, T. (2005). Communication as an element of service value. *International Journal of Service Industry Management*, *16*(2), 186–198.

Hoffman, D. L., & Novak, T. P. (1996). Marketing in hypermedia computer-mediated environments: Conceptual foundations. *Journal of Marketing*, *60*(3), 50–68. https://doi.org/10.2307/1251841.

Hollensen S. (2014). *Global Marketing* (6th ed.). Pearson Publ.

Johnston, W. J., Khalil, S., Le, A. N. H., & Cheng, J. M.-S. (2018). Behavioral implications of social media advertising: an investigation of intervening and contingency factors. *Journal of International Marketing*, *26*(2), 43–61.

Kaiser, C., Ahuvia, A., Rauschnabel, P. A., & Wimble, M. (2020). Social media monitoring: What can marketers learn from Facebook brand photos? *Journal of Business Research*, *117*, 707–717.

Kaplan A. M., & Haenlein M. (2010). Users of the world, unite! The challenges and opportunities of Social Media. *Business Horizons*, *53*(1), 59–68.

Katsikeas, C., Leonidou, L., & Zeriti, A. (2019). Revisiting international marketing strategy in a digital era: Opportunities, challenges, and research directions. *International Marketing Review*, *37*(3), 405–424. https://doi.org/10.1108/IMR-02-2019-0080.

Kemp, S. (2020). Digital use around the world in July 2020. https://wearesocial.com/blog/2020/07/digital-use-around-the-world-in-july-2020.

Kietzmann H. J., & Hermkens K. (2011). Social media? Get serious! Understanding the functional building blocks of social media. *Business Horizons*, *54*(3), 241–251.

Koul, S., Ambekar, S. S., & Hudnurkar, M. (2020). Determination and ranking of factors that are important in selecting an over-the-top video platform service among millennial consumers. *International Journal of Innovation Science*, *13*(1), 53–66.

Kumar, V., & Pansari, A. (2016). Competitive advantage through engagement. *Journal of Marketing Research*, *53*(4), 497–514.

Kushwaha, B. P., Singh, R. K., Varghese, N., & Singh, V. N. (2020). Integrating social media and digital media as new elements of integrated marketing communication for creating. *Journal of Content, Community and Communication*, *10*(6), 52–64.

Lee, I. (2014). *Integrating social media into business practice, applications, management, and models*. IGI Global Publ.

Lee, J., Park, D.-H., & Han, I. (2011). The different effects of online consumer reviews on consumers' purchase intentions depending on trust in online shopping malls: An advertising perspective. *Internet Research*, *21*(2), 187–206.

Li, Z. (2021). Marketing strategy of knowledge-based virtual community. *Advances in Intelligent Systems and Computing*, *1234*, 280–285.

Li, T., Berens, G., & De Maertelaere, M. (2013). Corporate Twitter channels: The impact of engagement and unforcedness on corporate reputation. *International Journal of Electronic Commerce*, *18*(2), 97–126.

Liu, L., Liu, R., Lee, M., & Chen, J. (2019). When will consumers be ready? A psychological perspective on consumer engagement in social media brand communities. *Internet Research*, *29*(4), 704–724. https://doi.org/10.1108/IntR-05-2017-0177.

Majumdar, A., & Bose, I. (2019). Do tweets create value? A multi-period analysis of Twitter use and content of tweets for manufacturing firms. *International Journal of Production Economics*, *216*, 1–11.

Morra, M. C., Ceruti, F., Chierici, R., & Di Gregorio, A. (2018). Social vs traditional media communication: Brand origin associations strike a chord. *Journal of Research in Interactive Marketing*, *12*(1), 2–21. https://doi.org/10.1108/JRIM-12-2016-0116.

Mukherjee, K. (2019). Social media marketing and customers' passion for brands. *Marketing Intelligence & Planning*, *38*(4), 509–522. https://doi.org/10.1108/MIP-10-2018-0440.

Okazaki, S., & Taylor, C. R. (2013). Social media and international advertising: Theoretical challenges and future directions. *International Marketing Review*, *30*(1), 56–71.

Olaniran, B. A. (2018). Social media as communication channel in emerging economies: A closer look at cultural implications. *Journal of Advances in Management Research*, *15*(2), 130–145. https://doi.org/10.1108/JAMR-04-2017-0050.

Porcu, L., Barrio-Garcia, S., & Kitchen, P. J. (2017). Measuring integrated marketing communication by taking a broad organisational approach. The firm-wide IMC scale. *European Journal of Marketing*, *51*(3), 692–718.

Prokofieva, M. (2015). Twitter-based dissemination of corporate disclosure and the intervening effects of firms' visibility: Evidence from Australian-listed companies. *Journal of Information Systems*, *29*(2), 107–136.

Sarin, P., Kar, A. K., & Ilavarasan, V. P. (2021). Exploring engagement among mobile app developers – Insights from mining big data in user generated content. *Journal of Advances in Management Research*, in print. https://doi.org/10.1108/JAMR-06-2020-0128.

Seran (Potra), S., & Izvercian, M. (2014). Prosumer engagement in innovation strategies. The Prosumer Creativity and Focus Model. *Management Decision*, *52*(10), 1968–1980. https://doi.org/10.1108/MD-06-2013-0347.

Simon, F., & Tossan, V. (2018). Does brand-consumer social sharing matter? A relational framework of customer engagement to brand-hosted social media. *Journal of Business Research*, *85*, 175–184.

Smith P. R., & Zook Z. (2016). *Marketing communications: Offline and online integration. Engagement and analytics*. Kogan Page Publ.

Šerić, M. (2017). Relationships between social Web, IMC and overall brand equity: An empirical examination from the cross-cultural perspective. *European Journal of Marketing*, *51*(3), 646–667.

Taiminen H. M., & Karjaluoto H. (2015). The usage of digital marketing channels in SMEs. *Journal of Small Business and Enterprise Development*, 22(4), 633–651.

Valos, M. J., Habibi, F. H., Casidy, R., Driesener, C. B., & Maplestone, V. L. (2016). Exploring the integration of social media within integrated marketing communication frameworks. *Marketing Intelligence & Planning*, *34*(1), 19–40.

Voramontri, D., & Klieb, L. (2018). Impact of social media on consumer behaviour. *International Journal of Information and Decision Sciences*, *11*(3), 1–25.

Whiting, A., & Williams, D. (2013). Why people use social media: A uses and gratifications approach. *Qualitative Market Research: An International Journal*, *16*(4), 362- 369.

Williams, D. L., Crittenden, V. L., Keo, T., & McCarty, P. (2012). The use of social media: An exploratory study of uses among digital natives. *Journal of Public Affairs*, *12*(2), 127–136.

Yu, Q., Yen, D. A., Cappellini, B., & Wang, C. L. (2019). From West to East: British sojourners' acculturation in China. *International Marketing Review*, in print. https://doi.org/10.1108/IMR-12-2018-0362.

Zhang, J., & Du, M. (2020). Utilization and effectiveness of social media message strategy: How B2B brands differ from B2C brands. *Journal of Business & Industrial Marketing*, *35*(4), 721–740. https://doi.org/10.1108/JBIM-06-2018-0190.

Zhang, S., Gosselt, J. F., & de Jong, M. D. T. (2020). How large information technology companies use Twitter: Arrangement of corporate accounts and characteristics of tweets. *Journal of Business and Technical Communication*, *34*(4), 364–392.

Zhao, H., Huang, Y. & Wang, Z. (2021). Comparison between social media and social networks in marketing research: A bibliometric view. *Nankai Business Review International*, in print. https://doi.org/10.1108/NBRI-12-2019-0072.

Part III

Innovation

7 Accelerating R&D with Knowledge and New Technological Solutions – From Innovation Cooperation to Translational Innovation

Puślecki Łukasz, Dąbrowski Marek, Czekajlo Michael, and Puślecki Mateusz

Introduction

Over the last 30 years, R&D cooperation has become a core aspect of innovation strategy for companies operating on both the domestic and international market. In the economic and management literature, there are a number of interesting works on R&D cooperation between companies regarding, among other things, the distinction between cooperation based on the transfer and exchange of technology, R&D arrangements, and joint-ventures (Auster, 1987; Casson, 1987; Contractor & Lorange, 1988). When analyzing technological agreements, they can be divided into those that are one-directional and are based on strong relationships between companies – e.g. joint-ventures, research corporations – and those that involve less organizational dependencies (contractual arrangements such as joint R&D agreements or technology exchange agreements). Taking into consideration different types of technological cooperation, they have different effects on the nature of the sharing of technology, the level of competitiveness, organizational aspects, and the possible economic consequences for the companies involved in cooperation (Auster, 1987; Contractor & Lorange, 1988; De Man & Duysters, 2007; De Man et al., 2009; Hagedoorn, 1990, 2002; Hagedoorn et al., 2000; Gomes-Casseres et al., 2006; Puślecki, 2010). Nowadays, technological cooperation is a very important channel of knowledge transfer in both the public and private sector. Companies are using global strategic partnerships in order to strengthen competitive position, enhance core competencies and skills, as well as acquire new technologies. Through development of R&D alliances, they can gain new opportunities to share the risk of the development of new technologies, particularly on new, emerging markets (Puślecki, 2010, 2012, 2015) and have better innovation cooperation performance (Puślecki et al., 2021a; Trąpczyński et al., 2018).

The main aim of this chapter is to verify how innovation cooperation can support the improvement of patient care, taking into consideration new

DOI: 10.4324/9781003204343-7

technological solutions – digital Health, medHealth, mobile health (mHealth), health information technology (IT), wearable devices, telehealth and telemedicine, and personalized medicine – and modern medical simulation. In addition, the authors will present how such innovative cooperation should be developed to bring about the required results. The authors will present examples of projects that use digital tools and artificial intelligence (AI) and are focused on the delivery of new solutions to protect healthcare workers and improve intensive care. In order to deliver these solutions to the market faster, we should not forget about the role of innovation cooperation. Taking this issue into account, the authors will share the results of one of the first quantitative primary research projects in the world that focuses on innovation cooperation in the biopharmaceutical industry in the Central and Eastern Europe (CEE) region (covering 18 countries), and qualitative research – focus group interview with representatives of the "ECMO (Extracorporeal Membrane Oxygenation)[1] for Greater Poland" regarding the development of successful innovation cooperation as an example of translational innovation. Finally, the authors provide a translational innovation model that can be extrapolated for every industry, social, and economic area.

The chapter is structured as follows. First, the authors present the development of R&D cooperation in the biopharmaceutical industry, taking into account different modes of cooperation as well as open innovation alliances. Implementation of joint activities between all partners, including appropriate alliance management tools and multiparty alliance strategies, can contribute to better use of research and the innovative potential of all parties involved in cooperation (Puślecki & Staszków, 2015; Staszków et al., 2017), in delivering new products, services, better therapies, and health care of patients. Next, the chapter presents how innovation cooperation can be boosted by digital health technologies (especially during the Covid-19 pandemic), as well as how modern medical simulation can be used to accelerate innovation cooperation to offer better therapies and treatment for patients. This can be well observed in the "ECMO for Greater Poland" program. In presenting this case study, the chapter suggests how such innovative cooperation should be developed, what kind of stakeholders should be included in the cooperation, how R&D can be accelerated using knowledge and know-how, and how knowledge can be transferred at different levels (regional, national, international) in order to improve the patient care. Finally, we offer a translational innovation model. It should be emphasized that the model of cooperation presented here not only refers to the health sector but can be successfully applied in other sectors (biopharma, IT) as well as in cross-industry cooperation. Indeed, it can be extrapolated for every industry, social, and economic area, including different entities: business to business, business-academia, public-private partnerships, etc., and modes of cooperation (open innovation alliances, cross-industry alliances, altruistic alliances, R&D alliances).

Development of R&D Cooperation in the Biopharmaceutical Industry

Biopharmaceutical (pharma and biotech) companies have developed cooperation with universities for many years. At the beginning, the cooperation mainly included individual, single projects from small research projects to large clinical trials. Subsequently, the companies started developing alliances with individual academic institutions, including a wider range of cooperation through, among other things, research programs, clinical trials, and translational research. Increasingly, companies began to use different models of R&D alliances, from individual links in research projects to multilateral agreements involving multiple research projects, including various models for open innovation, for example, where the main role of an academic institution was the coordination and sometimes funding of other institutions (Puślecki et al., 2021a). According to Chesbrough (2003) "open innovation" is the paradigm through which companies can and should use external and internal ideas, as well as internal and external paths to market. Taking into consideration the latest definition by Chesbrough, *open innovation* is "a distributed innovation process based on purposively managed knowledge flows across organizational boundaries, using pecuniary and non-pecuniary mechanisms in line with each organization's business model" (Chesbrough & Bogers, 2014, p. 17). The concept of open innovation can be applied in bilateral and multilateral alliances and is more dynamic than traditional alliances. Partners in the alliance are not identified in the conventional, purposeful way, and relationships are focused more on the exchange of knowledge and ideas during the period preceding the creation of the alliance. Open innovation alliances are aimed at supporting the free flow of knowledge and ideas, leading to the creation of partnerships aimed not only at joint innovation but also at risk and profit-sharing (Wilks & Prothmann, 2012). Analyzing the results of research on open innovation, we can see how companies manage both the inflows and outflows of knowledge and how they search for and select partners and the innovations they provide (Culpan, 2014; West, 2014). It can also be observed how companies in specific industries (like Biopharma) use the open innovation model to establish open innovation alliances not just with firms from the same or other industry but also with universities, individuals, communities, or other organizations (Academia-Institutions-Business relations) (DeWitt & Burke, 2012; Puślecki et al., 2021a, 2021b; Wilks & Prothmann, 2012). It should also be taken into account that the organizational fluidity of open innovation initiatives, as well as multiparty relations, increase the complexity in the alliance management. Here, the alliance management plays a central role, particularly in defining the alliance portal and framework. The open innovation model can significantly speed up the production process of new drugs and vaccines (Puślecki et al., 2021b), which are now in high demand because of the Covid-19 pandemic (Chesbrough, 2020a, 2020b). Having more interdisciplinary academic teams in a cooperation can also accelerate and support this process (Lavietes, 2012; Wilks & Prothmann, 2012). Open innovation has been implemented by companies in a number of ways, including innovations for users, crowdsourcing, creation of joint development alliances, and through building innovative ecosystems (Puślecki, 2015, 2016a, 2016b; Puślecki & Staszków 2015; Wilks & Prothmann 2012). Thanks to significant synergy effects, participation in innovative ecosystems enables the partners to access huge innovative potential and more market opportunities, which helps them to innovate, accelerate growth, and expand into new promising markets (Burke, 2020; De Man, 2018, 2020; De Man et al., 2019; De Man & Luvinson, 2019; Fraser, 2014; Puślecki et al., 2021a, 2021b).

Boosting Innovation Cooperation with Digital Health Technologies

In 2020, the Covid-19 pandemic contributed to the development of new strategic partnerships in the biopharmaceutical industry, including via use of open models (open innovation alliances). There was also considerable involvement of many companies from Biopharma in cooperation with IT companies in order to develop diagnostic tools using the latest technologies – the Internet of Things (IoT), AI, virtual reality (VR), machine learning, and Blockchain, along with the progressive overall digitalization of health care (telemedicine, medHealth, digitalHealth). Since the end of the 1980s, the world has seen more and more non-equity R&D alliances in the biopharmaceutical industry (Puślecki, 2012), which provide greater flexibility in the selection and possible change of partners, and also enable a faster change of technology than traditional equity alliances. The results of one of the first quantitative research projects in the world, focused on innovation cooperation in the biopharmaceutical industry in Central and Eastern Europe (CEE) in years 2015–2017 (conducted within a research grant entitled "Analysis of Open Innovation Alliances and Strategic Partnerships in the Biopharmaceutical Industry in Poland and CEE countries"), showed that over 80% of biopharmaceutical companies (n=107) from the 18 CEE countries mainly carried out non-equity R&D alliances in the development of innovation cooperation. The most important objective in the formation of these R&D alliances given by the CEE companies was gaining access to partners' knowledge and experience. However, only 19% of them have implemented innovation cooperation using new modes of cooperation, that is, open innovation alliances. This is less than in Western Europe, the United Kingdom, or in the United States, where especially in the last years, the development of partnerships in the biopharmaceutical industry using new modes of cooperation (open innovation alliances) have been observed. It should also be taken into account that more than 65% of companies from the CEE region are open to developing cross-industry alliances and altruistic alliances (non-profit) with companies or institutions in the biopharmaceutical industry and other industries. With more flexible modes of cooperation, it is possible to deliver new solutions and better patient treatment to the market faster, which is particularly germane to responses to the current Covid-19 pandemic, which aim to tackle the pandemic quickly.

The pandemic emphasized the need for high-quality data, digital health technologies, and AI analytics tools. Table 7.1 shows 15 selected projects (financed from IMI – Innovative Medicines Initiative and Horizon 2020), which use digital tools and AI to deliver new solutions to protect healthcare workers, quickly detect and prevent the spread of Covid-19, and improve intensive care. Such digital health technologies use computing platforms, connectivity, software, and sensors for healthcare and related uses and can be intended for use as a medical product, in a medical product, as companion diagnostics, or as an adjunct to other medical products (devices, drugs, and biologics). They can also be applied to develop or study other medical products. Within the next 24 months, the 15 selected projects will deliver solutions in five complementary areas:

1. Using telemedicine to assist intensive care in Covid-19 wards
2. Delivering new devices and tools for faster, cheaper, and easier diagnosis of Covid-19
3. Using telemedicine and AI to diagnose and monitor patients' safety and to reduce the burden of health systems
4. Protecting healthcare workers through new technologies
5. Supporting and fostering the uptake of innovative tools and technologies developed by small companies

The planned first prototypes as a result of innovation cooperation should be available in 2021.

Taking into account the 15 selected Horizon 2020 and IMI projects presented in Table 7.1, as well as existing Covid-19 vaccine projects (Puślecki, 2021; Puślecki et al., 2021b), the development of new partnerships between universities and research organizations and business–academia alliances can be observed, and the results will be helpful both for the world of science (new publications, scientific projects, scientific discoveries) and for the main beneficiaries – patients (new therapies, procedures in patient care, new drugs, vaccines, the use of existing drugs for new therapeutic purposes, faster products and drugs delivery to market – thanks to intellectual property (IP) release). Openness to cooperation through the use of digital health technologies will allow companies to develop new business strategies faster during and after the Covid-19 pandemic, share the risks and costs of R&D projects, and enable significant synergy effects in the development of better patient care.

Table 7.1 Digital health technologies addressing the Covid-19 pandemic in selected Horizon 2020 and Innovative Medicines Initiative (IMI) projects

Acronym/Title	*Description*	*Partners*	*Funding Body*
Using Telemedicine to Assist Intensive Care Against Covid-19			
ICU4Covid – Cyber-Physical Intensive Care Medical System for Covid-19	The Cyber-Physical System for Telemedicine and Intensive Care (CPS4TIC) enables existing or new ICU structures to transform and operate as one ICU hub with one central ICU and connected ICUs in peripheral hospitals.	**19 partners:** Austria (3), Germany (7), Greece (2), Luxembourg, the Netherlands, Portugal (5)	Horizon 2020
ENVISION – Intelligent plug-and-play digital tool for real-time surveillance of Covid-19 patients and smart decision-making in ICUs	Envision aims to advance an innovative digital tool, Sandman.MD – a real-time, plug-and-play monitoring app – to an intelligent decision-support system for monitoring, prediction, and treatment of Covid-19 patients in ICUs – the Sandman.ICU. The app will be integrated into an AI-driven data analytics suite with predictive modeling tools and enhanced with smart alert functionality.	**19 partners:** Belgium, Germany (4), Switzerland, Spain, Finland, Hungary (2), Italy (2), Lithuania, the Netherlands, Portugal, Romania, Slovenia (2), United Kingdom	Horizon 2020
Delivering New Devices and Tools for Faster, Cheaper, and Easier Diagnosis of Covid-19			
IRIS-COV – Market Release of a Portable Device for Covid-19 at the Point-of-Care; a Global Diagnostics Approach	IRIS-COV concerns the implementation of an existing and patented device and methodology based on isothermal LAMP amplification and real-time quantitative colorimetric detection, which has been proved to be able to detect SARS-CoV-2 in patient samples. The main objectives are the immediate deployment of the device following clinical validation and fast-track certification.	**8 partners:** Belgium, Switzerland, Greece (3), France, United Kingdom, South Africa	Horizon 2020

(*Continued*)

Table 7.1 (Continued)

Acronym/Title	*Description*	*Partners*	*Funding Body*
Covid-RED - Covid-19 infections – remote early detection	The project will combine expertise in clinical epidemiology with digital devices (e.g. wearables and mobile apps) to rapidly and reliably detect Covid-19 cases so that they can be prioritized for testing.	**9 partners:** Denmark (1), the Netherlands (4), Switzerland (3), United Kingdom (1)	IMI
COVIRNA – A diagnostic test to improve surveillance and care of Covid-19 patients	COVIRNA aims to develop a prognostic system based on cardiovascular biomarkers of Covid-19 clinical outcomes combined with digital tools and AI analytics. Complementary expertise of 15 EU partners from the healthcare sector, academia, associations, and industry will enable a large retrospective study on existing cohorts of Covid-19 patients. The project will quickly deliver a minimally-invasive, simple, yet robust and affordable prognosis tool that can be used during the current Covid-19 crisis as well as in further major health issues.	**15 partners:** Belgium, Germany (2), Spain, France, Hungary, Italy, Luxembourg (2), the Netherlands, Portugal, Slovenia, Bosnia and Herzegovina, United Kingdom (2)	Horizon 2020
CorDial-S – Portable and fast surface plasmon resonance point-of-care test for Covid-19	CorDial-S proposes a rapid, selective, and inexpensive solution by combining several technologies such as the use of Covid-19 specific nanobodies (VHH), magnetic nanoparticles with high magnetic strength, and VHH-modified interfaces, all integrated into a hand-held surface plasmon resonance-based point-of-care test for the screening of the presence/absence of the SARS-CoV-2 virus in nasal and saliva samples.	**7 partners:** Belgium, France (4), Ireland, Israel	Horizon 2020

(*Continued*)

Table 7.1 (Continued)

Acronym/Title	*Description*	*Partners*	*Funding Body*
VASCOVID – Portable platform for the assessment of microvasular health in Covid-19 patients at the intensive care	VASCOVID will deploy a portable, non-invasive, and real-time health monitoring platform that combines two bio-photonics technologies, time-resolved near-infrared spectroscopy and diffuse correlation spectroscopy. The platform will be adapted to meet the needs of a typical ICU dealing with Covid-19 and other patients requiring ventilation, as well as leverage large-scale testing of new treatment procedures and therapies aimed at addressing microvascular impairment and reducing extubation failure on ICU patients being weaned off mechanical ventilation life support.	**7 partners:** Spain (4), Ireland, Italy, the Netherlands	Horizon 2020
Using Telemedicine and AI to Diagnose and Monitor Patients' Safety and to Reduce the Burden of Health Systems			
PyXy.AI – Telehealth-ready AI-powered multi-parametric system for surveillance of Covid-19 and cardio-pulmonary chronic patients	This consortium presents a computerized auscultation device – the PyXy – which provides expert-level lung and heart check-up. The PyXy brings breakthrough capabilities in terms of sound and infrasound analysis, body temperature, blood oxygen levels, heart rate, and respiratory cycle, all analyzed by AI for accurate diagnostic data. The device recently showed very promising results in relation to managing Covid-19 disease.	**7 partners:** Germany (3), Israel (2), Norway (2)	Horizon 2020
ESSENCE – Emphatic platform to personally	ESSENCE aims to transform the lessons learned from the Covid-19 pandemic in a huge opportunity that	**9 partners:** Cyprus, Spain, France, Israel,	Horizon 2020

(*Continued*)

Table 7.1 (Continued)

Acronym/Title	*Description*	*Partners*	*Funding Body*
monitor, stimulate, enrich, and assist elders and children in their environment	exploits technology toward a deep evolution of the services targeting vulnerable populations: non- or pre-fail seniors, and children of the first years of primary school. To contribute to the public health response to the ongoing epidemic, and to preparedness for future emergencies, it aims to boost the creation of a new model of home-based care that relies on simulation, remote monitoring, tele-assistance, and connection between users, families, and professionals.	Italy (4), Slovenia	
DRAGON –Rapid and secure AI-imaging-based diagnosis, stratification, follow-up, and preparedness for coronavirus pandemics	The DRAGON project will apply AI and machine learning to deliver a decision support system for improved and more rapid diagnosis and prognosis. Citizens and patients will be involved in the development of the system.	**21 partners:** Belgium (4), China (4), Italy (1), the Netherlands (1), Switzerland (1), United Kingdom (10)	IMI
icovid – AI-based chest CT analysis enabling rapid Covid-19 diagnosis and prognosis	The icovid project aims to improve existing software, making it of greater value as clinical needs evolve, validating it in renowned academic centers, and its large-scale deployment across Europe. Icovid is expected to have a significant societal impact by increasing confidence when making CT diagnoses and providing accurate quantification of disease and prognostic information in patients with suspected Covid-19 disease.	**9 partners:** Belgium (5), Germany, the Netherlands, United Kingdom (2)	Horizon 2020

(*Continued*)

Table 7.1 (Continued)

Acronym/Title	*Description*	*Partners*	*Funding Body*
Protecting Healthcare Workers Through New Technologies			
PORSAV - Controlling viral aerosols in Covid-19 and beyond	Protecting healthcare staff is a key WHO priority area, both in the immediate-term during the Covid-19 pandemic, and also after peak crisis in the new practice landscape with population prevalence. Surgery is a key therapy for emergency patients as well as for cancer care and cardiac disease, among others. It is also the main aerosolizing intervention, risking viral transmission to many staff, not only during the procedure itself, but also during other interventional procedures, including bedside episodic procedures such as intubation for ventilation or nasogastric tube drainage. PORSAV will characterize the nature of these gas leaks using specialized imaging technology, develop vacuum devices to entrain and filter such leaks, validate the clinical effectiveness of the devices, complete CE mark certification, and deploy to surgery centers worldwide.	**5 partners:** France, Ireland (3), Poland	Horizon 2020
CleanAir – Lab to **Fab development of air decontamina-tion system for protecting health practitioners against Covid-19**	The CleanAir project relates to the application of an innovative and novel, geometrically extended electrode designed to be integrated into air ionizers. CleanAir's aim is to develop the technology to a market-ready level to protect practitioners and their patients against	**7 partners:** Austria (4), Germany, Ireland, Italy	Horizon 2020

(*Continued*)

Table 7.1 (Continued)

Acronym/Title	*Description*	*Partners*	*Funding Body*
	Covid-19 infections, and will be preferentially developed for use in dental treatment rooms, for medical personnel offices, and for patients' rooms in hospitals.		
Supporting and Fostering the Uptake of Innovative Tools and Technologies Developed by Small Companies			
INNO4COV-19 – Boosting Innovation for Covid-19 Diagnostic, Prevention and Surveillance	Europe needs to reinforce its technological leadership and rebuild an industrial sector capable of protecting its citizens' safety and well-being, and INNO4COV-19 will help in catalyzing this change. Accelerated uptake of innovative technologies to tackle Covid-19 is vital. In order to provide an efficient, rapid answer to this challenging situation, INNO4COV-19 aims to build an Innovation Hub for the addressed technologies.	**11 partners:** Austria, Belgium (2), Germany, Ireland, Spain (3), Italy, Portugal (2)	Horizon 2020
COVID-X – COVID eXponential Program	COVID-X will bridge the collaboration divide between eHealth solution providers – with an emphasis on lean startups and small and medium-sized enterprises (SMEs) – and professional healthcare systems to fight Covid-19. The purpose is to boost an end-to-end agile validation program using cutting-edge technology in three real-world clinical scenarios, with locations in Italy, Spain, and Sweden.	**10 partners:** Cyprus, Spain (4), Ireland, Italy, Luxembourg, Lithuania, Sweden	Horizon 2020

Source: Own elaboration based on: (European Commission, 2020, 2021; IMI, 2020; Puślecki et al., 2021b)

Furthermore, it is also important to highlight the international dimension of innovation cooperation in the above-mentioned projects: having international and interdisciplinary teams will make it possible to share knowledge from different countries and areas of science and business, create R&D innovation ecosystems with high innovative potential, utilize the resources, competencies, technology, and knowledge of partners, and thus respond more easily to changes in the environment. It is safe to say that these projects can be an inspiration for other entities in implementing and concluding innovation cooperation.

Medical Simulation as an Accelerator for Innovation Cooperation

The 1960s saw the development of revival manikins, i.e. prototypes for learning CPR (cardiopulmonary resuscitation), and in 1969, the first advanced Sim One Anesthesia patient simulator was developed, manufactured at the University of Southern California (USA).[2] However, despite these historical breakthroughs, medical simulation seems to have only started to find a permanent place in medical education in the late 20th century, and permanent use in the training of medical personnel only took place after 2000.

An important element – in a way, the essence – of a medical simulation is to obtain the highest possible level of reliability (HIGHFIDELITY[3]), which ensures an appropriate reflection of the simulated clinical conditions and makes them "believable". Additional realism comes from the use of standardized patients who are well-trained in their role as actors, or amateur actors who may also be medical personnel. They can simulate symptoms, communicate their health history, and show the many emotions that accompany such meetings between staff and patients during a medical examination. In this context, the following simulation methods can be identified: standardized patients, partial simulators for practicing medical activities, human patient simulators (HPS), computer simulators, and VR simulators.

The simulation process and method are based on creating an appropriate environment (realism) and preparing the participants to work in it (pre-briefing). The next step is to create and run a simulation scenario (case briefing and scenario). One of the fundamental elements of the simulation process is the process of analyzing and discussing medical events conducted by the learners, referred to as debriefing, which is a specially moderated extended feedback session, very often referred to as the "heart" of a medical simulation. In this process, the teacher acting as the moderator of the session challenges learners to self-reflect based on their autonomous decisions when participating in the scenario. Debriefing is particularly important because it enables the acquisition of knowledge through the description, analysis, and application phase in relation to the clinical or simulation experience based on the goals of the trained scenario. The aim of conducting a simulation session consisting of a scenario (realism and autonomy) and a debriefing session (self-reflection) is to achieve the correct individual value of the application (take-home message), which the participant will be able to use in clinical practice or in future simulation scenarios (Czekajlo et al., 2015).

It should be remembered, however, that simulation is a kind of bridge between the world of practical science and the clinical world. That is, this tool is a substitute that enriches the work with the real patients but does not, and cannot, replace it.

The 21st century has brought a new face to medical simulation. The role of medical simulation as an accessible and repeatable method of high-quality personal and procedural training is very well-known, especially in teaching emergency medical services or emergency procedures. In the case of rare, complicated, and expensive procedures, it allows for standardized and repeated training, skills improvement, and verification. Medical simulation – previously known as the skills, test, and educational tool – was merely an innovation tool. A new area of medical simulation, translational simulation, creates an innovative framework for cooperation in innovation, with use of more advanced and innovative tools (see Table 7.2). By significantly improving patient safety, medical simulation changes education centers into centers where the primary goal is to influence the quality of therapy for patients. Thus, Human Center and Patient Safety is becoming something more common and purposeful, not limited just to educating future generations of medical staff. Indeed, Medical Simulation Centers have started to become independent innovation centers for education, the creation of important trends and guidelines, and knowledge transfer (Czekajlo et al., 2015).

Moreover, the role of Medical Simulation Centers only increased during the recent pandemic. Because of the lack of training of medical personnel in clinical areas due to the Covid-19 pandemic, the greater use of medical simulation has been reported (high-fidelity iterations, with different techniques, including: trainers, HPS, BLS – Basic Life Support and ALS – Advanced Life Support computer simulation, SP – Standardized Patients). Most of the medical centers in the world affected by the pandemic situation also functioned as the most important centers offering training with the use of medical simulation for staff who were most exposed to Covid-19, and the pandemic forced changes in the area of critical care (new procedures and alghoritms), which is why there is a need to be more open to cooperation using local potential and partners in the development of better therapies for patients (Puślecki et al., 2021a).

Translational simulation is a dynamic process that integrates innovation, knowledge, skills, and institutional collaboration. Although the term was developed in the area of healthcare (Brazil, 2017), it is present in almost every developmental area of societies at the regional, national, and

Table 7.2 Simulation tools

Tool	*Description*
Hybrid simulation	Allows the use of various simulation means during an advanced scenario (actor, simulator, specific trainer). This type of simulation allows the use of a wide spectrum of activities in a scenario, limited only by the capabilities of the simulator or acting.
"In situ" simulation	Conducted in clinical conditions outside the area of the simulation center (ward, pre-hospital conditions, clinic or operating theater). In situ simulation is defined as one that takes place in a real environment – a patient care environment – to achieve a high level of fidelity and realism. It is an extremely valuable form of classes, carried out on the basis of transferring the simulation technology (simulator and video-recording system) to the workplace of medical personnel, in difficult working conditions due to space limitations and/or noise. Recently, it has been noticed that hospital systems have started to use in situ simulation to train healthcare workers and identify hidden security risks. This type of simulation helps the discovery of weak points in the organization and the ergonomics of both individual and team work. This model is devoid of limitations related to unfamiliarity with the work environment.
SimChallenge	Competitions are an opportunity for participants to use modern technology and science in the form of simulations in order to use all the information they have learned.
Virtual simulation (VR)	This innovation in education uses a wide range of VR products. These are both anatomical tables and decision tables containing a Virtual Patient Simulator (VPS) based on AI with physiological algorithms. Such models adopt a simulated environment where students develop advanced problem-solving and critical thinking skills based on pre-programmed and defined scenarios. In VR simulation settings, questions can be asked on a variety of topics while performing a patient medical assessment. Questions can be fixed for each scenario, but the answers change according to the patient's condition. Virtual patients may be aware, confused, moving, or unconscious. Such tools allow educators to save time and focus on the development of students and their practical results thanks to the decisions made. Other models using VR include simulation games or professionally prepared medical programs (advanced physiology or pathophysiology of life processes), imaging diagnostics programs using various types of goggles to show the medical environment, and laparoscopic trainers that allow the use of real tools with haptic properties.

(*Continued*)

Table 7.2 (Continued)

Tool	*Description*
Advanced simulation in the near future (up to 2030)	• In situ simulations with follow-up on a large scale – understanding self-improvement in the workplace • High-tech simulations – the highest bar ("brain transplants", operations on children's spines, 3D printouts) • Simulations in the field of plastic surgery, hybrid simulation – in short, a conversation with a living person, for whom a silicone cast of a part of the body for correction has been prepared. The surgeon, entering the operating theater, operates on the patient with whom he or she has just talked – albeit only a dummy/simulator. • AI-advanced simulation – simulator recognition of behaviors participating in training (in the scenario) – scan of facial expressions / voice timbre / tone and accentuation / movement and posture • Sewing simulations tailored to the needs of advanced projects, also in the field of artificial life support

international level. Translational simulation is used not only by public services but also companies, in a number of different industries, including: transport (rail, metro, aviation), the water industry, the military, etc. It can be treated in a universal sense as translational innovation (see Figure 7.1). Translational innovation (Tatnall, 2011) is the concept of innovation developed within Actor-Network Theory (ANT), a theory of innovation in which instead of using an innovation in the form it is proposed, potential adopters translate it into a form that suits their needs.

The term "translational innovation" describes a cooperation process focused directly on improving outcomes in the system through diagnosing potential obstacles and performance issues and delivering the proper intervention, irrespective of the location, modality, or local conditions. It offers a functional alignment with quality improvement activities in dedicated institutions/adopters while encompassing educational interventions targeting practice behavior or beneficial outcomes. Translational innovation requires close relationships with all partners, including governance and quality improvement services.

Development of Innovation Cooperation and Knowledge Transfer in the "ECMO for Greater Poland" Program – A Translational Innovation Example

Launched in 2016, the aim of the "ECMO for Greater Poland" program was to create systemic procedures for the identification, notification, and

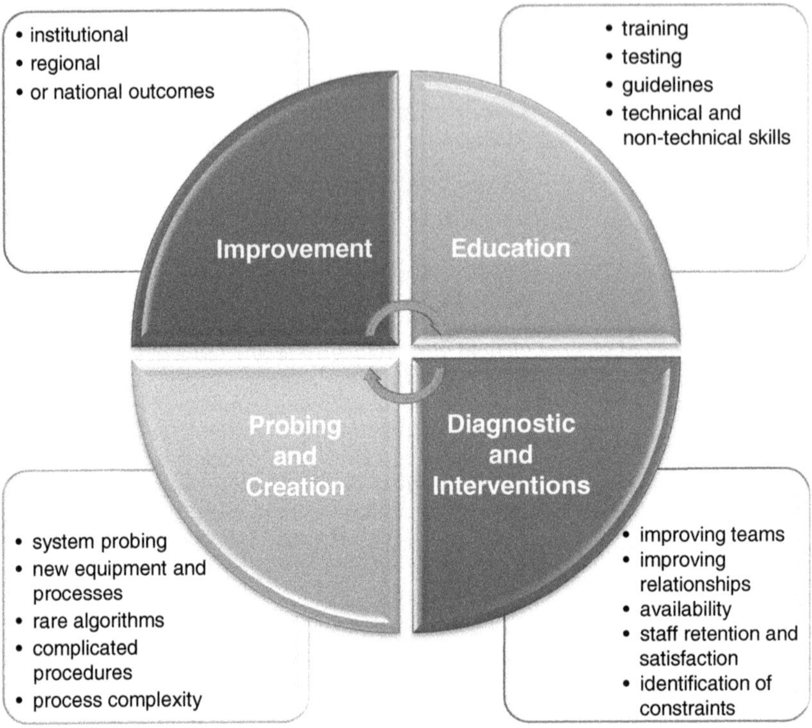

Figure 7.1 Translational innovation model.

Source: Based and developed on Translational Simulation (Brazil, 2017, p. 2)

transportation of potential candidates for extracorporeal support to conduct therapy at the highest possible level. The main tool for procedure creation was medical simulation, and this was possible with improvement of Medical Rescue System coordination, the sophisticated training of medical personnel, and creation of the ECMO team. It is worth emphasizing that this is a grassroots initiative by a dozen or so people, representing various medical professions, who can participate in the therapy of extracorporeal techniques "ECMO" and created the so-called "ECMO Team".

The main areas of the program are (Puślecki et al., 2017):

A. Use of ECMO in patients with hypothermia.
B. Use of ECMO to support reversible respiratory failure (RRF).
C. Use of ECMO to support other critical conditions (extended cardiopulmonary resuscitation – ECPR, poisoning, and other conditions resulting in cardiopulmonary failure).
D. Use of ECMO as a regional organ perfusion in the dead in the

mechanism of irreversible cardiac arrest (DCD – donation after circulatory death) in order to obtain potential donors of organs for transplantation.

Such a wide range of application of perfusion techniques marks the program out nationally, and places it among the best in the world. It is worth noting that in the case of the program, we are talking about the specific development of an ecosystem, from a bottom-up initiative developed by enthusiasts of extracorporeal techniques into a fully functioning hub, constituting a regulatory and educational role in a macroregion with 3.5 million inhabitants (see Figure 7.2), and thanks to the involvement of different partners from different levels, this unique program impacts the safety of patients in the region. The development of such a program can be a model for emerging hubs around the world, and it is important to note that with the use of translational innovation, the model of innovative cooperation is universal and can be applied in sectors with active partners wherever a common socially important topic can be identified. The role of such an innovative system can be vital in terms of creation, knowledge transfer, and self-improvement and may be directly translated into benefits and results (program outcomes) (see Table 7.3).

The most important concept for artificial support in critical states is adopted from the Extracorporeal Life Support Organization (ELSO) HandS (HUB and SPOKES) constellation. The role of the HUB is the coordination and integration of all external partners important for the knowledge transfer, especially by providing diffusion of knowledge, monitoring, management, and control of the ecosystem, continuous improvement of existing procedures, and improvement of qualifications and skills within a dedicated educational platform in order to develop mutual competencies necessary in the development of new therapies for patients (Puślecki et al., 2019).

Construction of the entire innovation ecosystem was initiated by volunteers and were responsible for selection of potential partners (taking into account potential benefits for HUB and partners) (Puślecki et al., 2021a) in the "ECMO for Greater Poland" program. As a part of the innovation ecosystem, an education center was established, which, thanks to effective training and the use of modern simulation medicine using the latest technological solutions, influenced subsequent volunteers enough for them to create new ECMO Teams in their cities, not only in Greater Poland but also (especially) in other parts of Poland, during the Covid-19 pandemic (from local/regional, to national levels). In addition, there were inquiries from other CEE countries about the construction of such ecosystems and training of personnel under ECMO, which points to the internationalization of the entire innovation ecosystem (from regional and national to international [CEE region] level). The role of the

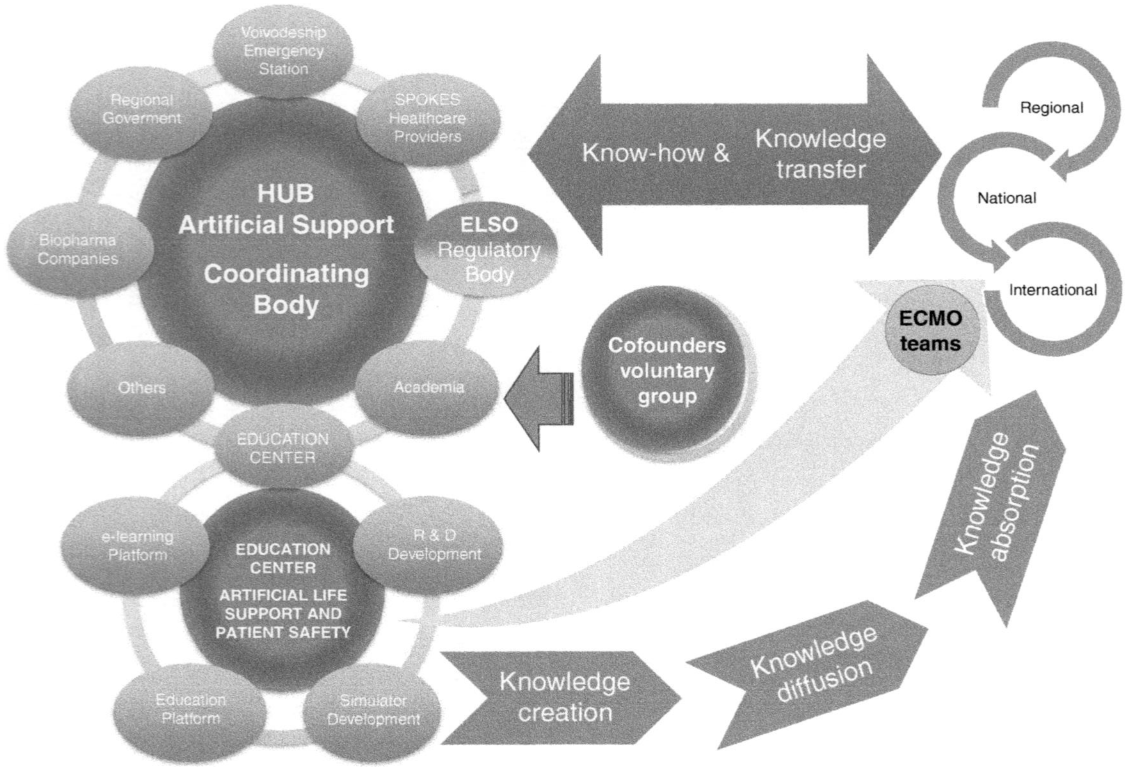

Figure 7.2 Ecosystem improvement and R&D Development: "know-how and knowledge transfer" in the Artificial Life Support and Patient Safety Education Center, part of the "ECMO for Greater Poland" Innovation Ecosystem (HUB).

Table 7.3 Outcomes of the innovation cooperation in the "ECMO for Greater Poland" HUB

Outcomes	*Description*
Education	• Know-how • National education program in extracorporeal support:a) development of "Artificial Life Support with ECMO", b) creation of "Center of Artificial Life Support and Patient Safety" within the University Medical Simulation Centre (CSM) • Staff skills improvement • ECMO teams, Mobile ECMO teams
Creation	• Algorithms for clinical implementation • Standard Operation Procedures (SOP) for transportation
Clinical	• Patient safety – 3.5m inhabitants
Knowledge	• Scientific publications • International impact in ALS • Staff self-improvement
Organizational	• HUB – Artificial Support Coordinating Body • Dedicated Mobile ECMO team
Cooperation	• ELSO • SPOKES Health Care Providers • Academia • Biopharma companies • Regional government • Regional emergency stations • Others

supervisory organization – ELSO – as the regulatory body has also been important in this process. In the coming years, it is expected that there will be more and more trained teams, as well as extensive innovative cooperation at the national and international level – where, thanks to the exchange of knowledge and experience, diffusion of innovation, and absorption at various levels (regional, national, international), it will be possible to develop procedures for the better care of patients (using the latest IT solutions), with the continuous development of innovation cooperation (constant improvement and R&D innovation ecosystem development).

Additional knowledge dissemination in the "ECMO for Greater Poland" program is realized mainly through different scientific articles (often working in interdisciplinary teams) in reputed scientific journals, presentations at different national and international conferences, as well as through organizing two "ECMO for Greater Poland" international conferences in Poznań (Poland), in 2017 and 2019, which met with high recognition in the community.

Innovation cooperation has also led to the creation of the education center under ELSO auspices and is unique to Poland and CEE. The national education program in extracorporeal support – "Artificial Life Support with ECMO" has been developed, and the "Center of Artificial Life Support and Patient Safety" was established within the University Medical Simulation Center (CSM).[4] The education center makes it possible to improve the existing procedures, monitor individual ECMO cases, and constantly improve the qualifications of all ecosystem participants. Moreover, as a part of the education center, there is ongoing R&D cooperation focused on developing an ECMO HPS and IT software (with dedicated mobile application, both for Android and IOS systems). The expertise of this organization managed to improve during this difficult, pandemic-blighted year and was able to publish guidelines for intensive and critical care of ECMO-supported patients. The HUB concept, including the regulatory body with ELSO, can be developed in every country, including individual conditions. Thanks to ELSO's trust, the project gained recognition from the ELSO organization, and during the first meeting in 2019, it was positively certified and obtained the status of an ELSO-endorsed course. Since 2019, more than 200 physicians from Poland have completed the course on extracorporeal techniques promotion.

In order to improve the quality of the education program, it is necessary to monitor, evaluate, and raise the competences in the face of the current challenging times. As the only ELSO-certified center in Poland and CEE, there is a huge demand for the course, both nationally and internationally, including countries such as Lithuania and Latvia, especially with regard to the Covid-19 pandemic.

As the superior method of program implementation, a role for the algorithms of conduct in individual program assumptions translational innovation was chosen for procedures that do not exist in Poland. For this purpose, innovative, unique, high-fidelity simulation techniques were used as a tool for both testing skills and for creating procedures and patterns of conduct that have never been performed by anyone before in Poland. The authors of the program discovered a new benefit of medical simulation, namely its use as a creating tool – they created and performed four high-fidelity simulations – simultaneously devising new algorithms for emergency procedures with the use of ECMO perfusion therapy in translational and probing simulation. Such an approach to the issues of medical simulation is worth imitating. It should also be emphasized that in each case, the attempts to reproduce the conditions given clinical situations in simulated algorithms – in terms of the involvement of human resources and resources, as well as the extent of space and time (e.g. transport of 80 km or the longest scenario lasting 48 hours) – were done for the first time in the world (Puślecki et al., 2019).

The benefit of the simulation and training activities of the program, during the first years of the project, was the creation of a unique ECMO-DCD algorithm, the first on a national scale, and the procedure for applying extracorporeal regional perfusion of organs (kidneys) in a donor who died as a result of irreversible cardiac arrest. This procedure was performed for the first time in Poland.

Another positive effect was the successful application of perfusion therapy to patients with cardiac arrest and hypothermia in two different hospitals in Poznań, where the temperature of patients was restored to normal values as planned. These were the first cases of using perfusion therapy in hypothermia in Greater Poland.

2017 brought a breakthrough in the treatment of acute respiratory failure in our region. Thanks to the use of high-fidelity simulation, it was prepared to transport a patient from a neighboring hospital connected to the ECMO system. Such preparation, in close cooperation with the Voivodeship Emergency Station and the Medical Simulation Center (CSM), made it possible to successfully carry out such transport several times in the following months. Throughout 2017, as part of the project, ECMO therapies were performed in patients with RRF for the first time in Greater Poland.

The concept of extended cardiopulmonary resuscitation (ECPR) for the Poznan agglomeration is a part of the development of the "ECMO for Greater Poland" program. The development of the ECPR concept was based on the experiences of predominantly single centers and was adapted to local protocols in 2019 as the first organized program in Poland – as Poznań Out-Of Hospital Cardiac Arrest (POHCA).

The created procedures allowed the establishment of dedicated ECMO teams that applied nearly 100 times extracorporeal techniques in critical patients conditions. In addition, a dedicated transport system for ECMO-supported patients was developed and was used more than 20 times, including for patients requiring isolation due to epidemiological reasons. These are the hard clinical outcomes of the regulatory HUB ecosystem and translational innovation concept realization (Puślecki et al., 2019; Puslecki et al., 2021).

The innovation ecosystem proved to be effective in times of crisis and disaster medicine, and ecosystem activity increased significantly during the pandemic (Covid-19 pandemic). The involvement of all partners in the cooperation, both from the local and regional level, from business and academia, is likely to have a positive effect on innovation cooperation performance of the whole "ECMO for Greater Poland" innovation ecosystem, as well as enable the development of new modes of cooperation, including, for example, R&D alliances, open innovation alliances, cross-industry alliances, and altruistic alliances (Czekajlo et al., 2020; Smereka et al., 2020).

Conclusions

Biopharmaceutical companies look for various forms of cooperation that will minimize the risk and share the costs of R&D investment. In addition to partnerships within the industry, they establish relationships with universities and research institutes as well as, more often, cross-industry alliances and public-private partnerships. In cooperating with academic institutions, particularly in the model of open innovation alliances, companies can significantly increase the likelihood of better medical therapy for patients. It should be noted, though, that as multi-party alliances they require greater competencies and skills of alliance managers and appropriate alliance management tools, particularly in the selection of potential partners, as well as in the creation and maintenance of alliance networks. Thanks to the diversity of modes of cooperation, new drug proposals can be developed (Burke, 2020; Wilks & Prothmann, 2012), as well as new vaccines (Puślecki, 2021; Puślecki et al., 2021b), which are currently in high demand in the fight against Covid-19.

The Covid-19 pandemic outbreak, a global critical situation in the whole healthcare sector, has forced the reorientation of existing procedures through the use of personal protection equipment (PPE), new and modified skills of medical staff, and the development of medical infrastructure and facilities. Taking into account the new challenges that will affect the healthcare system (new virus mutations, desire for new and modified vaccines), different stakeholders need to cooperate and share knowledge in order to tackle the Covid-19 pandemic faster. In order to improve patient care, new technological solutions (digital Health, medHealth, telehealth and telemedicine, and personalized medicine) should be taken into consideration that can be used to protect healthcare workers, quickly detect and prevent the spread of Covid-19, and improve intensive care.

In the future, it is almost certain that more cross-industry alliances (for instance, Biopharma-IT) in the biopharmaceutical industry can be expected, using more flexible modes of cooperation, digital health technologies, and new digital solutions to offer better patient care and new treatments. We can also expect the development of devoted R&D innovation ecosystems, including a variety of stakeholders (public/non-profit and private) on different levels (local, regional, national) from different industries (cross-industry alliances) and countries (multinational alliances). Openness to cooperation will allow companies to identify weak signals (e.g. subsequent epidemics) in order to react faster and prepare entire societies for new realities.

The dedicated R&D innovation ecosystem established in the "ECMO for Greater Poland" program, along with developed National Education Centers, plays a crucial role in knowledge and know-how transfer. Thanks in part to ELSO cooperation, the short-term results of the translational innovation in the "Center of Artificial Life Support and Patient Safety" are very promising. The implementation of similar cooperation programs in the Covid-19 pandemic accelerated the creation of specialized ECMO centers and specialized ECMO teams, including mobile teams, offering measurable benefits. In 2020 alone, the number of ECMO centers in the world increased from 700 to 1,000. It is important that, with the use of translational innovation, the model of innovative cooperation can be universal and can be applied in sectors with active partners, wherever a common socially important topic can be identified. The role of such an innovative system can be important in terms of creation, knowledge transfer, and self-improvement and may directly translate into benefits and results.

Acknowledgments

This chapter includes findings from the research project financed by the research grant of the National Science Centre (Poland) awarded based on the decision no. DEC-2015/19/D/HS4/00414 and project-awarded funding from a POWER competitive national grant no. POWR.05.04.00-IP.05-00-006/18 by the Polish Ministry of Health.

Notes

1 ECMO – Extracorporeal Membrane Oxygenation – is a technique of extracorporeal blood oxygenation, realized by an oxygenator, a gas exchanger and a pump that sets the blood flow. Depending on the method of connecting the cannulas to the patient, extracorporeal techniques are used to support patients with the most severe forms of respiratory or circulatory failure. In venous-venous cannulation, the work of the lungs is replaced, and the technique is a bridge during the most severe forms of reversible respiratory failure. In the case of venous-arterial cannulation, ECMO supports both the circulatory and respiratory systems. ECMO is a kind of temporary prosthesis that replaces the work of the lungs and/or the heart until the function of these organs improves, allowing them to work independently. The key criterion for therapy initiation, among other specific inclusions and exclusions, is the potential reversibility of the process that led to lung or heart failure. The duration of such therapy is also important, as it can be varied and last from a few days to a maximum of several weeks. A serious limitation of this technique is the progressive wave of complications associated with the use of an extracorporeal circulatory system and oxygenation. In patients undergoing therapy who, as a result of intensive therapy, respiratory therapy, pharmacotherapy, including antibiotics, manage to reverse the unfavorable processes responsible for the failure of key organs, i.e. the heart and/or lungs, ECMO therapy will be successful. Unfortunately, patients with irreversible organ damage will die when ECMO therapy is discontinued. For a select group of patients with heart failure, ECMO therapy will, however, be a bridge and an opportunity to use other, long-term support systems. There is no alternative for patients with respiratory failure. Only in extremely rare cases may an attempt to transplant a dysfunctional organ be considered.

2 The history of simulation goes back to ancient times, and models for the study of anatomy have been used since antiquity. It can be speculated, however, that the idea of a modern simulation in medicine was born in 1920, when doctor John Lundy, head of the anesthesiology department at the Mayo Clinic,

created a simulator and training program to educate residents in local anesthesia. After introducing his original idea, Lundy noticed a significant improvement in the preparation of doctors and residents in performing local anesthesia interventions in the operating theater. He also noticed that during the simulation, he was able to discuss well-performed activities as well as errors, for which there is no space or time in the operating theater.

3 High-fidelity simulation is a teaching methodology – a learning process that uses educational equipment from simple trainers for learning single tasks, through to advanced mannequins, the so-called patient stimulators faithfully imitating the human and its parameters. The main task of medical simulation is to educate and improve patient safety. Advanced human simulators can realistically cough, vomit, and bleed. Fake blood can cause medical staff real stress and the need for immediate action. The participants of high-fidelity medical simulation (using different techniques) can obtain better results and skills (mainly by learning-by-doing) than in traditional educational settings. A number of scientific reports have shown that the use of medical simulation in medical education is extremely useful for students‘ assimilation of the material and in the postgraduate education of medical personnel. Simulation also makes it possible to evaluate this process over time. The student community greatly appreciates the possibilities of education through medical simulation. They believe that it is an opportunity to use their knowledge and skills in safe conditions. The use of medical simulation in the first years of education allows students to better understand and assimilate basic medical contents, even physiology or pharmacology, because they learn about their functioning, interdependencies in science, and importance in contact with the patient.

4 The project will be implemented in 2019–2021 at the Poznan University of Medical Sciences and was awarded funding from a POWER competitive national grant (POWR.05.04.00-IP.05-00-006/18) by the Polish Ministry of Health for a total of USD 2,750,000 (PLN 10,974,708.60). The program will be offered to 264 physicians from Poland via an ELSO-endorsed Comprehensive Simulation Course.

References

Auster, E.R. (1987). International corporate linkages: Dynamic forms in changing environments. *Columbia Journal of World Business*, 22(2).

Brazil, V. (2017). Translational simulation: not 'where?' but 'why?' A functional view of in situ simulation. *Advances in Simulation*, 2(1), 1–5.

Burke, M. J. (2020). Ecosystems in motion. *Strategic Alliance Quarterly*, *Q1*, 10–19.

Casson, M. (1987). *The Firm and the market*. Blackwell.

Chesbrough, H. (2003). *Open Innovation: The new imperative for creating and profiting from technology*. Harvard Business School Press.

Chesbrough, H. (2020a). Open innovation in pandemic, Garwood Center for Corporate Innovation. Haas School of Business, University of California, webinar delivered on 10.11.2020.

Chesbrough, H. (2020b). To recover faster from Covid-19, open up: Managerial implications from an open innovation perspective. *Industrial Marketing Management*, *88*, 410–413.

Chesbrough, H., & Bogers M. (2014). Explicating open innovation: Clarifying an emerging paradigm for understanding innovation. In H. Chesbrough, W. Vanhaverbeke, & J. West (Eds.), *Open innovation: New frontiers and applications* (pp. 3–28). Oxford University Press.

Contractor, F. J., & Lorange, P. (1988). *Cooperative strategies in international business*. Lexington Books.

Culpan, R. (Ed.). (2014). *Open innovation through strategic alliances*. Palgrave Macmillan.

Czekajlo, M., Dąbrowski, M., Dąbrowska, A., Torres, K., Torres, A., Witt, M., Gąsiorowski, Ł., & Szukała, M. (2015). Medical simulation as a professional tool which affect the safety of the patient used in the learning process. *Polski Merkuriusz Lekarski*, *38*(228), 360–363. Polish. PMID: 26098659.

Czekajlo, M., Dabrowski, M., Puslecki, M., Drozd, A., & Szarpak, L. (2020). Using ECMO VV in the COVID-19 pandemic. *Disaster and Emergency Medicine Journal*, *5*(2), 114–115.

De Man, A. P., & Duysters, G. (2007). The second alliance management study 2007. Network Social Innovation (NSI). Masstricht University.

De Man, A. P., Duysters, G., & Neyes, I. (2009). The third alliance management study 2009, Network Social Innovation (NSI). Maastricht University.

De Man, A. P., Duysters, G., Luvison, D., & Krijnen, A. (2012). The Fourth State of Alliance Management Study 2011 – presentation at 2012 ASAP Global Alliance Summit in Las Vegas (USA), 5–8 March 2012, 1–14.

De Man, A. P. (2018), What does an ecosystem manager do? *Strategic Alliance Quarterly*, *Q4*, 35–40.

De Man, A. P., Koene, P., & Ars, M. (2019). *How to survive the organizational revolution: A guide to agile contemporary operating models, platforms and ecosystems*. BIS Publishers.

De Man, A. P. (2020). To be effective in an increasingly ecosystems world, It's vital to understand the different types of ecosystems and how they're governed and managed. *Strategic Alliance Quarterly*, *Q3*, 38–41.

De Man, A. P., & Luvinson, D. (2019). Collaborative business models: Aligning and operationalizing alliances. *Business Horizons*, *62*, 473–482.

DeWitt, J., & Burke, M. (2012). Alliances that could save the world. *Strategic Alliance Magazine*, *Q4*, 36–41.

Duysters, G., & Hagedoorn, J. (2000). A note on organizational modes of strategic technology partnering. *Journal of Scientific & Industrial Research*, *58*, 640–649.

European Commission. (2020). https://ec.europa.eu/info/research-and-innovation/research-area/health-research-and-innovation/coronavirus-research-and-innovation_en.

European Commission. (2021). https://ec.europa.eu/digital-single-market/en/digital-health-technologies-addressing-pandemic.

Fraser, R. L. (2014). Altruistic alliances: Business thrives when Biopharma companies partner with nonprofits. *Strategic Alliance Magazine*, *Q3*, 22-28, 41.

Gomes-Casseres, B., Hagedoorn, J., & Jaffe, A. B. (2006). Do alliances promote knowledge flows?. *Journal of Financial Economics*, *80*(1), 5–33.

Hagedoorn, J. (1990). Organizational modes of inter-firm cooperation and technology transfer. *Technovation*, *10*, 17–30.

Hagedoorn, J. (2002). Inter-firm R&D partnerships: An overview of major trends and patterns since 1960. *Research Policy*, *31*(4), 477–492.

Hagedoorn, J., Link, A., & Vonortas, N. (2000). Research partnerships. *Research Policy*, *29*(4), 567–586.

IMI. (2020). https://www.imi.europa.eu/news-events/press-releases/imi-announces-covid-projects-boosts-funding-pot-eur-72-million.

Lavietes, J. (2012). When the prof met Big Pharma. *Strategic Alliance Magazine*, *Q4*, 46–51.

Martinez-Noya, A., & Narula, R. (2018) What more can we learn from R&D alliances? A review and research agenda. *BRQ Business Research Quarterly*, *21*(3), 195–212.

Narula, R., & Martinez-Noya, A. (2015). International R&D alliances by firms: Origins and development. In D., Archibugi, & A. Filippetti (Eds.), *The handbook of global science, technology, and innovation* (pp. 148–173). Wiley-Blackwell.

Puślecki, Ł. (2010). Wpływ współpracy technologicznej krajów rozwiniętych gospodarczo na ich konkurencyjność międzynarodową. [The impact of technological cooperation of economically developed countries on their international competitiveness], Wydawnictwo Naukowe GRADO.

Puślecki, Ł. (2012). Sectoral analysis of strategic technology alliances in years 1980-2006. *Intercathedra*, *28*(4), Department of Economics and Wood Industry Management, Poznań University of Life Sciences, 79–83.

Puślecki, Ł. (2015). The development and management of alliance networks in the biopharmaceutical industry. In W. Sroka, & Š Hittmár (Eds.), *Management of network organizations: Theoretical problems and the dilemmas in practice* (pp. 199–213). Springer International Publishing. https://doi.org/10.1007/978-3-319-17347-4_14.

Puślecki, Ł. (2016a). Development of modes of cooperation: An opportunity for Open Innovation alliances in Polish biopharmaceutical industry. *Management*, *11*(1), 67–80.

Puślecki, Ł. (2016b). Diversity of relationships and alliances in biopharmaceutical industry. In W. Sroka, Š Hittmár, & J. Kurowska-Pysz (Eds.), *New trends in management and production engineering: Regional, cross-border and global perspectives* (pp. 127–137). Shaker Verlag.

Puślecki, Ł., & Staszków, M. (2015). New cooperation modes: An opportunity for Polish biotechnological clusters. *Managing Global Transitions: International Research Journal*, *13*(2), 171–188.

Puślecki, Ł. (2021). Challenges for innovation cooperation in the biopharmaceutical industry during the Covid-19 pandemic. In B. Jankowska, & E. Mińska-Struzik (Eds.) *Toward the "New Normal" after Covid-19: A post-transition economy perspective*. Wydawnictwo Uniwersytetu Ekonomicznego w Poznaniu.

Puślecki, Ł., Czekajlo, M., Puślecki, M. (2021a). How innovation cooperation supports the improvement of health care in the CEE region: The case of ECMO for Greater Poland. *European Research Studies Journal*, XXIV, 1, 1074–1095. https://doi.org/10.35808/ersj/2088.

Puślecki, Ł., Dąbrowski, M., & Puślecki, M. (2021b). Development of innovation cooperation in the time of COVID-19 pandemic. *European Research Studies Journal*, XXIV, 1, 1049–1073. https://doi.org/10.35808/ersj/2087.

Puslecki, M., Baumgart, K., Ligowski, M., Dabrowski, M., Stefaniak, S., Ladzinska, M., Goszczynska, E., Marcinkowski, P., Olasinska-Wisniewska, A., Klosiewicz, T., Pawlak, A., Zielinski, M., Puslecki, L., Podlewski, R., Szarpak, L., Jemielity, M., & Perek, B. (2021). Patient safety during ECMO transportation: Single center experience and literature review. *Emergency Medicine International*, *22*(2021),6633208. https://doi.org/10.1155/2021/6633208. PMID: 33688436; PMCID: PMC7920709.

Puślecki, M., Ligowski, M., Dąbrowski, M., Stefaniak, S., Ładzińska, M., Pawlak, A., Zieliński, M., Szarpak, Ł., Perek, B., & Jemielity, M. (2019). Development of regional extracorporeal life support system: The importance of innovative simulation training. *The American Journal of Emergency Medicine*, *37*(1), 19–26. https://doi.org/10.1016/j.ajem.2018.04.030. Epub 2018 Apr 18. PMID: 29699897.

Puślecki, M., Ligowski, M., Dąbrowski, M., Telec, W., Perek, B., & Jemielity, M. (2017). "ECMO for Greater Poland": A unique regional program for extracorporeal life support. *Polish Archives of Internal Medicine*, *127*(7-8), 567–568. https://doi.org/10.20452/pamw.4082. Epub 2017 Aug 7. PMID: 28817549.

Puślecki, M., Ligowski, M., Dąbrowski, M., Stefaniak, S., Ładzińska, M., Ładziński, P., Pawlak, A., Zieliński, M., Dąbrowska, A., Artyńska, A., Gezela, M., Sobczyński, P., Szarpak, Ł., Perek, B., & Jemielity, M. (2018). BEST Life - "Bringing ECMO Simulation To Life" – How medical simulation improved a regional ECMO Program. *Artificial Organs*, *42*(11), 1052–1061. https://doi.org/10.1111/aor.13332.

Smereka, J., Puslecki, M., Ruetzler, K., Filipiak, K. J., Jaguszewski, M., Ladny, J. R., & Szarpak, L. (2020). Extracorporeal membrane oxygenation in *COVID-19*. *Cardiology Journal*, *27*(2), 216–217.

Staszków, M., Puślecki, Ł., & Trąpczyński, P. (2017). Development of science and technology parks in Poland: Opportunities for new modes of cooperation in the biopharmaceutical industry. *Managing Global Transitions: International Research Journal*, *15*(1), 23–41. https://doi.org/10.26493/1854-6935.15.23-41.

Tatnall, A. (2011). Innovation translation, innovation diffusion and the technology acceptance model: Comparing three different approaches to theorising technological innovation. In A. Tatnall (Ed.), *Actor-network theory and technology innovation: Advancements and new concepts* (pp. 52–66). IGI Global.

Trąpczyński, P., Puślecki, Ł., & Staszków, M. (2018). Determinants of innovation cooperation performance: What do we know and what should we know? *Sustainability*, *10*(12), 1–32. https://doi.org/10.3390/su10124517.

West, J. (2014). Open Innovation: Learning from alliance research. In R. Culpan (Ed.), *Open innovation through strategic alliances* (pp. 1–14). Palgrave Macmillan.

Wilks, C., & Prothmann, C. (2012). Open Innovation Alliances, Novel alliance models accelerate the identification and advancement of breakthrough therapies. *Strategic Alliance Magazine*, *Q4*, 42–45.

List of Abbreviations

AI	artificial intelligence;
ALS	Advanced Life Support;
ANT	Actor –Network Theory;
AR	augmented reality;
BLS	Basic Life Support;
CEE	Central and Eastern Europe,
CSM	Medical Simulation Centre;
DCD	donor after circulatory death;
ECMO	extracorporeal membrane oxygenation;
ECPR	extended cardiopulmonary resuscitation;
ELSO	Extracorporeal Life Support Organization;
Covid-19	coronavirus disease;
HandS	HUB and SPOKE;
HPS	Human Patient Simulator;
R&D	research and development;
IMI	Innovative Medicines Initiative;
IoT	Internet of Things;
IP	intellectual property;
RRF	reversible respiratory failure;
SOP	standard operating procedure;
SP	standardized patients;
VR	virtual reality.

8 Family Business Responsibility – Allocation of Profit and Innovation Planning

Ewa Więcek-Janka and Alicja Hadryś-Nowak

Introduction

The effect of family, especially family ownership, on firm innovation has been controversial to date (Calabro et al., 2019), suggesting an "innovation paradox" in the case of family firms (De Massis et al., 2015; Forbes, 2018; Ingram et al., 2016). Inspired by agency theory, most empirical studies associate family ownership with conservative innovation strategies (Daily & Dollinger, 1992; Lopez-Fernandez et al., 2016) and lower levels of innovation (Block, 2012; Munoz-Bullón & Sanchez-Bueno, 2011; Nieto et al., 2015). There is still a need to focus on identifying the drivers of heterogeneity in innovation strategies among family firms (Chrisman et al., 2015; Filser et al., 2018). Observing behavioral patterns in members of a business family, both in family and business circles, leads to the conclusion that introducing a change, like succession or profit allocation, and introducing an innovation are difficult processes as they meet multi-layered resistance, irrespective of the kind of change. They are variables inscribed in the functioning of multi-generational family businesses. In this chapter, the authors take into consideration two aspects: allocation of profit and innovation planning. The positive course of profit allocation and planning of innovation are shaped by many factors (Aronoff & Ward, 1995; Cascio et al., 1997; Mandl, 2008; Rothwell, 2002). One of them, observed and defined by the authors, is the responsibility of the family business. This concept and analysis of the context of behavioral actions of family businesses led to the definition of the empirical objective. The main objective of the topic undertaken is to find factors related to the transfer of generational family businesses related to the responsibility of the family for the business sphere. Identification of factors was considered the specific objective to develop. The concept of the business responsibilities of the family as the main adhesive between the business sphere and the family sphere of family businesses as a distinguishing feature against non-family businesses is the context of the social exchange theory proposed by Homans (1967).

DOI: 10.4324/9781003204343-8

Behavioral Basis of Reflection

The ability to provide a sound theoretical explanation as to why family-owned businesses may hold contradictory positions of adopting more or less innovative strategies than their nonfamily counterparts is arguably the main contribution of innovation studies using a behavioral approach.

Behaviorism, as a trend in psychology in the 20th century, assumes that all analyses of phenomena should stem from the observation of human and animal behavior. Management sciences borrowed from behavioristic concepts, particularly utilitarian ones, the notion of reinforcements, i.e. reward and punishment. The modification of basic behaviorism ideas by theorists such as Frazer, Malinowski, Mauss, and Levi-Strauss allowed to develop an exchange theory in sociological terms, which is expressed in a few generalizations (Turner, 1991). One of them is the idea of creating welfare that in a given situation organisms will exhibit a behavior that brings as many rewards and as few punishments as possible. Another paradigm of the behavioral attitude is reward satiation. The more rewards an organism gets as a result of a specific behavior, the less rewarding this kind of behavior becomes due to reward satiation. An organism will be more likely to exhibit an alternative behavior to seek other rewards (Turner, 1991). Both of the presented research generalizations may be implemented in the area of research on family businesses. If the operation of a business is viewed in the same way as it is viewed by organists, then family businesses, as observed by the author, record a tendency towards establishing welfare (1) between family and business spheres, when one sphere expects the other to provide reinforcements connected with two types of goods: financial means and time. An example might be the choice of the direction of financial means allocation (geared towards a business vs. geared towards a family or devoting time towards meeting business needs vs. family needs). The key factor out of those listed for effecting succession in family businesses is to maintain equilibrium between allocating profit to business expansion and satisfaction of family needs. Type two behavior (2) pertains to the issue of gathering positive reinforcements geared towards the satisfaction of both spheres of family business activity, which may result in lowering interest in co-participating in the development of both spheres. In the situation where owners of a firm do not gain financial or non-financial benefits out of managing a firm, they may seek the satisfaction of their needs outside the business sphere. It may bring about a relaxation of internal relations and transfer of managerial responsibility to other people. The situation when the family sphere expects a continuous increase in outlays for ever-growing needs may lead to consuming the profit and in consequence to lowering the competitive edge through the lack of developmental investments. In both cases, the consequence might be the dissolution of a firm or inability to effect succession.

Family Business Responsibility

In the opinion of researchers, a deciding factor in the discussion about family businesses is processes that take place in family-business areas and that allow allocation of profit and planning for innovation; they are often considered as the *sine qua non* condition for defining a business as a family one (Safin, 2007). A clear definition of factors responsible for allocation of profit and innovation planning becomes a challenge that is hard to deal with, not only due to a wide variety of businesses but also due to different personalities of owners, family members, and successors. Moreover, what also needs to be taken into account is a broadly defined context of a business: the close one – employees, clients, and competitors – and the distant one – local and national policies, legal and economic conditions, regional culture, etc. (Safin, 2015).

Analyzing the course of allocation of profit and innovation planning processes is connected with the mutual interaction of internal forces of a family business. Lansberg and Astrachan (1994) point to two systems: family and business, where the family interest being at one with the business interest leads to activities for the benefit of innovation. In the model, featuring three systems apart from the two systems listed above, there is a system of individual interests. According to the authors, taking no heed of personal needs, aspirations, and value systems may destroy not only the succession process but also the functioning of the remaining two areas of a family business. The third area of a family business may be considered in relation to a successor or successors, which is often connected with trust they can inspire in founders (Więcek-Janka, 2013) and their willingness to retain decision-making power and control over business activity (Kujawińska et al., 2015). Such a conservative behavior may be a result of apprehension that decisions concerning the firm's transfer might turn out to be erroneous, which raises psychological costs on both parties involved (Sharma et al., 2003). There are also more complex concepts. The approach by Bienert and his team (Safin, 2015) is of particular importance to this paper. The approach states that the functioning of a family business, its success and chance of a good allocation of profit and innovation planning, lies in harmony and convergence of business aims with individual aims of family members. While conducting research on the so-understood harmony, success factors responsible for harmony in family businesses were identified. They include: economic factors, psychological factors, legal factors, and fiscal factors (Hamrol et al., 2010; Safin, 2015; Więcek-Janka et al., 2016).

The harmony factor was recognized by the author of the article as particularly important, especially in the context of the exchange theory, which became a basis for tackling research problems and refers to "the exchange theory" considered in the way it is treated by Homans and Blau (Turner, 1991). It specifies a mutual influence of benefits and costs in a given exchange relation. If the operating norms are thrown out of balance, the party experiencing dissonance may show passive behavior or even aggression. Similar situations are encountered by observers of those processes in family businesses when decisions related to allocation of profit and innovation planning are taken without due preparation, are excessively prolonged, or become complex because of relating to a large group of successors. Blau also notes the possibility of conflict emergence when the development of equilibrium in one type of relation may disturb the harmony of the other. The authors analyze the allocation of profit and innovation planning experiences of family businesses when there is difficulty maintaining appropriate relations with all stakeholders of the business during generational change (Więcek-Janka, 2011).

One can notice in succession processes the existence of another regularity connected with the exchange theory, namely "social attractiveness" (Turner, 1991), which has a strong bond with perceiving the benefits of remaining and rendering services to a given unit or group. The owner's decision to transfer the business, and the successor's decision to accept it, bear the symptoms of social exchange encumbered with additional expectations connected with family-business culture and observing the value system developed by predecessors. Both the doyen and the successor hope that the exchange transaction will bring them expected fruits. Blau (Turner, 1991) presents the hierarchy of the benefits of exchange, which include: power, respect, social acceptance, and money. Exercising power allows a person to subject others to his or her own aims, which, in the case of succession, is of great significance as beneficiaries (successors) may not use coercion measures or opposition toward benefactors (at least not during the succession process). There may also be another type of behavior connected with the business owner's inability to give up managing the business and transferring it to next generation. The process getting increasingly long causes the potential successor to cease being interested in taking over the family business. The remaining benefits mentioned by Blau (social acceptance, money, and respect) may be relatively easily obtained outside work in a family business. Hence, according to the authors, the possibility of making other people compliant and thus exercising control over them is a decisive factor in lengthy succession processes in family businesses.

Dwelling on the rule of reciprocity, which says that "we are obliged to return favors after people do favors for us", we can state that:

1. The multi-annual upbringing process in business families allowing for family values and entrepreneurial behavior requirements may contribute to successors perceiving benefits resulting from taking over family businesses.
2. The development and implementation of ethical business models in the operation of family businesses will increase the value of succession in the eyes of successors.

The analysis of the collected premises allowed the author to present and analyze a preliminary model of family business responsibility (FBR). The authors assume that there is awareness of activities, both business-related, i.e. operational and strategic activities contained in business models, and family-related, which should be understood as conscious decisions and educational activities accounting for social norms and universal and family values. Figure 8.1 presents a model treatment of FBR.

FBR should be regarded as the behavior of a conscious balance between the sphere of family life and business operations. The combination of two areas of decisions and activities, including requirements of individuals and the remaining stakeholders, will be possible through the implementation of FBR postulates. The concept of FBR shows intellectual debt towards the accomplishments of the exchange theory as treated by Homnes and Blau (Safin, 2015). According to the author, a responsible family, in the accepted upbringing model,[1] voluntarily takes account of the developmental aims of a business model[2], hoping that it will obtain particular benefits (e.g. financial, security, succession of ownership and power). Meeting such assumptions becomes a basis for building a multi-generational family business.

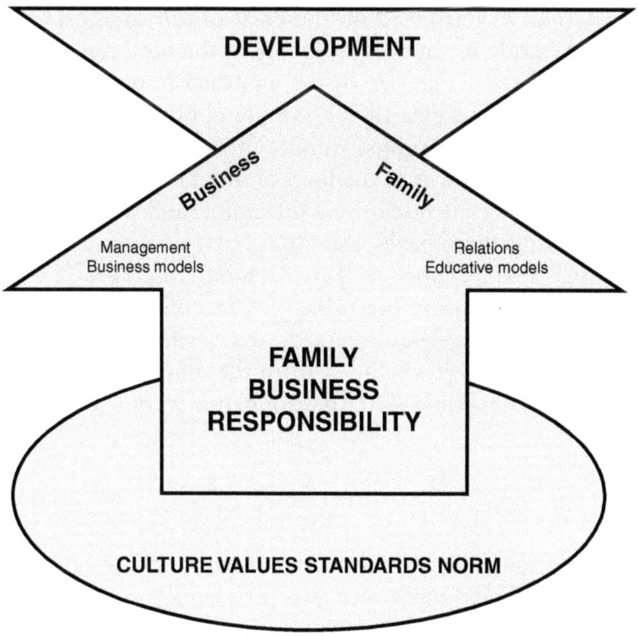

Figure 8.1 Model treatment of family business responsibility.

Research Methodology

Undertaking research on FBR became a basis for developing a methodology adjusted to the specific character of family businesses. The research was conducted in two stages: an expert interview and a survey (Więcek-Janka, 2015).

The first stage comprised an interview with six experts.[3] The aim of the study was to identify variables affecting FBR in family businesses. The selection of experts for the interview was intentional.

The second stage aimed to assess variables affecting the shape of FBR in family companies.

The population unit represented by the analyzed sample was a family business understood as:

1. The majority of votes are held by the person who established or acquired the firm (or their spouses, parents, child, or child's direct heirs).
2. At least one representative of the family is involved in the management or administration of the firm.
3. In the case of a listed company, the person who established or acquired the firm (or their families) possesses 25% of the right to vote through their share capital, and there is at least one family member on the board of the company (PWC, 2018).

The analyzed population was assessed on the basis of information concerning the number of family businesses as 41.4% of the total number of firms in Poland (Jeżak, 2014). The size of the analyzed population was 172,400 family businesses. The size of the sample obtained during the research was greater than the assumed minimum one, which allowed generalization of analyses[4] and was at the level of 422 family businesses. In order to efficiently conduct the research, a survey method was adopted and was carried out along three paths using CATI (*Computer Assisted Telephone Interview*),[5] PAPI (*Paper & Pen Personal Interview*)[6], and CAII (*Computer Assisted Internet Interview*).[7] The collected material was analyzed in the form of tables, discussed, and verified. Two questionnaires containing errors were excluded from the whole set of questionnaires collected. The remaining 420 questionnaires were used in the statistical analysis.

Results Analysis

During the first stage of the study, six in-depth expert interviews in three rounds were conducted. Their main aim was to identify variables allowing family businesses to combine family and business areas with the perspective of successful allocation of profit and innovation planning in

Table 8.1 Results of the first stage of the research – expert interview.

Abbreviated	*Marking a Feature in the Research*
Allocation of profit to business development	APED
Allocation of profit to family development	APFD
Family decision-making takes into account the interests of the business	FDB
The family takes the time to improve business organization	FTO
Employing on the basis of merit	EBM
Engaging the family in the construction of the business's strategy	EFbS
Raising children in entrepreneurship	RCE

the future. The list of variables obtained[8] comprised several points, which were narrowed down to a few ones in discussions with the experts. Table 8.1 contains variables singled out in the first stage of the study, which allow – in the experts' opinion – for coexistence and synergy in the development of family businesses.

The preliminary analysis of the collected material – in the second stage – concerned (apart from the main aim) the recognition of the studied population structure. A particular interest was attached to the following features: size of the business, type of business, legal form, generation managing the business, and gender of the person managing the business.

One of the research assumptions was to secure the representative character of the study. The research was conducted in all regions in Poland,[9] and the results are presented in Figures 8.2–8.8.

In Jeżak's research (2014), one can note a similar distribution of the sample in relation to family business activity. Services were identified as the most frequently realized form of family business activity (46.9%). In the research conducted, a "pure" form of services was declared by 32% of respondents, but the other 26% stated that services were an important part of business activity. Commercial activity in the presented sample was declared by 21%, but the remaining 30% realize it as an additional activity. In Jeżak's research (2014), close to 40% of respondents declared commerce as the main business activity. Manufacturing activity and industrial processing were declared by 8% of respondents, which exactly reflects the distribution of results in Jeżak's research (2014).

The representative sample accounted for differences in the size of a firm, understood as the number of people employed. Jeżak's research comprised firms that did not have any people employed (50%). The present paper had this category classified as microenterprises, which made up 60% of the analyzed firms (number of people employed – up to 9). In turn, 28% were small firms employing from 10 to 49 people, 10% were medium-sized firms

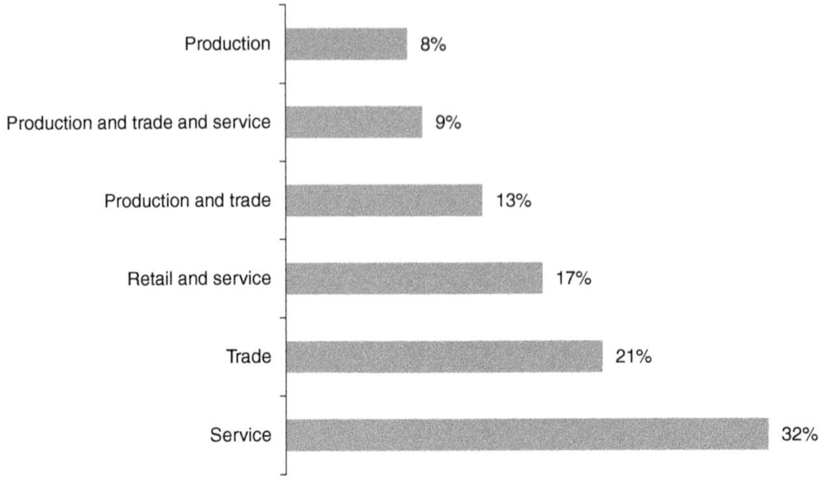

Figure 8.2 Declared business line in the studied sample (n = 420).

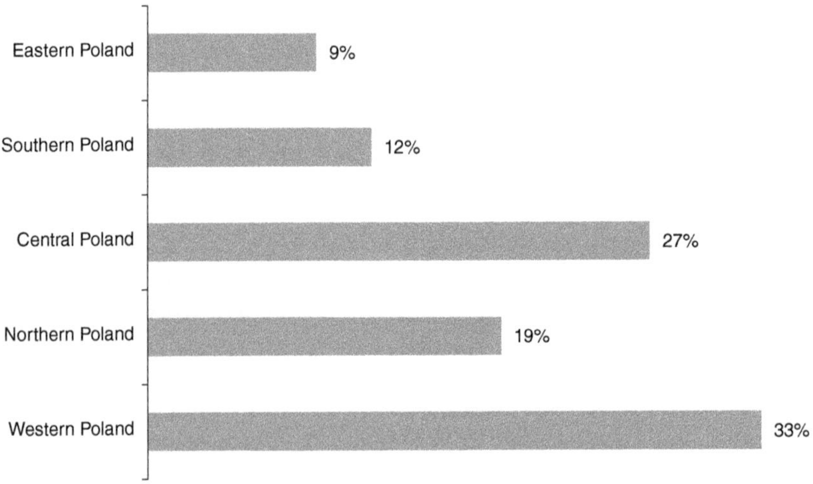

Figure 8.3 Distribution of analyzed family businesses in Poland (n = 420).

employing from 50 to 249 people, and 2% were large firms employing over 250 people.

In accordance with the distribution of businesses operating in Poland, small and medium-sized business were represented by 98% of firms. The most popular legal form declared by respondents was a registered business activity run by a natural person (55%), limited liability

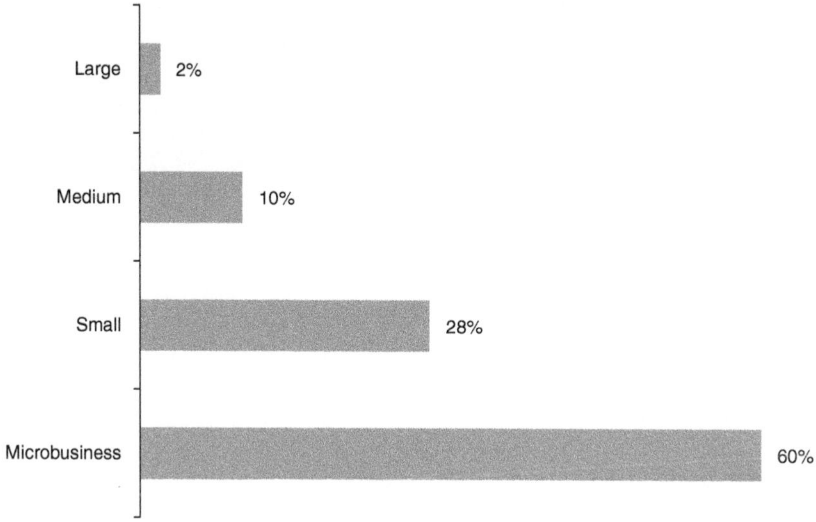

Figure 8.4 Size of family businesses in the analyzed sample (n = 420).

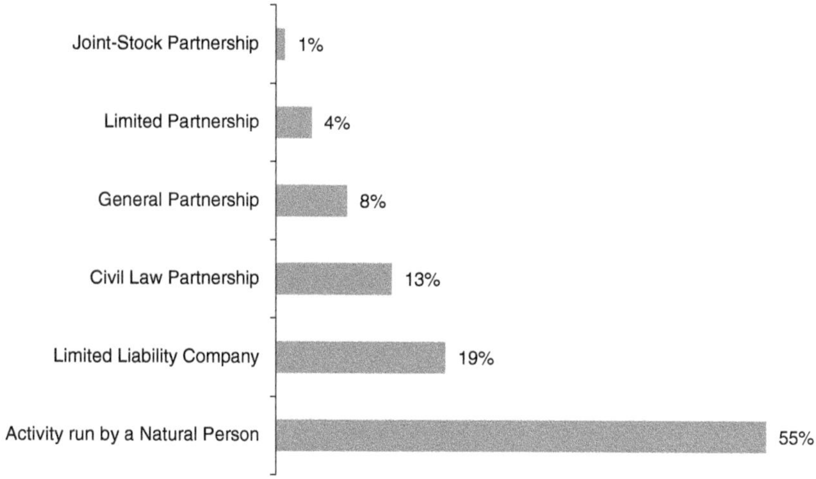

Figure 8.5 Legal form of business activity declared in the analyzed sample (n = 420).

company (19%), civil law partnership (13%), registered partnership (8%), limited partnership (4%), and joint-stock partnership (1%).

A large percentage (68%) of legal forms, such as a business run by a natural person or a civil law partnership, are a sign of lack of knowledge about possible benefits and losses resulting from a given legal form. As it

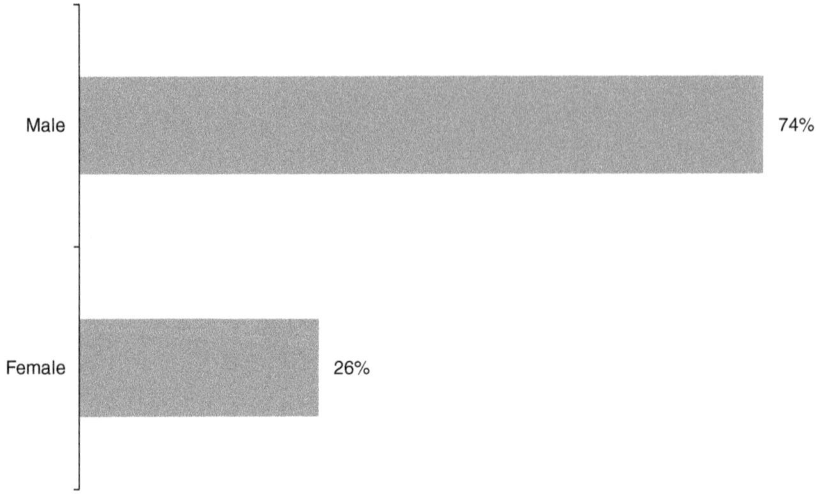

Figure 8.6 Managers in the studied sample according to gender (n = 420).

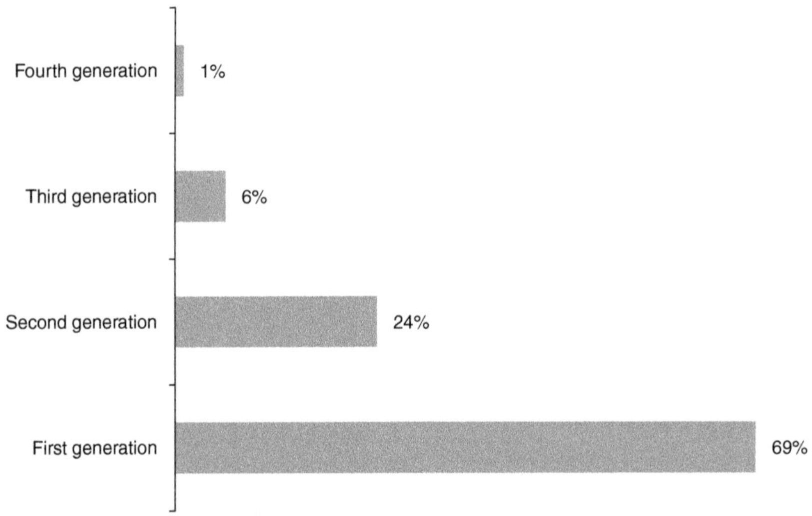

Figure 8.7 Managing generation in the studied sample (n = 420).

is shown by the quoted data, most often an entrepreneur is a natural person as it is the easiest way of running a business.

Another important feature that was analyzed was the gender of the current owners of family businesses. The structure of the obtained data is illustrated in Figure 8.6. Female owners made up 26% of the sample.

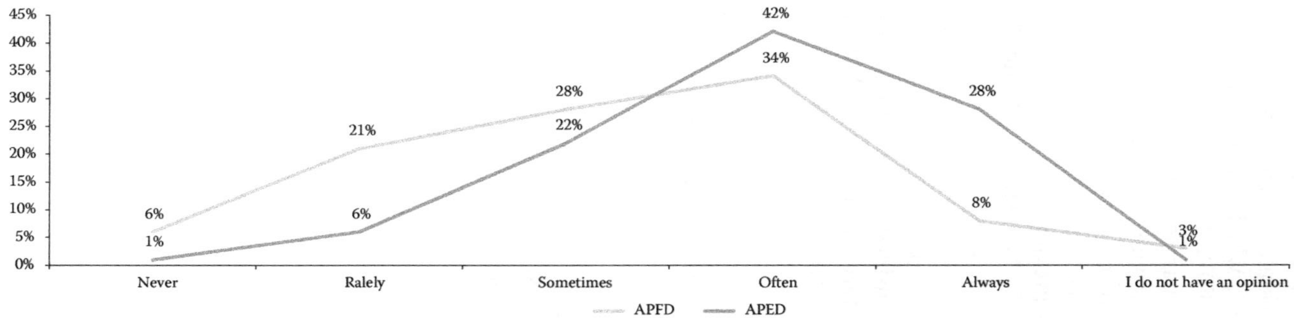

Figure 8.8 Distribution of answers for one of the variables describing family business responsibility (profit allocation, n = 420).

Another important feature specifying family businesses in Poland is the generation exercising authority in family businesses. A large majority of businesses has not gone through succession yet (69%). It turns out that 24% of family businesses are run by the second generation, 6% by the third generation, and 1% by the fourth generation.

The excerpted sample has a similar structure to the material that Jeżak and his team obtained in 2014, which allows the author to draw statistical conclusions regarding FBR. In the detailed analysis – for the purpose of this study – particular attention was paid to the first two features of FBR, which were activities connected with profit allocation (*APFD, APED*). The activity of owners and chief managers of family businesses were evaluated on the scale ordering the frequency of their occurrence. The following expressions were used as parameters: "it never happens to me", "rarely", "sometimes", "often", "always", and "I do not have an opinion". One of the factors singled out by experts that has an influence on the stable development of both spheres of a family business is the way of dividing profit between family needs and developmental needs of a business. The results are presented in Figure 8.8. Only 7% of the analyzed businesses declare that they never or rarely spend profit on business development, which corresponds with the results of 27% of firms in which it is declared that revenue is never or rarely spent on meeting family needs. Almost 28% of entrepreneurs declare that they sometimes invest acquired profit in family development, whereas 22% of owners sometimes invest in business development.

Data collected in this part of the analysis should not raise doubts. It should be remembered that a great majority of respondents were owners of microbusinesses where the border between the business sphere and family sphere is sometimes very narrow. Hence, the differences in the obtained answers were so small. Significant differences, however, may be observed in declared behavior for results *often* and *always* (*...spend the profit made on the development of a business/family*). Namely, 70% of entrepreneurs stated that they allotted profit to the development of the business sphere, whereas 42% stated they allotted it to the development of the family sphere.

Discussion

Trying to provide a fuller explanation of activities connected with profit allocation in family businesses, an attempt was made to identify interdependencies between dependent variables and independent variables (Hamrol et al., 2010).

The main hypothesis, which became an introduction to further analyses, assumes that family businesses consciously allocate profits to company development and satisfy family needs. This assumption is complemented by seven auxiliary hypotheses in which it was essential to recognize relationships between dependent variables (allocating profit to the development of the business sphere/satisfying family needs) and independent variables (business metrics):

1. Profit allocation (PA) is connected with the age of a business (AB).
2. Profit allocation (PA) is connected with the size of a business (SB).
3. Profit allocation (PA) is connected with the owner's gender (OG).
4. Profit allocation (PA) is connected with conscious innovation planning (IP).
5. Profit allocation (PA) is connected with children's entrepreneurial engagement in the business sphere (EE).
6. Profit allocation (PA) is connected with business-related conflicts (B-RC).
7. Profit allocation (PA) is connected with family-related conflicts (F-RC).

Each of the auxiliary hypotheses made was broken into two detailed ones connected with the place of profit allocation (here: business – B or family – F). A chi-squared test was used as a verifying tool of the hypotheses made. As a result of that, each detailed hypothesis was divided into the next two ones: the null hypothesis stating there is no relationship between the analyzed variables and the alternative hypothesis stating there is a relationship between them (Więcek-Janka, 2015). The test results for the detailed hypotheses are contained in Table 8.2.

The analysis of the detailed hypotheses allowed us to single out relationships between the variables of family businesses. The first of the detailed hypotheses assumed a relationship between the forms of profit

Table 8.2 Test results for auxiliary hypotheses ($\alpha = 0.05$; n = 420).

Auxiliary Hypothesis		*Relationship between*	*Chi-squared Test*	*df*	*p*	*V-Cramer*
H.1	1.1	PA-B/AB	19,583	15	,189	,124
	1.2	PA-F/AB	21, 457	15	,123	,112
H.2	2.1	PA-B/SB	50,702	15	**<,001**	,256
	2.2	PA-F/SB	18,87	15	,220	,023
H.3	3.1	PA-B/OG	8,345	4	,080	,111
	3.2	PA-F/OG	9,276	4	,055	,121
H.4	4.1	PA-B/IP	63,216	25	**<,001**	,173
	4.2	PA-F/IP	24,363	25	,498	,012
H.5	5.1	PA-B/EE	45,026	20	**,0012**	,238
	5.2	PA-F/EE	46,726	20	**,001**	,216
H.6	6.1	PA-B/B-RC	87,750	25	**<,001**	,204
	6.2	PA-F/B-RC	16,837	25	,888	,023
H.7	7.1	PA-B/F-RC	46,398	25	**,006**	,259
	7.2	PA-F/F-RC	19,365	25	,0779	,121

distribution and the age of a business. No relationship with the age of a business was recorded either in the case of allocating profit to business development or securing family needs (H.1). It may mean that, regardless of the length of duration of a business, the directions of revenue allocation are similar. Common observations of family businesses and their decision-making processes may indicate another type of behavior, e.g. "consuming" profit in the first years of business operation. Statistical results unequivocally exclude the influence of this independent variable on the directions of financial means allocation.

The second hypothesis underlined the relationship between the analyzed variable and the size of a business. The obtained results of statistical testing indicate the lack of relationship between profit allocation to family needs and the size of a business, which may signify a balanced distribution of such support irrespective of the size of a business (H.2.2). However, in the case of activities connected with profit allocation to business development, there is a link with the size of a business (H.2.1). It means that businesses, along with their development, invest profit earned (or part of it) into progressive measures.

The third hypothesis tested the relationship of gender with the selected directions of profit allocation. The analysis made did not show connection between gender and the selected direction of financial means distribution (H.3). The obtained result disclaims the stereotypes of female managers making decisions in a more emotional way and directing profit to be consumed in the family.

Another testing area comprised relationships between the analyzed dependent variables and innovation planning. A relationship between allocating profit to business activity and planned innovations was confirmed (H.4.1). At the same time, the hypothesis regarding interdependency between using profit to satisfy family needs and implementing innovation plans in the business sphere was rejected (H.4.2). Such results are in keeping with the logic of management, which states that profit (or its specific part) should be spent on business developmental activities (profit reinvestment). It testifies to family business owners' and managers' business maturity.

An appropriate preparation of future successors is an essential problem of family business responsibility. The fifth detailed hypothesis assumed a relationship between profit allocation directions and children's entrepreneurial engagement in the company's business activity. Testing the hypothesis revealed that both in the first case (allocation in the business) and the second case (allocation in the family) there is a connection with children's entrepreneurial engagement in business matters (H.5). The presented relationship between the researched variables may have different origins. First, it may result from adopted family models and values that oblige children to help their parents. Second, according to the exchange theory, children, observing the business development

Table 8.3 Results of testing the main hypothesis ($\alpha = 0.05$; $n = 420$).

The Main Hypothesis	*Relationship between*	*chi-squared test*	*df*	*p*	*V-Cramer*
	PA-B/PA-F	215,7982	25	<,001	,34

and growth in family living standards, notice the benefits of running the business and commit themselves more willingly to work in it. Third, according to the exchange theory, young people see their commitment to work for the good of the business as an opportunity to obtain more quickly benefits such as: power, respect (of both family members and people from outside), and social acceptance.

While conducting the research, attention was also paid to the emergence of conflicts in family businesses. Two of the hypotheses made (H.6 and H.7) concerned the analysis of the relationship between profit allocation directions and conflicts that were subdivided into business- and family-related. The existence of relationships between allocating profits to business company development and the emergence of business- and family-related conflicts was confirmed. Using profit to meet family needs does not give rise to conflicts. Such an outcome may be explained by the lack of co-deciding by other family members about detailed plans connected with financing the business area and family. Table 8.3 presents results of testing the main hypothesis.

The main hypothesis concerning activities connected with the conscious allocation of profits in both business and family spheres was confirmed. In accordance with the results contained in Table 8.3, it can be stated that family entrepreneurs consciously divide profit into business development and innovation planning and satisfaction of needs signaled by the family.

The results of the multiple-path analysis justify the conviction that: first, owners of family businesses show great awareness and maturity in harmonizing activities undertaken for the sake of the development of both spheres of a family business, second: the postulate of shaping *business responsibility* in regards to activities related to the direction of profit allocation should be acknowledged as fulfilled.

Conclusion

In search of theoretical bases for developing the concept of FBR, the behavioral perception of social exchange was adopted. It allows us to analyze the activity of family businesses as a system created by at least two players (business and family), whose present and future welfare is contingent on developing and satisfying mutual considerations.

In the course of the preliminary research, a few variables were singled out that may influence FBR. The chapter featured and thoroughly analyzed one of the variables singled out by experts, namely *the direction of profit allocation andand innovation planning*. The main hypothesis, verified during the interpretation of statistical data, pointed to the ability of owners of family businesses to effect a harmonious division of profits between the development of a business and the needs of the family. Moreover, a few dependencies were proved to be linked to the analyzed variable, and the findings of this study also offer practical recommendations to family business owners and family advisers:

1. The bigger the business, the more often profit is earmarked for business development.
2. Innovative (or aspiring to be innovative) businesses earmark profit for business development more often.
3. Raising children in the entrepreneurial spirit and engaging them in making business decisions is tied with a harmonious profit allocation.
4. Family-related conflicts are connected with a higher frequency of allocating profits in the sphere of business development.

The result of the development of a complete business model on family responsibility will be to indicate the actions that should be taken by the family company seeking to maintain longevity. Our study also contributes to the connection between theoretical constructs and measures in family firm studies that follow a behavioral approach. There are some limitations of this study. First, the owner of the firm, who is most frequently the largest stockholder, answered the survey. This is the person who sets the strategy for the business and determines the importance of family goals for the firm, besides having the proper information to answer all the questions in our survey. Another potential limitation of our study is that it was conducted among Polish family-owned businesses. This context may also have influence on the results. Thus, studies from other countries are needed.

Certain characteristics of family firms can work against business innovation. They may include limited exposure to innovative ideas from other industries, particularly in families where business leaders have not worked anywhere else. Lack of willingness to adopt outside ideas due to a feeling that family members, who may have been in the business for decades, know more than anyone else about what it takes to succeed. Limited desire to take risks because "all of the family's eggs are in one basket": the business. Despite such factors, many family-owned businesses are among the most innovative in their industries. Family businesses can leverage the fact that decisions can be made quickly in an environment where management and ownership generally overlap to bring innovations to market quickly. Innovation in family business does not need to be tied to size of the company as much as the management's knowledge and creativity and the owners' passion to succeed. A long-time horizon that allows for investments that may not pan out in the next year helps, as does the desire to keep the business going – which may mean that ideas are evaluated not purely on an economic basis.

The obtained results clearly indicate that family businesses allocate the obtained profits, taking into account two spheres: the family sphere and the business sphere. The concept of FBR relates precisely to this particular characteristic of family businesses, which "orders" the owners of the business to protect the interests of the family, often more than the interests of the business. Family business is often a source of income for the family; therefore, the development of the business should be the main area of interest for family business owners. Hence, profit (or its specific part) should be spent on business developmental activities (profit re-investment). In today's dynamically changing environment, the development of the company is often inextricably linked with the introduction of innovations – innovations understood not only through the context of new products or services, but also marketing or process innovations. The introduction of innovations should be properly planned. In the context of family businesses that are constantly balancing between meeting family needs and business development, family businesses consciously divide profit into business development and innovation planning and satisfaction of needs signaled by the family; innovation planning becomes extremely important. As the research results show, only the awareness of the challenges related to the development of a company and its significance for family development allows for a responsible approach to planning innovation in a family business. Therefore, owners of family businesses should realize that business responsibility is not only responsibility for the family, but also for the business and the people working in it. An important characteristic of family business is the transition of the company to the next generation, i.e. the matter of the succession process. The succession process is a very complex process, requiring both family and business involvement. It is often also a financially demanding process. Hence, when planning to introduce innovations in a family business, one should also take into account the possible transfer of the company to the next generation. As indicated by the results of the conducted research, preparing the successors to take over and run a family business is also important from the point of view of business responsibility. Therefore, owners of family businesses should take into account the importance of the succession process when planning innovation in the business.

Taking care of both basic spheres of influence in family businesses becomes particularly important in times of global crisis, like the Covid-19 pandemic, especially from the strategic perspective. Systematic observations and interviews with owners of family businesses indicate changes in current planning, i.e. more often safety and the so-called safe development. This means that in the perspective of 2030, greater emphasis will be placed on business security that guarantees the maintenance of the family of founders and owners, as well as the safety of the families of the company's employees. The choice of such a path for some industries will lead to a reduction in investment (HORECA); for others, the opposite (Industry 4.0) will result in opening new markets and investments not only on a regional or national scale, but also the internationalization of family businesses. It seems that the help of the first group is necessary, which should not rely only on one-off support, but also on the development of systemic support tools at the local and regional level with the help of central authorities.

Notes

1 The upbringing model is understood as a process of shaping human personality, which covers social culture (including family culture), social structure, personality, adopted (also imposed) social roles, attitudes, needs, self-evaluation, and the resulting behavior.
2 The business model is understood as a long-time strategy, which covers the use and expansion of resources in order to obtain and maintain a competitive advantage.
3 The experts were involved both academically and practically in family business activity: three scientists and three family entrepreneurs. The first stage of the research was carried out in January and February 2015.
4 The minimum sample was 383 firms, with $\alpha = 0.05$, $b=0.05$ and $p=0.5$.
5 The CATI method was used to conduct research with 75 respondents.
6 The PAPI method was used to conduct research with 67 respondents.
7 The CAII method was used to conduct research with 280 respondents.
8 Variables understood by the author as features, behavior, and decisions, which can be generalized and which are observed in family businesses.
9 The regional division was as follows: eastern Poland (Podlaskie Region, Lublin Region, Subcarpathian Region), southern Poland (Opole Region, Silesian Region, Małopolska Region), central Poland (Kuyavian-Pomeranian Region, Masovian Region, Świętokrzyskie Region), northern Region (West Pomeranian Region, Pomeranian Region, Warmian Masurian Region), western Poland (Wielkopolska Region, Lower Silesian Region, Lubuskie Region).

References

Aronoff, C. E., & Ward, J. L. (1995). Family-owned businesses: A thing of the past or a model for the future?. *Family Business Review*, *8* (2), 121–130.

Block, J. H. (2012). R&D investments in family and founder firms: An agency perspective. *Journal of Business Venturing*, *27*(2), 248–265. https://doi.org/10.1016/j.jbusvent.2010.09.003.

Calabro, A., Vecchiarini, M., Gast, J., Campopiano, G., De Massis, A., & Kraus, S. (2019). Innovation in family firms: A systematic literature review and guidance for future research. *International Journal of Management Reviews*, *21*(3), 317–355. https://doi.org/10.1111/ijmr.12192.

Cascio, W. F., Young, C. E., & Morris, J. R. (1997). Financial consequences of employment-change decisions in major US corporations. *Academy of Management Journal*, *40*(5), 1175–1189.

Chrisman, J. J., Chua, J. H., De Massis, A., Frattini, F., & Wright, M. (2015). The ability and willingness paradox in family firm innovation. *Journal of Product Innovation Management*, *32*(3), 310–318. https://doi.org/10.1111/jpim.12207.

Daily, C. M., & Dollinger, M. J. (1992). An empirical examination of ownership structure in family and professionally managed firms. *Family Business Review*, *5*(2), 117–136. https://doi.org/10.1111/j.1741-6248.1992.00117.x.

De Massis, A., Di Minin, A., & Frattini, F. (2015). Family driven innovation: Resolving the paradox in family firms. *California Management Review*, *58*(1), 5–19. https://doi.org/10.1525/cmr.2015.58.1.5.

Filser, M., De Massis, A., Gast, J., Kraus, S., & Niemand, T. (2018). Tracing the roots of innovativeness in family SMEs: The effect of family functionality and socioemotional wealth. *Journal of Product Innovation Management*, *35*(4), 609–628. https://doi.org/10.1111/jpim.12433.

Forbes. (2018). The world most innovative companies. http:// www.forbes.com/innovative-companies/list/.

Hamrol, A., Kowalik D., & Kujawińska A. (2010). Impact of selected work condition factors on quality of manual assembly process. *Human Factors and Ergonomics in Manufacturing & Service Industries*, *21*(2), 156–163. https://doi.org/10.1002/hfm.20233.

Homans, G. (1967). *The nature of social science*. Harcourt, Brace & World.

Ingram, A. E., Lewis, M. W., Barton, S., & Gartner, W. B. (2016). Paradoxes and innovation in family firms: The role of paradoxical thinking. *Entrepreneurship Theory and Practice*, *40*(1), 161–176. https://doi.org/10.1111/etap.12113.

Jeżak, J. (2014). Przedsiębiorstwa rodzinne w Polsce. Znaczenie ekonomiczne oraz strategiczne problemy rozwoju [Family businesses in Poland. The economic importance and strategic development problems]. Wydawnictwo Uniwersytetu Łódzkiego.

Kujawińska, A., Vogt, K., & Wachowiak, F. (2015). Ergonomics as significant factor of sustainable production. In P. Golińska, & A. Kawa (Eds.), *Technology management for sustainable production and logistic* (pp. 193–203). Springer.

Lansberg, I., Astrachan, J. H. (1994). Influence of family relationships on succession planning and training: The importance of mediating factors. *Family Business Review*, 7(1), 39–59.

Lopez-Fernandez, M. C., Serrano-Bedia, A. M., & Gomez- Lopez, R. (2016). Determinants of innovation decision in small and medium-sized family enterprises. *Journal of Small Business and Enterprise Development*, *3*(2), 408–427. https://doi.org/10.1108/JSBED-02-2015-0028.

Mandl, I. (2008) *Overview of family business relevant issues, final report, project on behalf of the European Commission*. Austrian Institute for SME Research.

Munoz-Bullón, F., & Sanchez-Bueno, M. J. (2011). The impact of family involvement on the R&D intensity of publicly traded firms. *Family Business Review*, *24*(1), 62–70. https://doi.org/10.1177/0894486510396870.

Nieto, M. J., Santamaria, L., & Fernandez, Z. (2015). Understanding the innovation behavior of family firms. *Journal of Small Business Management*, *53*(2), 382–399. https://doi.org/10.1111/jsbm.12075.

PWC. (2018). Transforming family businesses. https://www.pwc.com/sg/en/publications/assets/epc-transform-family-businesses-201805.pdf, (access: 02.11.2020).

Rothwell, W. J. (2002). Putting success into your succession planning. *The Journal of Business Strategy*, *23*(3), 32–37.

Safin, K. (2007). *Przedsiębiorstwa rodzinne – istota i zachowania strategiczne* [Family businesses - the essence and strategic behavior]. Wydawnictwo Akademii Ekonomicznej.

Safin, K. (2015). Potencjał sukcesyjny polskich przedsiębiorstw rodzinnych [The potential of Polish succession of family businesses]. *Przedsiębiorczość i Zarządzanie*, *16*(7), Publisher Social Sciences Academy, Łódź, 9–23.

Sharma, P., Chrisman, J. J., & Chua, J. H. (2003). Succession planning as planned behavior: Some empirical results. *Family Business Review*, *16*, 145–178.

Sułkowski, Ł., & Marjański, A. (2009). *Firmy rodzinne* [Family Businesses]. Poltext.

Szacki, J. (2006). *Historia myśli socjologicznej* [History of sociological thought]. PWN.

Turner, J. H. (1991). *The structure of sociological theory*. Wadsworth Publishing Company.

Więcek-Janka, E. (2011). *Games and decisions*. Publishing House of Poznan University of Technology.

Więcek-Janka, E. (2015). *The essentials of marketing research*. Publishing House of Poznan University of Technology.

Więcek-Janka, E. (2013). *Wiodące wartości w zarządzaniu przedsiębiorstwami rodzinnymi* [The leading value in the management of family businesses]. Publishing House of Poznan University of Technology.

Więcek-Janka, E., Mierzwiak, R., & Kijewska, J. (2016). Competencies' model in the succession process of family firms with the use of grey clustering analysis. *The Journal of Grey System*, *28*(2), 121–131.

Looking Ahead 2030

Rafał Śliwiński and Łukasz Puślecki

Predicting the Future

The future is extremely difficult to accurately predict, mostly because it is so complex and because random situations can change a lot. As we saw, for example, with Covid-19, unforeseen events such as pandemics make the world an unpredictable place. However, based on trends and analysis of progressive changes, we can try to predict with a certain probability what the near future may look like until the end of this decade. Earlier chapters dealt with business and consumer strategy and innovation in the context of changes brought about by technological, economic, environmental, and social megatrends, and the related megatrends of demographics, political change, and globalization. After reading the chapters of this book, the question remains of how the discussed issues will develop. The aim of this chapter is to bring the vision of development of the above-mentioned megatrends in the context of strategic and consumer challenges until 2030.

Demographic Increase and the Rise of the New Middle Class

Man is the basis of economic development. Therefore, megatrends resulting from demographic changes are of fundamental importance. Currently, the world is inhabited by 7.8 billion people. In 2030, this number is expected to increase to about 8.55 million people (Gaub, 2019). The greatest dynamics will be in African and Asian countries. The expansion of large urban agglomerations is also expected. It is estimated that by 2025, 2 billion people, or about 25% of the world's population, will live in the 600 largest cities in the world, providing $64 trillion of GDP, which will account for 60% of global GDP (McKinsey, 2011). As McKinsey points out, it will be profitable for companies to take into account these trends and rethink their expansion plans, considering major global cities more than leading countries. Moreover, the migration trend from the countryside to the cities is still strong. In 440 emerging cities in

DOI: 10.4324/9781003204343-102

2025, 1 billion new consumers will appear in relation to 2010, and the consumption level in these cities will amount to $10 billion by 2025 (McKinsey, 2012). The share of the middle class in society in low- and middle-income countries will increase from 5% in 2005 to 25% in 2030. China alone will be responsible for one billion consumers in the new middle class (Torre & Rigolini, 2020), and globally it will be 5.5 billion middle-class people, 87% of which will be from Asia (European Commission, 2021). The strategic challenge for businesses will be to find places where dynamic growth will take place from the point of view of their offer. Undoubtedly, the sooner investment decisions are made, the better. By 2030, we can expect a sustained increase in global welfare, and the proportion of people living in extreme poverty will decrease in the coming years in favor of the growth of the middle-income population. This is due to easy access to communication, artificial intelligence (AI) supporting many areas of our lives, education and medicine, and digitization of everyday goods and services (Diamandis, 2020; Diamandis & Kotler, 2012, 2020). Such a rapidly growing middle class creates room for dozens of new multinational firms. In addition, the growing needs of an increasing population will mean a lack of productive resources, and by 2030, we are likely to witness the first space expeditions for natural resources (Mallick & Rajagopalan, 2019). For consumers, the dynamic demographic development will mean more difficult and costly access to resources, including those necessary for life, such as clean water, air, and healthy food. On the other hand, more emphasis will be placed on the environment, and hence on renewable energies. Continuous advancement in solar, wind, geothermal, hydroelectric, nuclear, and indigenous farms will lead humanity towards ubiquitous, worldwide, cheap, renewable energy (Diamandis, 2020; Diamandis & Kotler, 2020).

Transforming Globalization

In the context of globalization, a number of changes that have been gaining momentum for some time should be expected by 2030. First, global supply chains are changing significantly for several reasons. One of them is a significant increase in consumption in developing markets, by as much as 50% since 2007 (McKinsey, 2019), and consequently a significant increase in internal consumption in the largest markets in the world, such as China, India, Indonesia, and Brazil, satisfied mainly with local production. Another change is the relative reduction in the volume of international trade, and the increase in the international exchange of services. Increasing digitization also contributes to these changes, which means that many types of services can be provided over the Internet. This is evidenced by the significant increase in data transmission. Only between 2005 and 2014, the transfer increased 45 times from 4.5 Tbps to 211.3 Tbps (McKinsey, 2016), and in 2020 to over 600 Tbps (Telegeography,

2021). As a result, we can speak of a transformation of globalization from material (goods) to non-material (services, data). This trend will continue to develop. Another change that can be expected by 2030 will be a radical improvement in access to the market of small and medium-sized enterprises (SMEs), which thanks to online platforms, such as Amazon, Alibaba, Flipkart, and eBay, gain access to global customers. In addition, automation, robotization, and additive technologies have made it profitable for companies to build several highly automated, medium-sized factories close to outlets instead of one factory in a place with low labor costs (Śliwiński & Śliwińska, 2020). This will gradually change the geography of goods flows, which will be visible in the next decade. For businesses, these changes create a great opportunity as they enable not only large but also small and medium-sized enterprises to internationalize quickly and cheaply. Thanks to the Flipkart platform, Xiaomi entered the Indian market, gaining $1 billion in sales revenue and an 11% share in the smartphone market within two years. This is a fantastic result considering the relatively low cost of gaining a new market (Bhattacharya et al., 2017). Certainly, the strategic challenge for businesses, resulting not only from the megatrend of globalization, but also from the megatrend of technology, will be digitization and the operational use of the latest technologies. For the consumer, in turn, these changes should bring about lower prices and access to a greater variety of products, also thanks to the overall decline in transport prices, which will also change the situation for real estate, finance, insurance, material management, and urban planning markets.

Artificial Intelligence: The Paramount Technology

The technology megatrend plays a key role in transforming the world. It consists of a number of key technologies, but only those covered in the chapters of this book will be discussed. Starting with AI, it should be noted that by 2030 there will be a significant boom in this amazing technology, which, thanks to its enormous potential, especially in combination with automation and robotization, will create the possibility to significantly reduce costs and increase production efficiency (Cordes & Stacey, 2017), to predict the future (Agrawal et al., 2019), and to increase the overall possibilities and help gain a competitive advantage (Śliwiński & Śliwińska, 2020). However, it also causes fear and hesitancy due to the possibility of replacing both manual workers and knowledge workers (Naveen, 2018), and the risk of succumbing to more technologically developed competition if firms are not supported by AI or supported by less developed AI algorithms. Combining AI technology with the Internet of Things (IoT) will result in the creation of many of the aforementioned highly automated factories supervised by AI by 2030. In conjunction with the digitization of AI communication, it will significantly affect the purchasing decisions of consumers (see Chapter 1); the method of customer acquisition; the type and level of investment, e.g. on the stock exchange, largely controlled by AI bots; or the type of e-entertainment, in many cases also related to with AI bots (e.g. chess, GO, Starcraft2).

AI is able to accumulate knowledge acquired over generations and multiply it, and there is a hope that it will solve important problems of mankind, like polluted seas and oceans, limited drinking water resources in the face of growing demographics, and health problems like cancer or many other diseases. With regard to health, the World Economic Forum indicated that AI will improve disease recognition by 2030 and recommend preventive measures in advance. Moreover, it will shorten the patient's waiting time for a medical service in national health systems (Kriwet, 2020). AI is also expected to improve understanding of the human genome and extend the treatment of genetic diseases by 2030 (Denny & Collins, 2021). Thanks to the development of AI, the period of human health can be extended by as much as 10 years. It will be possible to completely cure many diseases, including congenital defects and genetic diseases, or to regain fitness in people after spinal cord injuries. In this decade, dozens of biotechnological and pharmaceutical breakthroughs, currently in the first, second, or third phases of clinical trials, will reach patients with new therapies and medical solutions (Diamandis, 2020; Diamandis & Kotler, 2020; Karpa, 2019; Puślecki et al., 2021). AI will also influence education by helping to assimilate and test knowledge in students, responding to emerging boredom or fatigue, which will be read by AI from the students' faces. AI face reading will probably be massively introduced to human resources departments in the near future, in order to select suitable candidates for work from the available pool of applicants and to verify during the interview whether a candidate for a job is suitable or not (Harwell, 2019), or banks may use it to grant customers a loan or not (Duszczyk, 2021).

The cooperation of AI with people in the workplace will increase rapidly, and the platform "Artificial Intelligence as a Service" (AIaaS) will be created. The use of autonomous systems and AI in various areas of social life will become more and more frequent. AI will be embedded in everyday business operations, serving employees as collaborators in order to support creative tasks, generate new ideas, and deal with previously unattainable innovations. AI in the media, agriculture, medicine, and robotics is already changing each of these areas in a more revolutionary than evolutionary way (Diamandis, 2020; Diamandis & Kotler, 2020). AI will probably achieve intelligence on a human level by 2030, as Ray Kurzweil (2014) claims. As a technologist and futurologist, he predicted that AI will achieve human performance in this decade. In the 2020s, AI algorithms and machine learning tools will increasingly be made available on the cloud as open-source software, allowing anyone connected to the Internet to supplement their cognitive abilities, increase their ability to solve problems, and build new ventures. Every industry will be impacted, including industrial design, healthcare, education, and entertainment (Castrounis, 2019; Diamandis, 2020; Diamandis & Kotler, 2020; Kurzweil, 2005, 2014; Lee, 2018). In terms of transport, by 2030, it is highly likely that autonomous cars and trucks will appear on the streets in greater numbers as a means of wheeled transport (Thomas, 2021). These are just a few of the groundbreaking changes that the application of AI technology will bring to the economy and other areas of social life.

Unfortunately, there is also a dark side of AI's potential, which in the hands of the wrong people can lead to a significant restriction of individual freedom. This is what many Chinese residents say, who are tracked by AI-linked cameras in every public place. On the one hand, these cameras have led to a significant reduction in crime, but at the cost of depriving privacy. Other governments, like the United States, also want to take advantage of this application of AI technology (Lesman, 2019a). AI is already able to write books, edit messages, and even create movies. The potential is as much fantastic as it is terrifying. More and more often, one gets the impression that while developing AI, we as humans play with matches while sitting on a powder keg. A telling example is the fact that the creators of the GPT2 algorithm, the OpenAI company, seeing how AI quickly learned to manipulate and fabricate "fake news" and to add continuations of world-famous books, decided to close this program (Lesman, 2019b), probably for fear of the negative effects of dissemination of this algorithm. In practice, this may mean that it will no longer be possible to recognize whether text in a newspaper or a book is written by a human or by AI. What about fake news that can destroy people's lives? What if such a tool becomes the object of a political battle? These are all difficult questions, but they need to be asked right now. You have to ask yourself, for example, what will happen to people who will not get a job or a loan due to a negative assessment from AI? Is AI infallible, condemning some people to a lack of work, credit, and perhaps other privileges or goods? Certainly, the disadvantage of AI may be the impact on limiting people's privacy and obtaining excessive amounts of detailed information about a given person. For example, AI analyzing the likes of Facebook users can quite accurately assess the personality of a given person, sometimes to an extent exceeding the knowledge of that person (Hodson, 2015; Tandera et al., 2017). As long as it is used for marketing targeting, it is not as harmful as, for example, the use of this knowledge and the influence of social media in the US presidential election or the Brexit decision, as shown by the example of Cambridge Analytica (Ball, 2020; Cadwalladr, 2020). From the point of view of corporate strategy (Ciszewska-Mlinarič et al., 2015), the general conclusion is that without AI, at the end of this decade, a company may not be able to survive for too long, so investment in this technology should definitely be a priority. Moreover, the scope of using AI in business can significantly reduce costs and increase productivity, so the more areas in the business that are supported with AI tools, the greater the effects will be. The more data companies collect and intelligently process with the help of AI, the greater their competitive advantage. Keep in mind that data allows a different level of competition, and Ant Financial is the best example of this. Experts from the World Economic Forum indicate that as early as 2026, AI will also start to sit on the boards of corporations.

From the consumer's point of view, AI can allow you to quickly find the things you are looking for on the Internet, provide convenient personalization, offer relief from driving a car, provide better healthcare, or offer interesting entertainment. On the other hand, it means limited privacy; it could be a potential barrier to obtaining a loan or work; and, as seen by the case of fake news targeting specific people, it can be an enemy that surpasses a single consumer in intelligence so they cannot deal with it. Therefore, we are now dealing with a key moment when the increased role of AI in all spheres of social life should be included in the education system of the young generation. It is humanity's preparation, knowledge, and awareness that will determine whether this technology will bring harm or good.

Extended Reality: A Revolution in Work and in Education

Another key technology is augmented and virtual reality (AR and VR), the marketing aspects of which were described in Chapter 4. It is expected that this technology will revolutionize several areas of the global economy by 2030. First of all, this technology will allow the display of spatial images with any content, which can be especially useful for education. Thanks to this, students at medical or technical universities will be able to see any object in space, even in motion, visualizing things like, for instance, the preservation of the left ventricle during its work. What's more, such an image can be rotated, selected elements can be enlarged, and additional systems can be added or subtracted, e.g. nervous or blood systems. By 2030, AR and VR should largely replace 2D images and descriptions in books, and science confirms that this method of presentation will radically accelerate the assimilation of knowledge and the durability of remembered images in human memory.

Remote collaboration will be another area that will become popular by the end of this decade thanks to AR and VR. The possibility of meeting in virtual 3D and cooperation on strategic, design, operational, and many other issues will spread. Everyone from their place in the world can be present in a shared virtual room, where it will be possible to work on any project, repair a machine remotely, or carry out any other tasks. In this way, it will be possible to carry out remote operations, in which, for example, a specialist doctor will participate in a patient's operation in a virtual way. Another doctor located in a different location will perform the operation with the specialist's advice. Thanks to the advances in robotics and AI, it is predicted that at the end of this decade, doctors will operate on patients remotely, with the assistance of a nurse (Feussner et al., 2018; Solbiati, 2021). The development of these technologies will completely change the importance of surgery in the future, which will largely rely on telemedicine (tele-surgery).

The use of AR and VR in factories will also increase significantly by 2030. In the factory, AR can train employees and prompt or monitor the sequence of actions, like signaling a mistake or helping an employee to make repairs (Syberfeldt et al., 2016). As Barmak Heshmat, former MIT researcher and technology conceiver, points out, in the years 2020–2025 VR and AR will merge in such a way that VR will absorb AR as a more promising platform, creating an extended reality, i.e. a reality with comments, hints, and correspondence constantly seen in glasses, with additional fully customizable screens. Special glasses will therefore replace the screen of a monitor, and finger pads will allow us to touch various types of objects in the virtual world. In addition, special bracelets or smartphones will be coupled with the glasses. In the period 2025–2030, we should expect an evolution and a reduction in the size of relatively large VR glasses, which we will wear even if we do not have a vision defect for functional reasons. These glasses will read the commands of our mind directly, helping us to answer our questions in real time and deal with various matters in any situation (Heshmat, 2019). It will probably be based on a new type of sensor capable of direct communication with the brain and digital devices, developed, for example, by the company Neurolink (www.neurolinkglobal.com). The scale of practical use of AR in online stores will increase, allowing you to try on various types of clothing in a virtual way, test virtual makeup, or try furniture for a room or equip an empty office space with new furniture. From the point of view of the corporate strategy, the attractiveness of this technology is so great that its use may significantly increase the effectiveness of communication and cooperation productivity, and also ensure repeatability in production, or significantly accelerate the introduction of a new employee to the workplace. From the marketing point of view, this technology significantly brings the company's offer closer to the consumer, so in practice it affects the level of sales. As long as this technology does not become too commonplace too quickly, it can provide the company with a temporary or longer-lasting competitive advantage. From the point of view of the consumer, AR and VR significantly break the limits of imagination during shopping, work, and leisure. They allow the consumer to experience learning, entertainment, and even travel in new, virtual ways. The only drawback of this technology may be the feeling of confusion immediately after use and the physical reactions of the body in the form of headache (~75%), nausea (~70%), dizziness (~70%), drowsiness (~50%), hallucinations (~10%), and vomiting (~1%) (Lee et al., 2017).

The Internet of Things Makes the Machines Speak and Act

The IoT is an important basis for the development of technologies such as AI, big data, and AR. Although the increase in the number of sensors in the second decade of the 21st century radically increased the number and availability of data enabling the development of AI, the third decade will transfer the intensive development of the number of sensors in the world from approximately 1 trillion in 2021 to approximately 25.5 trillion in 2030 (Statista, 2021a). Progress in data transmission thanks to 5G technology will allow sending more data per unit of time and an increase in the number of devices that can communicate with each other. Consequently, it will allow for greater use of data in production, services, trade, medicine, and many other areas of the economy and life. In practice, therefore, by 2030 we will observe the emergence of more and more intelligent ecosystems in cities, homes, fields, and workplaces (offices, factories). In practice, in this decade, progress can be expected in each of the four key areas for the IoT. First, the number of new connections between various IT systems and devices will increase, including those that were not previously covered by this technology. Second, the collection of data obtained from devices will improve. Third, in the field of advanced computing, there will be an increased ability to transform advanced data into new opportunities. Finally, there will be unique creation of new interactions, business models, and solutions (IHS Markit, 2017). By 2030, the number of autonomous vehicles will increase dramatically. As a consequence of increasing the number and new types of sensors, driving safety will be improved for both passengers and pedestrians. Agriculture will be able to significantly increase its yields due to constant monitoring and intelligent, autonomous responses from irrigation or specialized spraying systems. In medicine, remote monitoring of the patient's health will certainly improve, especially as today's devices allow for the transmission of key information, if necessary, such as stopping or slowing down the heart rate, or dangerous reduction of the oxygen saturation level in the blood, which is especially important for patients with Covid-19. The popularity and importance of telemedicine will also increase thanks to the IoT, and thanks to the link with AR, also remote rehabilitation. In the future, a 6G network appears, which can realistically be introduced in 2030 with the task of further increasing the possibilities of the communication potential of IoT sensors. From a strategic point of view, companies increasing the involvement of the IoT can receive multiple benefits related to easy traceability in time and space of part or all of the production, as well as savings, increased productivity, etc. AI will also synergistically invest in the IoT, but the challenge here is overcoming the managers' traditionalist way of thinking (Jarosiński & Winch, 2017). Nevertheless, in view of the achievements of Industry 4.0, it is difficult to imagine a company's competitive advantage without the IoT. From the consumer's point of view, the IoT brings many amenities, such as the aforementioned health monitoring, smart homes, children's safety through constant monitoring, and many other applications. Unfortunately, as mentioned in Chapter 5, the loss of privacy can be a major downside. For example, Activision Blizzard, by tracking the health of its employees, knows exactly the phase of the female menstrual cycle, what their mood is at the moment, and even when they have sex (Duszczyk, 2019). This example shows the level of dilemmas that arise.

Sustainable Development: The Rescue for the World

Another key megatrend is the growing consensus on the need for sustainable development, which is partly addressed in Chapter 2. It is based on three pillars: environmental, social, and economic. In terms of the environment, civilization pressure should be significantly reduced by 2030. In terms of agriculture, it can be assumed with a high probability that the use of pesticides will decrease significantly in favor of biological plant protection products and natural fertilizers. The rules of cutting trees will be more regulated in the world in order to maintain regeneration growth. The seas and oceans will be partially cleared of plastic and other debris by 2030, and people will massively use biodegradable packaging. The main issue polluting the air are the sources of heat and propulsion energy. Different polices will try to solve that issue (Wach et al., 2021). In this regard, it should be assumed that by 2030 there will be infrastructure for hydrogen to fuel cars, buses, trucks, and airplanes. Huge investments are already being made to produce hydrogen. Denmark has decided to build an artificial island in the North Sea with a huge wind farm surrounding it that will produce electricity for electrolysis to produce hydrogen. Hydrogen will be transported to the continent, enabling environmentally friendly fuel consumption, or energy consumption in general (FuelCellsWorks, 2021). A consortium composed of the German firm RWE, the British-Dutch firm Shell, and the Russian firm Gazprom wants to replicate the Danish idea by building wind farms in the North Sea and a group of giant electrolysers with a capacity of 10 GW, transporting hydrogen via an underwater pipeline to the European continent (Kublik, 2021). The pipeline is expected to be ready by the end of this decade, and the entire installation by 2035. This means the beginning of the race for new, ecological energy sources that will significantly reduce the level of air, water, and land pollution.

In the social dimension, it can be expected that in the next decade, thanks to social movements like Fair Trade and other multi-stakeholder initiatives, as well as increasing national and international regulations, slave labor of children and adults in the Global South will be increasingly eliminated and will improve working and living conditions for the poorest producers. In the next decade, more and more global companies will commit to supporting sustainable development. Starbucks has gradually embarked on the path of supporting farmers by providing coffee producers with new trees to be planted as part of its sustainability strategy (Starbucks, 2019). These are small but important steps in a big cause, particularly in a setting where climate change and environmental pollution are causing coffee tree disease and the loss of part of the harvest. Such an attitude of multinational companies is of great importance for the poorest market participants.

In the economic dimension, it can be hoped that by 2030 the economic growth measure will be officially adopted, which, apart from the economic dimension on which GDP is currently focused, also measures environmental protection, quality of life, and social cohesion. This need is indicated by many scientists, including Nobel Prize winners (Ciszewska-Mlinarič & Obłój, 2014; Gorynia, 2019; Stiglitz et al., 2018), but also the European Commission, which adopted the "Beyond GDP" initiative (European Commission, 2013), understanding the issue that what is measured affects what is done, so bad metrics are causing bad outcomes. By 2030, many new business models can be expected to counteract excessive consumerism related to, among other things, excessive moral wear and tear of many products, or deliberate deterioration of the quality of products, etc. At present, devices, cars, machines of deliberately lower quality, or items programmed to break down after a specified period of time are often produced for the consumer to buy again. In this way, natural resources needed to make new products go to waste, rather than creating a product that is of high quality and rarely breaks down, and if it breaks down, it will be repaired. This shift in attitudes is crucial to halt the gradual degeneration of our planet due to the excessively fast use of resources, and consumers who expect specific behaviors from businesses can play a key role in this process. This change also means creating a global economy that recovers resources and reduces waste. For a real breakthrough in recovery and minimization of resource use, it is essential to maximize the use of biological materials that provide biodegradability to products that account for the highest percentage of waste, such as nylon bags. By 2030, it can be assumed with high probability that the waste will be fully biodegradable, and the plastic bag will be replaced, for example, by a cassava starch bag of plant origin, which can completely dissolve in water and is neutral to the environment. From a strategic point of view, companies should now completely change their approach to sustainability, if they have not already done so. The political will of the most important countries in the world in this regard is clear. Therefore, it is worth using sustainable development strategies (see Chapter 2) to take advantage of humanity's need in this regard. For consumers, sustainable development means clean air, uncontaminated water, healthy food, endless resources, and their economic availability. So, from the point of view of the consumer and the people of the world, this is clearly a very positive megatrend.

Digitalization Will Spread Even Faster

The technologies described above (AI, AR, VR, the IoT), combined with the progressive degree of computerization of society, the widespread use of smartphones, and the growing percentage of society constantly online – currently around 4.32 billion people (Statista, 2021b) – represent the digitization megatrend. As presented in Chapter 3, these processes can pose significant challenges and barriers to management. It should be assumed that the dynamic development of digitization will be a constant challenge for many managers, somehow embedded in the digital economy. Until 2030, progress will be intensive, which means that managers of companies constantly overcome existing barriers as well as newly emerging ones. For this reason, particularly desirable features for managers are the ability to learn quickly; the ability to appropriately shape business models and strategies (Chapter 2); the capacity to take entrepreneurial responsibility, which in the context of family businesses is presented in Chapter 8; the capability for innovation and cooperation with various partners (Chapter 7); and the desire to appropriately use modern technologies for sales (Chapter 1) and image shaping, e.g. through social media, which is one of the most effective tools in this area (Chapter 6). It should not be expected that by 2030 the barriers resulting from dynamic technological changes will decrease. Rather, it can be assumed that they will increase. From a strategic point of view, businesses should, on the one hand, take care of appropriately educated staff and, on the other hand, use appropriate tools for the above-mentioned technologies in order to effectively overcome the accumulating difficulties and successfully transform the business into a firm based on modern technologies, and at the same time, focused on sustainable development, which these technologies should serve.

For the consumer, on the one hand, digitization brings significant facilitation and increased opportunities, and on the other hand, a loss of privacy and a split personality between life in the physical world and life in the virtual world (Facebook, Instagram, etc.). Therefore, as in the case of managers, by the end of the decade, the problems related to digitization will increase, and as indicated in Chapter 3, people will increasingly want to simplify their lives, even at the cost of giving up some technological achievements. Therefore, the challenge for the present decade seems to be learning how to properly use the fruits of megatrends for personal and professional development.

It should be remembered that the megatrends responsible for changes are neither bad nor good in themselves; it all depends on how humanity will use them, and it depends on what will be the prevailing values, e.g. economic calculation or social values. As indicated above, even the question of the economic growth measure in economic calculus is of significant importance. The effect of the changes also depends on how we prepare ourselves for them. What is needed is the education of society at every age stage, not only technical, but also moral. Widespread awareness of the needs of sustainable development, which new technologies should serve in overcoming global economic, social, and environmental challenges, is crucial.

References

Agrawal, A., Gans, J. S., & Goldfarb, A. (2019). Artificial intelligence: The ambiguous labor market impact of automating prediction. *Journal of Economic Perspectives*, *33*(2), 31–50.

Ball, J. (2020, October 11). The real story of Cambridge Analytica and Brexit. *The Spectator*. https://www.spectator.co.uk/article/were-there-any-links-between-cambridge-analytica-russia-and-brexit-.

Bhattacharya, A., Reeves, M., Lang, N., & Augustinraj, R. (2017). New Business Models For A New Global Landscape. *Boston Consulting Group*. https://www.bcg.com/publications/2017/globalization-new-business-models-global-landscape.

Cadwalladr, C. (2020, January 4). Fresh Cambridge Analytica leak 'shows global manipulation is out of control'. *The Guardian*. https://www.theguardian.com/uk-news/2020/jan/04/cambridge-analytica-data-leak-global-election-manipulation.

Castrounis, A. (2019). *AI for people and business: A framework for better human experiences and business success*. O'Reilly Media.

Ciszewska-Mlinarič, M., & Obłój, K. (2014). Systemic effects of the internationalization of Polish companies. In G. W. Kołodko (Ed.), *Management and economic policy for development* (pp. 73–94). Nova.

Ciszewska-Mlinarič, M., Obłój, K., & Wąsowska, A. (2015). *Strategia korporacji*. Wolters Kluwer.

Cordes, F., & Stacey, N. (2017). *Is UK industry ready for the fourth industrial revolution? BCG*. Retrieved from, https://media-publications.bcg.com/Is-UK-Industry-Ready-for-the-Fourth-Industrial-Revolution.pdf.

Denny, J. C., & Collins, F. S. (2021). Precision medicine in 2030—Seven ways to transform healthcare, Cell, *184*(6), 1415–1419.

Diamandis, P. H. (2020, January 5). 20 Metatrends for the roaring 20s. https://www.diamandis.com/blog/20-metatrends-2020s.

Diamandis, P. H., & Kotler, S. (2012). *Abundance: The future is better than you think*. Free Press.

Diamandis, P. H., & Kotler, S. (2020). *The future is faster than you think: How converging technologies are transforming business, industries and our lives*. Simon and Schuster Ltd.

Duszczyk, M. (2019). Ten pracodawca wie, kiedy uprawiasz seks. *Rzeczpospolita*. https://cyfrowa.rp.pl/it/33603-ten-pracodawca-wie-kiedy-uprawiasz-seks.

Duszczyk, M. (2021). AI przewidzi, czy spłacisz pożyczkę. Polski pomysł robi furorę. *Rzeczpospolita*. https://cyfrowa.rp.pl/biznes/62644-ai-przewidzi-czy-splacisz-pozyczke-polski-pomysl-robi-furore?utm_source=rp&utm_medium=teaser_redirect.

ESPAS. (2017). Welcome to 2030. The Mega-Trends. ESPAS. https://ec.europa.eu/assets/epsc/pages/espas/chapter1.html.

European Commission. (2013). Commission Staff Working Document Progress On 'Gdp And Beyond' Actions. *European Commission*, SWD(2013) 303 final.

European Commission. (2021). *Developments and forecasts of growing consumerism*. https://knowledge4policy.ec.europa.eu/foresight/topic/growing-consumerism/more-developments-relevant-growing-consumerism_en.

Feussner, H., Ostler, D., & Wilhelm, D. (2018). Robotik und "augmented reality" Aktueller Entwicklungsstand und Zukunftsperspektive. *Chirurg*, *89*, 760–768. https://doi.org/10.1007/s00104-018-0697-z.

FuelCellsWorks. (2021, February 4). Denmark decides to construct the world's first wind energy hub as an Artificial Island in the North Sea: To include green hydrogen. *FuelCellsWorks*. https://fuelcellsworks.com/news/denmark-decides-to-construct-the-worlds-first-windenergy-hub-as-an-artificial-island-in-the-north-sea-to-include-green-hydrogen/.

Gaub, F. (2019). Global trends to 2030. Challenges and choices for Europe. *ESPAS*. https://ec.europa.eu/assets/epsc/pages/espas/ESPAS_Report2019.pdf

Gorynia, M. (2019). Competition and globalisation in economic sciences. Selected aspects. *Economics and Business Review*, *5*(3), 118–133.

Harwell, D. (2019). A face-scanning algorithm increasingly decides whether you deserve the job. *The Washington Post*. https://www.washingtonpost.com/technology/2019/10/22/ai-hiring-face-scanning-algorithm-increasingly-decides-whether-you-deserve-job/.

Heshmat, B. (2019). *Augmented reality and the future of marketing*. http://tctechnology.com.pe/cgi-bin/content/view.php?data=augmented_reality_and_the_future_of_marketing&filetype=pdf&id=5f7180054926fbb8ddbc0c7abffd3b43.

Hodson, H. (2015, January 12). What you 'like' on Facebook gives away your personality. *Technology*. https://www.newscientist.com/article/dn26781-what-you-like-on-facebook-gives-away-your-personality/.

Howell, J. (2017, October 24). The Internet of Things: A movement, not a market. IHS Markit. https://cdn.ihs.com/www/pdf/IoT_ebook.pdf.

Jarosiński, M., & Winch, S. (2017). Schematy myślenia barierą internacjonalizacji przedsiębiorstw: wyniki badań. *International Entrepreneurship Review*, 3(2), 9–22.

Karpa, W. (2019). *Osobliwość Innowacji Medycznych. Analiza Ekonomiczna. [The singularity of medical innovation. Economic analysis]*. Wydawnictwo Poltext.

Kriwet, C. (2020, January 07). Here are 3 ways AI will change healthcare by 2030. *World Economic Forum*. https://www.weforum.org/agenda/2020/01/future-of-artificial-intelligence-healthcare-delivery/.

Kublik, A. (2021). Niemcy planują rurociąg na wodór z Morza Północnego. Wraz ze spółką Gazpromu. *Wyborcza*. https://wyborcza.biz/biznes/7,177151,27028265,niemcy-planuja-rurociag-na-wodor-z-morza-polnocnego-wraz-ze.html.

Kurzweil, R. (2005). *The singularity is near, when humans transcend biology*. Viking.

Kurzweil, R. (2014). *How to create a mind. The secret of human thought revealed*. Bloomsbury Trade.

Lee, K-F. (2018). *AI superpowers: China, silicon valley, and the new world order*. Houghton Mifflin Harcourt.

Lee, J., Kim, M., & Kim, J. (2017). A study on immersion and VR sickness in walking interaction for immersive virtual reality applications. *Symmetry*, *9*(78), 1–17. https://doi.org/10.3390/sym9050078.

Lesman, U. (2019a, April 15). Udziałowcy Amazona: Nie dawajcie aplikacji do totalnej inwigilacji rządowi. *Rzeczpospolita*. https://cyfrowa.rp.pl/technologie/sztuczna-inteligencja/33379-aplikacja-amazona-moze-umozliwic-totalna-inwigilacje.

Lesman, U. (2019b, March 5). Groźne oblicze SI. To mistrz konfabulacji i fake newsów. *Rzeczpospolita*. https://cyfrowa.rp.pl/technologie/sztuczna-inteligencja/32144-grozne-oblicze-sztucznej-inteligencji-to-mistrz-fake-newsow.

Mallick, S., & Rajagopalan, R. P. (2019, January 24). If space is 'the province of mankind', who owns its resources?. *Observer Research Foundation Occasional Paper*. https://www.orfonline.org/research/if-space-is-the-province-of-mankind-who-owns-its-resources-47561/.

McKinsey. (2011). Urban world: Mapping the economic power of cities. *McKinsey Global Institute*. https://www.mckinsey.com/~/media/McKinsey/Featured%20Insights/Urbanization/Urban%20world/MGI_urban_world_mapping_economic_power_of_cities_full_report.pdf.

McKinsey. (2012). Urban world: Cities and the rise of the consuming class. *McKinsey Global Institute*. https://www.mckinsey.com/~/media/McKinsey/Business%20Functions/Operations/Our%20Insights/Urban%20world%20Cities%20and%20the%20rise%20of%20the%20consuming%20class/MGI_Urban_world_Rise_of_the_consuming_class_Full_report.pdf.

McKinsey. (2016). Digital globalization: The new era of global flows. *McKinsey Global Institute*. https://www.mckinsey.com/~/media/McKinsey/Business%20Functions/McKinsey%20Digital/Our%20Insights/Digital%20globalization%20The%20new%20era%20of%20global%20flows/MGI-Digital-globalization-Full-report.ashx.

McKinsey. (2019). Globalization in transition: The future of trade and value chains. *McKinsey Global Institute*. https://www.mckinsey.com/~/media/mckinsey/featured%20insights/innovation/globalization%20in%20transition%20the%20future%20of%20trade%20and%20value%20chains/mgi-globalization%20in%20transition-the-future-of-trade-and-value-chains-full-report.pdf.

Naveen, J. (2018). Goldman Sachs has replaced 99% of its traders with robots. Are robots now taking over the white-collar jobs?. *Allerin*. https://www.allerin.com/blog/goldman-sachs-has-replaced-99-of-its-traders-with-robots-are-robots-now-taking-over-the-white-collar-jobs. Perspective on Augmented Reality, Proceedings from the 6th CIRP Conference on Assembly Technologies and Systems (CATS), CIRP, *44* (2016), 108–113.

Puślecki, Ł., Dąbrowski, M., & Puślecki, M. (2021). Development of innovation cooperation in the time of COVID-19 pandemic. *European Research Studies Journal*, *XXIV*(1), 1049–1073. https://doi.org/10.35808/ersj/2087.

Śliwiński, R., & Śliwińska, M. (2020). Współczesny model globalizacji – konsekwencje dla strategicznego zarządzania przedsiębiorstwem międzynarodowym. In R. Śliwiński (Ed.), *Strategiczne Zarządzanie Przedsiębiorstwem Międzynarodowym* (pp. 13–50). Difin.

Solbiati, L. A. (2021). Augmented reality: Thrilling future for interventional oncology?. *Cardiovasc Intervent Radiol*, *44*, 782–783. https://doi.org/10.1007/s00270-021-02801-9.

Starbucks. (2019). Global social impact report. *Starbucks*. https://stories.starbucks.com/uploads/2020/06/2019-Starbucks-Global-Social-Impact-Report.pdf.

Statista. (2021a). Number of Internet of Things (IoT) connected devices worldwide from 2019 to 2030. *Statista.* https://www.statista.com/statistics/1183457/iot-connected-devices-worldwide/.

Statista. (2021b). Global digital population as of January 2021. *Statista.* https://www.statista.com/statistics/617136/digital-population-worldwide/

Stiglitz, J. E., Fitoussi, J. P., & Durand, M. (2018). *Measuring what counts for economic and social performance.* OECD. https://doi.org/10.1787/9789264307292-en.

Syberfeldt, A., Holm, M., Danielsson, O., Wang, L., & Lindgren Brewster, R. (2016). Support systems on the industrial shop-floors of the future – Operators' perspective on augmented reality. *Procedia CIRP*, *44*, 108-113.

Tandera, T., Hendro, D., Suhartono, D., Wongso, R., & Prasetio, Y. L. (2017). Personality prediction system from Facebook users. *Procedia Computer Science*, *116*, 604–611.

TeleGeography. (2021, February 16). 2021 Global internet map tracks global capacity, traffic, and cloud infrastructure. TeleGeography Blog. https://blog.telegeography.com/2021-global-internet-map-tracks-global-capacity-traffic-and-cloud-infrastructure.

Thomas, M. (2021). The future of AI: How artificial intelligence will change the world. 7 ways AI can change the world for better… or worse. *Builtin.* https://builtin.com/artificial-intelligence/artificial-intelligence-future.

Torre, A., & Rigolini, J. (2020). MIC Forum: The rise of the middle class. *The World Bank.* https://www.worldbank.org/content/dam/Worldbank/document/MIC-Forum-Rise-of-the-Middle-Class-SM13.pdf.

Wach, K., Głodowska, A., Maciejewski, M., & Sieja, M. (2021). Europeanization processes of the EU Energy Policy in visegrad countries in the years 2005–2018. *Energies*, *14*(7), 1802. https://doi.org/10.3390/en14071802.

Index

Note: Page numbers in *italics* and **bold** indicate figures and tables, respectively.

actor-network theory 189
advanced life support 187
agency theory 203
alliance management 176–177, 196
artificial intelligence 1, 3, 5, 7, 15–30, 176
artificial life support **189**, *192*, **193**
augmented reality 4–5, 7, 105, 108, *111*, **113**, **116–117**, **119**
automation 225

B2C 152–153, 157–158, 160, 165
behavioral approach 204, 218
Big Brother effect 140
Big data 5–7, 134, 137, 143
biopharmaceutical industry 176–179
born sustainable business/business model / born sustainables 37, 40–42, 47, 49–53, 61–63, 66
business development 204, 206, 207, 209, 214, 215, 216, 217, 218, 219, 220, 221
business model 36–37, 40–54, 58, 60–62, 65–68

Central and Eastern Europe (CEE) 176, 178–179, 191, 193–194
chatbot 23–24
co-creation value *122*, 123–125, 127
communication 151–152, 154–155, 157, 159
communication instruments 151
competition 2–4
competitive advantage 3, 16–19, 47, 49, 53, 65
competitive position 35–37, 42, 46, 47, 49–50, 53, 55, 61, 63, 66–68
competitiveness 2, 36–37, 43, 49, 53, 61
consumer-perceived value 106–107, *122*, 125–126
corporate strategy 7
Covid-19 4, 6, 176, 178–179, **180–185**, 187, 191, 194–196
customer recommendations 25, 26
customer-oriented search 19

data security 137
demographics 1, 223, 226
demography 1, 10
digital 7–8
digital health technologies 176–179, **180**, 196
digital hygiene 8
digitalization 7–8, 151

early adopters 140–143
e-commerce 3, 16–19, 19
ecosystem 4–7, 178, 186, 191, *192*, 193–196
effects 152–153, 156–157, 162, **163**, 164–166
ethical markets 37–38
Extracorporeal Life Support Organization (ELSO) 191, *192*, **193**, 193–194, 196, 198n4
Extracorporeal Membrane Oxygenation (ECMO) 176, 189–191, *192*, **193**, 194–197, 197n1

Facebook 152, 155–156, 159, 160, **161–163**, 165
fair markets 37, 39
fair trade 9, *55–58*, 60–65
Fairtrade International *55–57*, 64
fake product reviews 28, 29
family business 9, 203–222
family business responsibility 203, 204, 205, 207, 209, 211, *213*, 215, 216, 217, 218, 219, 221
family goals 218

G7 2
G20 2
generational transfer 203, 206
global changes 1, 2
globalization 1, 10

Haenlein, M. 154, 157
HandS 191
hedonic value **113**, **116**, 120–123
Homans and Blau 203, 205, 221
Horizon 2020 179, **180–185**
human patient simulator 186

inclusive business models 47
Industry 4.0 6
innovation 203, 204, 205, 206, 208, 215, 216, 217, 218, 219, 220, 221
innovation cooperation 179
innovation resistance 135–6
innovations 109, **114**
innovative cooperation 7, 176, 179, 191, 193
Innovative Medicines Initiative 179, **180**, **183**
Instagram 152, 155–156, 159, 160, **161–163**, 164, 167
instant messengers 155–156
intellectual property 179
intelligent agent 26
international marketing communication 151–153, 155, 157–158, 160, **161**, 162, **163**, 164–166
internet of medical things 5
Internet of Things 5–7, 133–145, 178
interpersonal communication 154
inventory management 26, 27, 28

Kaplan, A.M. 154, 157
knowledge transfer 175, 187, 189, 191, *192*, 196–197

Kotler, Ph. 108

local social media (LSM) 159, 160, **161–163**, 165
Lusch, R.F. 105, 108

machine learning 138
marketing activities 105–107, 121, *122*, 124–125
marketing communication 151–157, 160
marketing orientation 135
medical simulation 4, 7, 176, 186–187, 190, 194, 198n3
medical simulation centre 187, **193**
megatrend 1, 3, 7–9, 8–10
middle class 223, 224
modern slavery 36, 50, 64–65

needs 108–109, 125
new technologies 105, **118**, 126–127, 166
next generation 206, 219

open innovation 7, 177–178
open innovation alliances 176–178, 195–196
organic 38–40, 49, 51, *55–56*, 62, 64
owner 203, 204, 205, 207, 212, 214, 216, 217, 218, 219, 220, 221
ownership 203, 218, 221

perceived value 139
personalization 22–23, 25
Polish companies 159
predictive marketing 20
privacy 136–145
privacy paradox 138, 141–142
products 108–109, 112, 120–121, 124–126
profit 203, 204, 205, 206, 208, 209, *213*, 214, 215, 216, 217, 218, 219

qualitative research 153, 156, 166

R&D alliances 175–178, 195
R&D cooperation 176–178
resources 1–3, 7–8
robotization 225

sales process 20
scarce resources 2, 3
services 108–109, 112, 120–121, 125

simulation **183**, 186–187, **188–189**, 191, 194–195, 197n2, 198n3, 198n4
smart home 140–1
shift of political and economic balance of power 2
social exchange theory 203, 206, 207, 217
social media 151, 154, 159, **161–163**, 166
social media marketing 165
standardized patients 186–187
succession 203, 204, 205, 206, 207, 214, 219, 222
sustainability 35–42, 44–47, 49, 51, 53–55, 59–61, 65–68
sustainable business model (SBM) 36–37, 40, 42, 44–48, 50, 53–54, 61–62, 66–68
sustainable certification schemes 37, 40, 49, 53–54, 59, 66–67
sustainable development 8–10, 47–51, 54–55, 59–60, 64–66
sustainable development goals (SDGs) 8, 35–36, 38–39, 44, 65, 68
sustainable markets 35–44, 48–49, 51, 53–54, 66–68
sustainable markets definition 42
sustainable markets determinants 37, 39–43, 48–49, 53, 66
sustainable strategy 48–50, *59*

technological cooperation 175
technological development 1
technological progress 3
technology 1, 3–5, 7–10
technology acceptance 135, 142
translational innovation 7, 176, 189, 190–191, 194–195
translational innovation model *190*
translational simulation 177, 179
Twitter 152, 155–156, 159, 160, **161–163**, 164

utilitarian value **113**, 120–121, 123

Valos, M.J. 155, 157
Vargo, S.L. 105, 108
virtual assistant 20, 24
virtual reality 4–7, 105, **117**, 178, 188
voice assistant 139–140

Web 2.0 154
WhatsApp 155–156
Woodruff, R.B 108
World Fair Trade Organization (WFTO) 40, 56–57, 61–62

YouTube 152, 155–156, 159, 160, **161–163**, 164, 165

For Product Safety Concerns and Information please contact our EU representative GPSR@taylorandfrancis.com
Taylor & Francis Verlag GmbH, Kaufingerstraße 24, 80331 München, Germany

www.ingramcontent.com/pod-product-compliance
Ingram Content Group UK Ltd.
Pitfield, Milton Keynes, MK11 3LW, UK
UKHW022352190926
475702UK00015B/2239

* 9 7 8 1 0 3 2 0 6 8 9 2 3 *